D1564438

Yeats's VISION and the Later Plays

Yeats's VISION
and the Later Plays

HELEN HENNESSY VENDLER

HARVARD UNIVERSITY PRESS

Cambridge, Massachusetts

Publication of this book has been aided by a grant from the Ford Foundation

Library of Congress Catalog Card Number 63-9565

FOR MY PARENTS

Preface

"My head is all frozen hard because of a morning of mystic geometry," Yeats wrote in 1928, "and I am trying to melt it." Sometimes, at least, Yeats had a sense of humor when he contemplated *A Vision*; usually he treated it with a solemn gravity that most of his commentators have imitated. Parts of *A Vision* deserve gravity, but others must be taken with a grain of salt, and not even the most admiring critic can swallow *A Vision* whole. But the choice is not between accepting the "mystic geometry" wholesale and shrugging it off as one of Yeats's dotages. There is a middle course, and that is to see *A Vision* as a symbolic statement, somewhat cluttered up with psychic paraphernalia, which yields itself quite well to reasonable interpretation.

Readers of Yeats usually come to *A Vision* by way of something else — the poetry, the essays, or the plays. To understand most of the essays and a good part of the poetry it is not essential to know *A Vision*, but for the late plays I think it is. So I propose, before coming to the plays which led me to my own reading of *A Vision*, to define what Yeats's "system" is, and how it should be read; to relate, as clearly and as simply as I can, what is contained in each of the five books of *A Vision*, not in terms of esoteric doctrine, but in terms of experience, especially aesthetic experience. Once this is done, it becomes possible to offer a reading of Yeats's late dramatic work which will save the plays from the charge of incomprehensibility.

From time to time I will have recourse to the poems when they shed light on the topic at hand.

In the end, I would like to redeem both *A Vision* and the plays for the reader who cares enough for Yeats's poetry to want to read him entire. Yeats dedicated his *Autobiographies* "To those few people, mainly personal friends, who have read all that I have written." Those few have multiplied into many, but even so, *A Vision* remains (to use Bridges' phrase about "The Wreck of the Deutschland") a great dragon lying folded at the entrance to all of Yeats's later work. When it is vanquished, most of the difficulties of the late plays disappear; at least, I have found it so. I am not attempting an artistic rehabilitation of either *A Vision* or the plays since they fall far short, in general, of Yeats's lyric poetry. They deserve, nevertheless, a better hearing than they have had, and until they are understood, the fine poetry in the late plays will go unappreciated.

ACKNOWLEDGMENTS

I owe special gratitude to Professor John V. Kelleher of Harvard University, who first taught me to know and value Yeats's *Vision* and the late plays. He and Professor Reuben Brower conducted an amicable prosecution of my first draft; their comments helped me to unwind Yeats's winding paths. Colonel Russell K. Alspach kindly read my manuscript and offered encouragement; Professor Paul de Man let me read his notes on the manuscript drafts of *The Player Queen*; and Professor Stephen Parrish allowed me to use the forthcoming Cornell concordance to the poetry of Yeats while it was still in proof. My greatest debt is to Marguerite Moloney, who shared my days and hours with Yeats.

The Alice Freeman Palmer Fellowship of Wellesley College and a National Fellowship from the American Association of University Women made possible the free time in which this book was first written. The Department of English of Cor-

nell University provided a grant-in-aid from the Clark Fund
to cover secretarial help and fees for the use of copyright
material. The libraries of Harvard College, Radcliffe College, and
Cornell University have been of service very often. I am particularly glad to have been given permission to use and to
quote from the Yeats manuscripts in the Houghton Library
at Harvard.

I am grateful to the following for permission to quote from
works protected by copyright: Mrs. W. B. Yeats, Messrs.
Macmillan & Company, Ltd., and the Macmillan Company for
the quotations from the poetry and prose of W. B. Yeats;
Oxford University Press for the quotations from the poetry
of Gerard Manley Hopkins; and Alfred A. Knopf, Inc., for
quotations from the *Collected Poems* of Wallace Stevens
(copyright 1923, 1931, 1935, 1936, 1937, 1942, 1943, 1944,
1945, 1946, 1947, 1948, 1949, 1950, 1951, 1952, 1954 by Wallace Stevens), as follows: "Angel Surrounded by Paysans,"
"A Primitive like an Orb," "Peter Quince at the Clavier,"
"Notes toward a Supreme Fiction," "Sunday Morning,"
"Asides on the Oboe."

HELEN HENNESSY VENDLER

Ithaca, New York
June 1962

Contents

Yeats's VISION and the Later Plays

Introduction

Yeats saw a vision and wrote it down; but what, in Yeats's terms, is the visionary faculty? The difference between Vision and sight is a Blakean one, and Blake's definition of Vision, quoted repeatedly by Yeats,[1] is the one that should be adopted in defining Yeats's title. For Blake, Vision is a species of poetry: "The Last Judgment is not Fable or Allegory, but Vision. Fable or Allegory are a totally distinct & inferior kind of Poetry. Vision or Imagination is a Representation of what Eternally Exists, Really and Unchangeably."[2] Yeats's book is about imagination, about the truer seeing which may be said, in some sense, to be a revelation or a vision.

At times, in the twenty years that *A Vision* was in the making, Yeats was interested only in the skeleton of his scheme, but when the work was finally done it was the dream itself enchanted him, not only the mathematics of it. "The mathematical structure, when taken up into imagination, is more than mathematical . . . seemingly irrelevant details fit together into a single theme."[3] That statement, which prefaces the completed *Vision*, may reassure us as we begin this difficult book, but we still wonder how seriously we should take the "mathematical structure." Of course any abstract scheme taken up into the imagination ceases to be abstract; in Blake's terms, it ceases to be seen with the corporeal eye and is seen with the eye of the imagination.

"What," it will be Question'd, "When the Sun rises, do you not
see a round disk of fire somewhat like a Guinea?" O no, no, I see an
Innumerable company of the Heavenly host crying 'Holy, Holy,
Holy is the Lord God Almighty.' [4]

We might have preferred Yeats to say outright that the "mathematical structure" was a work of imagination rather than
of scholarly history or philosophy; but he has told us as much
in his title and his final statement:

Some will ask whether I believe in the actual existence of my cir-
cuits of sun and moon . . . Now that the system stands out clearly in
my imagination I regard them as stylistic arrangements of experience
comparable to the cubes in the drawings of Wyndham Lewis and to
the ovoids in the sculpture of Brancusi.[5]

It is as a stylistic arrangement of experience — a poet's experience — that *A Vision* must be seen if it is to shed light
on Yeats's poetry and plays. It is not simply a mathematical
structure, which, taken up into imagination, acquires a the-
matic unity; it is a structure which never had anything to do
with the corporeal eye at all. Yeats was not, in spite of his
occasional wishful thinking, either a metaphysician or a historian. To follow *A Vision*, the reader must "Enter into these
Images in his Imagination, approaching them on the Fiery
Chariot of his Contemplative Thought" [6] — a method which
Yeats himself recommended, quoting Blake, for all interpreting of symbolic art.[7]

Those instructors who came so opportunely in 1917 to
give Yeats metaphors for poetry expressly warned him not to
systematize their revelations,[8] a warning he could not always
bring himself to observe. And so we are indeed faced with a
system and a doctrine, but our reaction to them should be the
reaction of Yeats's father to Blake's system, that "mysticism
was never the *substance of his poetry, only its machinery*."
In fact, all that J. B. Yeats wrote to his son about Blake applies
just as well to *A Vision*:

You need not be a believer in his mysticism to enjoy his poem, 'Oh

Rose, thou art sick.' The substance of his poetry is himself, revolting and desiring. His mysticism was a make-believe, a sort of working hypothesis as good as another. He could write about it in prose and contentiously assert his belief. When he wrote his poems it dropped into the background, and it did not matter whether you believed it or not, so apart from all creeds was his poetry . . . Out in the world, among his enemies and his friends, Blake was a polemical mystic. In his poetry, it was only a device, a kind of stage scenery, and a delight to understand and to think about, and yet all the time a something apart, that helped but was never more than a help.[9]

We do not have Yeats's answer to this long passage; but Yeats collaborated with Pound in choosing the extracts from his father's letters to be published by the Cuala Press,[10] and being Yeats he probably would not have printed an opinion on Blake unless he concurred with it. Even so, we cannot rely on this passage alone, but must take into account what Yeats himself thought *A Vision* was and what function it was supposed to perform.

Yeats explicitly disclaimed any mystical orientation in *A Vision*: "there was nothing in Blake, Swedenborg, Boehme or the Cabbala to help me now." It seems from this statement that *A Vision* is something not supernatural in its concerns, but natural; and Mrs. Yeats's admission that her automatic writing was deliberately undertaken in order to distract her moody husband offers at least a partial explanation of the "unknown instructors." Neither is *A Vision* primarily a philosophical compilation. Although Yeats, contrary to the commands of his "instructors," read Berkeley, Thomas Taylor, and Plotinus before revising his system, he tells us that he turned to philosophy not for new notions (thereby keeping to the spirit of the prohibition) but for confirmation of what he already knew: "the more I read the better did I understand what I had been taught." Philosophy became a support to the given metaphors. And finally, although Yeats kept up the fiction of the "instructors" even after he had discarded most of the mumbo-jumbo surrounding the first edition of *A*

Vision, he admits that it is not to spirits but to his own Daimon that the book is due. "Spirits," Yeats's instructors announced, "do not tell a man what is true but create such conditions, such a crisis of fate, that the man is compelled to listen to his Daimon." Again and again, says Yeats, the instructors insisted that the whole system was "the creation of my wife's Daimon and of mine." [11] The Daimon will be defined by Yeats in Book I of *A Vision*, but for the moment, he leaves the term unexplained and passes on to two statements about poetry which conclude his introduction to the system.

The first statement defends system as a basis for art or for any attempt to unite the conscious with the unconscious: "An arbitrary, harsh, difficult symbolism . . . has almost always accompanied expression that unites the sleeping and waking mind." For lack of a system accompanying his poetry, Blake remains, says Yeats, almost unintelligible, while Dante, on the other hand, profited by having a system at hand — one familiar to his readers, but subtle enough to form the substratum of his poetry. Once "those hard symbolic bones" are under the skin, we can "substitute for a treatise on logic the *Divine Comedy*, or some little song about a rose." [12] Every small fact, in relation to a universal system, takes on auras of meaning of the sort which Yeats desired, believing as he did that any poetry needs behind it a network of interrelations in which the several worlds of experience are bridged. In such a system, a given metaphor drawn from one area will cause a poetic resonance from other sectors. The reader deprived of this resonance by ignorance of "those hard symbolic bones" will miss all but the surface of the poem; and a poet deprived of a matrix will be able to write only superficial poetry.

It is necessary here to make a distinction between the desirability of a "belief" (Arnold's *glaube*) and the desirability of a "system." Yeats had little true interest in the former, but a good deal of missionary spirit for the latter. Religious "faith" is not an element in Yeats's theory as it is, for instance, in Wallace Stevens' remarks on the Supreme Fiction. Rather, Yeats's peculiar attraction was to something he thought Dante had found in the medieval synthesis — an elaborately conceived group of concepts distinguishing and dividing both mental and physical experience. The "ghostlier demarcations, keener sounds" which poetry continually attempts are fostered by such intellectual discrimination. If, then, *A Vision* has its own equivalent of the legendary debates about angels dancing on pins, it has too the corresponding virtue of subtlety in analyzing human activity, especially in the aesthetic realm.

Yeats's second statement about poetry fills out his theory, which might have seemed too harsh if it had contained nothing but metaphorical bones. "Muses resemble women who creep out at night and give themselves to unknown sailors and return to talk of Chinese porcelain . . . except that the Muses sometimes form in those low haunts their most lasting attachments." It is the old assertion that the poet must "lie down where all the ladders start," but it is more than that: it is a characteristically Yeatsian assertion of a rhythm of violence followed by elegance. "Virginity renews itself like the moon," [13] and the Muse is not only not inviolable, she thrives on spoliation. Like Yeats's poetry, *A Vision* oscillates between two poles — human "complexities of mire or blood" and aesthetic "porcelain," remembering that the one begets the other. Even in his most metaphysical moments, Yeats does not forget the physical source.

A Vision, then, exists to provide a "systematic" background against which Yeats's poetry and plays must be read to acquire their proper resonance. Seemingly theoretical and abstract, like the Pythagorean numbers from which Phidias planned his statues, it is in truth only another statement of the human experience we find embodied in Yeats's work; it revolves around the same concerns, it comes to the same conclusions. But to describe the experiences "arranged" in *A Vision*, we must translate Yeats's esoteric metaphors into the human terms from which they originated, an undertaking sometimes easy, sometimes almost impossible.[14]

Chapter I

The Great Wheel

T HE tales which preface *A Vision* — the "Stories of Michael Robartes and His Friends" — now have a faded antiquarian savor in their remoteness, their rather perverse and precious humor, and their artificial tone. They serve as a fictional frame for the system, linking it to that elusive compilation of Giraldus, the *Speculum Angelorum et Hominum*, which it so mysteriously resembles. Yeats must have enjoyed the elaborateness of his stage scenery, and the tales hint at the spirit in which the book is to be taken.

Book I proper is by far the longest, the most crowded, and the best known of the five books of *A Vision*. It is divided into three unequal parts: two give introductory material and the third contains the heart of the book. The first two parts are chiefly glossaries of terminology, and nowadays Yeats's terminology is no longer so forbidding as it was in 1925, when *A Vision* first appeared. The phases of the moon and the gyres are familiar symbols, at least in their general meaning, but what we sometimes forget is the precision of their use by Yeats. We usually need to be reminded that the gyres are always double, that there is no separating subjective and objective, aesthetic and moral, emotional and rational. As one diminishes, the other increases, and consequently no statement about these or other qualities is made absolutely. If the antithetical cone expresses "our inner world of desire and imagination," that world flows from and into the primary world of "outward things and events." [1]

Likewise, in the definition of the Four Faculties [2] (Will, Mask, Creative Mind, and Body of Fate) the familiar idea of what the symbols imply should be sharpened by a realization that for Yeats these Faculties are not so much things in themselves as ways of looking at the world: "Everything that wills can be desired, resisted, or accepted, every creative act can be seen as fact, every *Faculty* is alternately shield and sword." [3] The transformation of one Faculty into another is one aim of the aesthetic act — to transform the desired into the real, the Mask into the Body of Fate. The protean quality of the Faculties helps to keep Yeats's system from stasis, and explains why he uses words like "whirl" and "drag" in describing the interplay of the Faculties.

One more caution; the Great Wheel is not only a historical figure. It represents every cyclical process, whether momentary or lengthy, whether interior or exterior, whether controllable or unpredictable. In speaking of the Wheel, Yeats uses the copula of metaphor and not the language of schematic representation: "This wheel is every completed movement of thought or life, twenty-eight incarnations, a single incarnation, a single judgment or act of thought." [4] The Wheel *is* what it represents, as only a poetic reality can be.

Almost at once, at the beginning of Book I, Yeats betrays the point of primary interest in the Wheel. The entire Wheel is described as a process culminating in its high point, Phase 15; this is the phase of the attained object, where Sun is consumed in Moon and all is beauty. [5] No other phase has value in itself except Phase 15, which incarnates the ideal, and in some sense it is true to say that all of *A Vision* is written to explain the central phase. All other phases are seen in relation to it, whether as struggles to attain it or as recessions from it once achieved. There are of course reasons for this, and some of them will be discussed later when Phase 15 is considered in detail.

Given the multiple meanings of the Wheel, we might have

thought that Yeats would begin his description with the historical sense, which is after all the interpretation to which he seems to give the most attention. As a matter of fact, he does not. He begins with the Wheel as an allegory of the individual life, and we have proof in the Dedication of the first edition of *A Vision* that he conceived of his system in terms of the individual, not in terms of political or cultural history. "I wished for a system of thought," he wrote, "that would leave my imagination free to create as it chose and yet make all that it created, or could create, part of the one history, and that the soul's." [6] It seems natural that this should have been his central intuition, the sense of the Wheel as metaphor for his own experience. "We are dealing always," Yeats begins, "with a particular man." [7]

The Four Faculties are defined in terms of that "particular man," and I quote the definitions from the first edition because they are given there in an elementary and simple form: [8]

> By *Will* is understood feeling that has not become desire because there is no object to desire . . . By *Mask* is understood the image of what we wish to become, or of that to which we give our reverence. Under certain circumstances it is called the *Image*. By *Creative Mind* is meant intellect, as intellect was understood before the close of the seventeenth century — all the mind that is consciously constructive. By *Body of Fate* is understood the physical and mental environment . . . the stream of Phenomena as this affects a particular individual.[9]

In the second edition a more elaborate and more symbolic definition is given, oddly enough in terms of memory. And not the man's memory, but the memory of his Daimon (an entity yet to be fully defined). It is the simpler definitions that have become most familiar, and no wonder; but Yeats rewrote the definitions with a purpose. Too often we think of the Mask as an exterior object of desire or as a disguise assumed; we think of the Body of Fate as events in the physical world; Yeats wants to leave us no excuse for doing so. These are all mental in origin, and spring from a mental record.

The *Four Faculties* are not the abstract categories of philosophy, being the result of the four memories of the *Daimon* or ultimate self of that man. His *Body of Fate*, the series of events forced on him from without, is shaped out of the *Daimon's* memory of the events of his past incarnations; his *Mask* or object of desire or idea of the good, out of its memory of the moments of exaltation in his past lives; his *Will* or normal ego out of its memory of all the events of his present life, whether consciously remembered or not; his *Creative Mind* from its memory of ideas — or universals — displayed by actual men in past lives, or their spirits between lives.[10]

Leaving out of consideration for the moment the idea of re-incarnation (we can see more clearly what it represents for Yeats in Book III of *A Vision*) we can realize from this passage the central position held by the Daimon in Yeats's symbolism. If we are to understand what the Wheel as an allegory for a particular man meant to Yeats, we must discover what the Daimon of the self represents. It is in *Per Amica Silentia Lunae*, that early foretaste of *A Vision*, that Yeats first writes of the Daimon:

Daemon and man are opposites; man passes from heterogeneous objects to the simplicity of fire, and the Daemon is drawn to objects because through them he obtains power, the extremity of choice. For only in men's minds can he meet even those in the Condition of Fire who are not of his own kin . . . Always it is an impulse from some Daemon that gives to our vague, unsatisfied desire, beauty, a meaning and a form all can accept.[11]

The Condition of Fire is familiar to us from "Sailing to Byzantium," and there, in the realm of art, Yeats located that self with whom we quarrel. "We make out of the quarrel with others, rhetoric, but of the quarrel with ourselves, poetry." The quarrel is represented by all the phases of struggle, but the Daimon presides perfectly only over Phase 15, where the vague desire is finally given "that sudden luminous definition of form which makes one understand almost in spite of oneself that one is not merely imagining." [12]

The role of the Daimon is most nearly expressible in sexual

imagery, and the Daimon is in part Yeats's barbaric recasting
of the image of the Muse, which he amalgamates with the
femme fatale of the 1890's:

> My imagination runs from Daemon to sweetheart, and I divine an
> analogy that evades the intellect. I remember that Greek antiquity
> has bid us look for the principal stars, that govern enemy and sweet-
> heart alike, among those that are about to set, in the Seventh House
> as the astrologers say; and that it may be "sexual love," which is
> "founded upon spiritual hate," is an image of the warfare of man and
> Daemon; and I even wonder if there may not be some secret commu-
> nion, some whispering in the dark between Daemon and sweetheart.[13]

In fact, the relation of poet to Daimon is symbolically a "demonic parody" (in Northrop Frye's terms) of the mystical
marriage — a resemblance which Yeats emphasizes by quoting from St. John of the Cross shortly after the above description of the Daimon, as well as by adopting the motto, "Demon
est Deus Inversus." The Daimon is even referred to by female
pronouns in the first edition of *A Vision*, where Yeats says
unequivocally that the Daimon is of the opposite sex to that of
the person possessed, and that "this relation . . . may create
a passion like that of sexual love." He adds that when a man
becomes passionate "this passion makes the *Daimonic* thought
luminous with its peculiar light — this is the object of the
Daimon — and she so creates a very personal form of heroism
or of poetry." [14] Before we get too deeply entrenched in
mythology, Yeats reminds us in the same passage that the Daimon is a part of our mind, the part which to us is "dark," or
unconscious. The struggle between man and Daimon is part
of the quarrel with ourself that yields poetry.

The most fruitful of all symbols for Yeats in describing the
activity of the Daimon will be the image of sexual intercourse.
The other symbol Yeats uses (one which comes to mind especially in thinking of *The Player Queen*) is an image from
the world of the theater:

> When I wish for some general idea which will describe the Great

Wheel as an individual life I go to the *Commedia dell'Arte* or im-
provised drama of Italy. The stage-manager, or *Daimon*, offers his
actor an inherited scenario, the *Body of Fate*, and a *Mask* or rôle as
unlike as possible to his natural ego or *Will*, and leaves him to im-
provise through his *Creative Mind* the dialogue and details of the
plot.[15]

This is a much more "comic" description of creation than the
sexual description, which always bears elements of the tragic,
and we can see in the plays how each is appropriate in its
place. What we must grant at this stage of interpreting *A
Vision* is that the scheme of lunar phases, whatever historical
or religious symbols it may employ, is essentially individual,
personal, and mental. It is a pattern for the expression of
Yeats's interior evolution, and by extension, a pattern for that
same unfolding in his readers. As for his Daimon, it is not an
irresponsible mythical creation, but, on the contrary, it is
"the necessary angel of earth" who describes himself in Wallace Stevens' lines:

> Am I not,
> Myself, only half of a figure of a sort,
>
> A figure half seen, or seen for a moment, a man
> Of the mind, an apparition apparelled in
>
> Apparels of such lightest look that a turn
> Of my shoulder and quickly, too quickly, I am gone? [16]

The "sudden lightning" [17] of the Daimon's visit corresponds,
in Yeats, to that momentary apparition of Stevens' angelic
visitant.

2

The definitions which Yeats makes at the beginning of *A
Vision* become trying even to the devotee, but a good many
of them never turn up again, and therefore can be fairly
safely ignored. Some comment is needed, though, on the central distinction between antithetical and primary, repeated in
all of Yeats's work. There are many definitions of these terms

given by Yeats, of which the shortest is peculiarly Miltonic —
"The *primary* is that which serves, the *antithetical* is that
which creates." [18] This is more of an aphorism than a definition, and it may be clearer to give Yeats's earliest description
from the 1925 edition of *A Vision*: "All men are characterised
upon a first analysis by the proportion in which these two
characters or *Tinctures*, the objective or *primary*, the subjective or *antithetical*, are combined." [19] The primary is objective and also solar, the antithetical is subjective and also
lunar, and thus we attach the human character to the two
central astrological symbols of *A Vision*. It is evident where
Yeats's sympathies lie, since it is the light of the moon that he
glorifies and praises, not the sunlight. Actually the primary
world and primary man have only one function in his system
— to serve as the dark background upon which the antithetical
vision may shine more brightly. (There is a dramatic correlative in *The King of the Great Clock Tower*.)

The other definitions, the tables of rules, and the associations of terms which occupy pages 90 to 104 of *A Vision*
can best be invoked (those which are intelligible, at least)
when they become useful to this commentary. For the moment, they remain abstract skeletal statements, but in the detailed pages of "The Twenty-Eight Incarnations" some of
them begin to take on imaginative flesh.

Since the twenty-eight incarnations making up the Great
Wheel are the heart of *A Vision*, remaining almost unchanged
through all revisions, it is in considering them that the genetic
questions first arise. What possessed Yeats to undertake the
book; and to what disciplines should we have recourse to understand it? The first fact about the genesis of *A Vision* is
that it did not come only through Mrs. Yeats's automatic
writing. Four months before that memorable afternoon of
October 24, 1917, Yeats wrote to his father:

Much of your thought resembles mine in *An Alphabet* [later titled
Per Amica Silentia Lunae] but mine is part of a religious system more

or less logically worked out, a system which will I hope interest you as a form of poetry. I find the setting it all in order has helped my verse, has given me a new framework and new patterns. One goes on year after year gradually getting the disorder of one's mind in order and this is the real impulse to create.[20]

Clearly, then, *A Vision* was the product of a conscious "impulse to create" and was to be both a religious system and a form of poetry.

We recognize the familiar nineteenth-century identification of religion and art as we see Yeats following the more exotic of the two paths open to the unconventionally religious poets of his generation. They could either, like Baudelaire and his English imitators, create a Catholicism embodying new aesthetic perceptions and stressing the demonic; or they could, like Gérard de Nerval and Yeats, take all religion as their province and form an eclectic synthesis of myths from the East and West. Nineteenth-century studies in comparative religion made available so much poetic material that it is hard to overestimate the freedom of the imagination refreshed by floods of new mythological images. *The Golden Bough* was only the English representative of a movement embracing all of Western Europe, beginning in Germany, continuing in France and Italy, and taken up with enthusiasm in England. Yeats's debt to this mass of data appears in one of his early diagrams, described by Donald Pearce:

> In one of Yeats's unpublished notebooks for the years 1896–98 there is a drawing of a twenty-two petalled Cabbalistic rose, each petal marked with a Hebrew letter, and a Rosicross at the centre. Beside it is a corresponding geometrical diagram in which zodiacal and occult symbols have been substituted for the Hebrew letters. A schematic table follows in which Yeats correlated each of these symbols with: (a) classical deities, heroes and powers, (b) Celtic divinities and heroes, (c) forms of evocation and magical rites, (d) character and personality traits, (e) philosophic formulae concerning fate, death, birth, justice, etc., (f) elements and colors of magical and occult tradition, (g) symbolism of the Tarot cards. From this rose, whose numbered petals represented divinities and astrological and philosophical prin-

ciples, to the lunar system of gyres and cycles is surely a direct step. Essentially it is a step of abstraction and amplification. One may indeed see in the symbolic Rose of the Nineties the nucleus of *A Vision*.[21]

This diagram, drawn almost twenty years before *A Vision* was begun, bears witness to Yeats's magpie fascination with collecting into correspondences all sorts of symbols and myths. This is what lies at the heart of *A Vision*. A serious historian or philosopher could not have conceived of such a diagram; only to a poet could it make sense. In the light of nineteenth-century discoveries in several fields — anthropology, comparative religion, comparative literature — a total synthesis of human imaginative activity seemed for the first time possible. Universal histories like Herbert Spencer's are only another offshoot of the delighted imagination scanning new hemispheres. Theosophy and mystical orders, enormously attractive in the nineties, presented two seductive ways of penetrating the Eastern mysteries. Our present discomfort in imagining Yeats at Madame Blavatsky's arises from our feeling that there are more respectable ways of approaching the esoteric, forgetting that a concrete encounter is the only one likely to appeal to a mind peculiarly attuned to words and visual symbols. The poetry always precedes the system which, in Yeats's words, is its "prose backing." [22]

Yeats's choosing of a system came primarily from the impulse to participate in a more universal imaginative tradition, but it had religious roots as well. The bitterness against Huxley and Tyndall in the *Autobiographies* suggests that almost any flight to religion might have occurred in reaction to their hated scientific rationalism. *A Vision* is described in embryo, if one reads between the lines, in Yeats's description of what he substituted for "the summer dream beneath the tamarind tree": [23]

I am very religious, and deprived by Huxley and Tyndall, whom I detested, of the simple-minded religion of my childhood, I had made a new religion, almost an infallible church of poetic tradition, of a fardel of stories, and of personages, and of emotions, inseparable from their first expression, passed on from generation to generation by poets and painters with some help from philosophers and theologians . . . I had even created a dogma: "Because those imaginary people are created out of the deepest instinct of man, to be his measure and his norm, whatever I can imagine those mouths speaking may be the nearest I can go to truth." [24]

It is a very short step from this recollection of youth to the system of *A Vision*, dogma and all. *A Vision* is a natural, foreseeable, and inevitable production of Yeats's maturity, an integral part of his work — not an irresponsible compilation of his declining years.

The origins of *A Vision* are not only poetic and religious, but also psychological. Writing to Ethel Mannin in 1938, Yeats distinguished his "public philosophy" (*A Vision*) from his "private philosophy" which, he said, was "the material dealing with individual mind which came to me with that on which the mainly historical *Vision* is based." [25] This letter would seem to separate the historical dogma from the personal, but other statements indicate that one is only the type or figure for the other: "I begin to see things double," Yeats wrote in 1937, "doubled in history, world history, personal history." [26] Again and again we find the doctrines of *A Vision* springing out of Yeats's interior discoveries. Because he found other epochs more congenial than his own, he devised the doctrine of phases, and saw a disruption of interior being when a man finds himself out of phase.[27] He describes the genesis of the doctrine of Creative Mind and Mask with remarkable fidelity to his psychological deductions about himself:

As life goes on we discover that certain thoughts sustain us in defeat, or give us victory, whether over ourselves or others, and it is these thoughts, tested by passion, that we call convictions. Among subjective men (in all those, that is, who must spin a web out of their own bowels) the victory is an intellectual daily re-creation of all

that exterior fate snatches away, and so that fate's antithesis; while
what I have called "the Mask" is an emotional antithesis to all that
comes out of their internal nature. We begin to live when we have
conceived life as tragedy.[28]

In some ways, we could wish that Yeats had left his theories
in such plain language, but we forget the convenient short-
hand of symbols, and the consequent compression of *A Vision*
once the symbols are established. It is simply necessary to recall, when faced with a page of Yeats's pseudo history, that it
is pseudo history because it is metaphorical; that its genesis is
religious, poetic, psychological; and that it demands an interpretation based on one of these three areas rather than a reading based on a philosophy of history. Yeats's own analogies
with Spengler are misleading in the extreme, and are mostly
a case of his naïve delight in having apparently accomplished
something verifiable — which he never set out to do. If
Spengler had not published at just that crucial moment, we
should probably have heard a lot less about historical validity.
The fact was that Yeats was afraid in 1925 (as he was again in
1937) of the reaction of his acquaintances to the book: "Will
so-and-so think me a crazed fanatic?" [29] Any claim to intellectual respect was for Yeats, at that point, something to be
loudly voiced.

Magic, like esoteric doctrines and rituals, presents an odd
problem to the reader of *A Vision*. Yeats's defiant statement
to John O'Leary in 1892 was somewhat modified in later life,
but nonetheless it shows the central position of magic in
Yeats's early work:

Now as to Magic. It is surely absurd to hold me "weak" or otherwise because I chose to persist in a study which I decided deliberately
four or five years ago to make, next to my poetry, the most important
pursuit of my life . . . If a had not made magic my constant study
I could not have written a single word . . . It holds to my work the
same relation that the philosophy of Godwin held to the work of
Shelley.[30]

If we look at Yeats's essay on Shelley we find him refuting with indignation those critics who thought that *Prometheus Unbound* was Godwin's *Political Justice* put into rhyme,[31] but the precise relation of Godwin to Shelley is something Yeats himself never wishes to define.[32] We are warned by the essay not to make any too literal connection between systematic magic and Yeats's poetry, since the true function of magic is a suggestive one.

It is only by ancient symbols, by symbols that have numberless meanings beside the one or two the writer lays an emphasis upon, or the half-score he knows of, that any highly subjective art can escape from the barrenness and shallowness of a too conscious arrangement, into the abundance and depth of nature.[33]

This is what magic can do: it can give an extended control over the use of images, which is, after all, what any poet aims at. The only perennial philosophy, says Yeats, is one that has been made into poetry,[34] and magic is the wedding of the two. "I cannot now think symbols less than the greatest of all powers," Yeats writes, "whether they are used consciously by the masters of magic, or half unconsciously by their successors, the poet, the musician and the artist." [35] A symbolic system arising out of magical practice is simply an attempt to make conscious what had been formerly unconscious, and Yeats is the poet *par excellence* of the conscious nineteenth-century, envying the "unconscious" poet of an earlier day. His wishful thinking that invisible gates would open for him as for Blake and Swedenborg and Boehme no doubt helped to invite and welcome the voices of the mysterious instructors. From magic, Yeats took mainly the great concept of the *Anima Mundi* which, transfiguring as it does the scholarly idea of poetic tradition, makes that tradition a holy presence and provides for a new Urania. The visitations from the Daimon required an explanation, not simply out of curiosity, but out of devout gratitude:

Surely, at whatever risk, we must cry out that imagination is always seeking to remake the world according to the impulses and the patterns in that Great Mind, and that great Memory? Can there be anything so important as to cry out that what we call romance, poetry, intellectual beauty, is the only signal that the supreme Enchanter, or some one in His councils, is speaking of what has been, and shall be again, in the consummation of time? [36]

This call to a crusade ends the essay on magic, and makes unmistakably clear how deeply veined with the vocabulary of magic Yeats's theory of inspiration had become, so much so that it could scarcely exist without it. That sense of being a holy speaker, of descending from Mount Sinai with revelation on one's lips, was what Yeats looked for and found in the poets he admired, and it was that authority which he wanted his readers to sense in his own writing. In 1931, he acknowledged what he had done and for what reasons, and this statement, better than all the others, accounts for the genesis of his remarkable book:

I have really finished *A Vision* . . . I write very much for young men between twenty and thirty, as at that age, and younger, I wanted to feel that any poet I cared for — Shelley let us say — saw more than he told of, had in some sense seen into the mystery. I read more into certain poems than they contained, to satisfy my interest. The young men I write for may not read my *Vision* — they may care too much for poetry — but they will be pleased that it exists . . . I have constructed a myth, but then one can believe in a myth — one only assents to philosophy.[37]

Yeats's remark about belief embodies one of the new facts of psychology with which the Victorians and their successors had to make their peace. Newman, for instance, had come to the same conclusion as Yeats — "Many a man will live and die upon a dogma: no man will be a martyr for a conclusion." [38] If we treat the statements in *A Vision*, then, as assertions in mythical form of what we are to believe about poetry rather than as "philosophy," we will be reading them as Yeats intended them to be read, and using them somewhat as he used them himself, when he wrote of *A Vision*, "I am longing to put it out of reach that I may write the poetry it seems to have made possible." [39]

Writing on Poe's *Eureka*, Paul Valéry reflected on the literary form to which *A Vision*, as well as *Eureka*, belongs. Most of what I have said above is summed up in his definition of what he chose to call the Cosmogony:

> The Cosmogony is one of the oldest of all literary forms. It belongs to a department of literature remarkable for its persistence and astonishing in its variety . . . Just as tragedy borders on history and psychology, the cosmogonic form verges sometimes on religion, with which it is confused at many points, and sometimes on science, from which it is necessarily distinguished by the absence of experimental proof. It includes sacred books, admirable poems, outlandish narratives full of beauties and absurdities, and physico-mathematical researches often so profound as to be worthy of a less insignificant subject than the universe. But it is the glory of man, and something more than his glory, to waste his powers on the void. Often these crackbrained researches are the cause of unexpected discoveries. The rôle of the nonexistent exists; the function of the imaginary is real; and we learn from strict logic that *the false implies the true*. Thus it would seem that the history of thought can be summarized in these words: *It is absurd by what it seeks; great by what it finds*.[40]

I do not claim greatness for *A Vision*, but I do deny that it is absurd. Following Valéry's insight, we may find "The Twenty-Eight Incarnations" less of a puzzle and more of a "sacred book," deciding that it seems less important to reconcile its synoptic passages than to sense the revelation behind its gospel, a revelation which comes at Phase 15.

3

The Fifteenth Phase is the phase of the full moon, and the best way of defining it is to look at the texts which describe it, whether they occur in *A Vision* or in the poems. (For the time being, I will disregard the plays.) The phase absorbed Yeats's thought from 1914 on, turning up poetically for the first time in *The Wild Swans at Coole* (1919), appearing systematically in "The Phases of the Moon," and incidentally in several other poems. Although "The Phases of the Moon" shares the faults of most doctrinal poems — a certain predictability and monotony of progression — it comes to eloquence in speaking of Phase 15, in which

> All thought becomes an image and the soul
> Becomes a body: that body and that soul
> Too perfect at the full to lie in a cradle,
> Too lonely for the traffic of the world:
> Body and soul cast out and cast away
> Beyond the visible world.[41]

The Fifteenth Phase is a time of perpetual incarnation, says Yeats, when experience, "fed with light," is transmuted into image, and the inapprehensible into the visible. Whatever is poetically incarnated springs like Minerva full-grown: the image is not embryonic or unformed, but adult and solitary. Strangely enough, it is when thought becomes housed in a visible image that embarkation beyond the visible world takes place, since the visible image and the visible world cannot coexist. A species of death descends, so that death and incarnation are for a moment identified. The originating experience vanishes in the creation of the dream, as Yeats says in one of the essays:

It may have been his enemy or his love or his cause that set him dreaming, and certainly the phoenix can but open her young wings in a flaming nest; but all hate and hope vanishes in the dream, and if his mistress brag of the song or his enemy fear it, it is not that either has its praise or blame, but that the twigs of the holy nest are not easily set afire.[42]

The immolation of experience to image which is the characteristic "death" of Phase 15 is seen most clearly in the last plays.

Yeats describes the creatures of the full moon in "The Phases of the Moon":

When the moon's full those creatures of the full
Are met on the waste hills by countrymen
Who shudder and hurry by: body and soul
Estranged amid the strangeness of themselves,
Caught up in contemplation, the mind's eye
Fixed upon images that once were thought;
For separate, perfect and immovable
Images can break the solitude
Of lovely, satisfied, indifferent eyes.[43]

The eyes are those of the tranced figures of the Fifteenth Phase. In perfect ecstasy, they are inhumanly remote from earthly concerns, and the only things intruding upon their solitude are images, which embody the one aspect of mental activity not alien to their "lovely, satisfied, indifferent" state. "Nothing is apparent but dreaming *Will* and the Image that it dreams," [44] says Yeats in the prose description of the phase. Conflict has become superfluous, because Chance and Choice (or Body of Fate and Mask) are now one. Not only have image and event coincided; desire has become thought (as Will and Creative Mind become absorbed in each other). The mind no longer despairs at the lack of congruence, for as image meets experience in perfect appropriateness, the zodiac at last becomes a sphere.

When Yeats looks for analogies to the phase (or we should rather say, looks for the realities to which the phase is analogous) he finds two — love and art. Love is perhaps the perfect analogy theoretically, but art provides the only experience in which a true union actually occurs. The converging of will and thought, Yeats continues, can best be described by adjectives like "musical" and "sensuous," and finally he finds the terms of the analogy: "Thought has been pursued, not as a means but as an end — the poem, the painting, the reverie has been sufficient of itself." [45] This is the central sentence in all the descriptions of the Fifteenth Phase, and from it we are justified in assuming that the mental states which Yeats describes so minutely in *A Vision* are primarily the mental states attendant upon aesthetic activity — reverie ending in creation. The heightened pitch reached by the artist exceeds in its success all other human ecstasies.

The earlier phases preceding the Fifteenth are the approach to artistic creation: "Since Phase 12 the *Creative Mind* . . . has more and more confined its contemplation of actual things to those that resemble images of the mind desired by the *Will*. The being has selected, moulded and remoulded, narrowed its circle of living, been more and more the artist." [46] This narrowing of the heterogeneous physical world into a small and intense collection of obsessive images is characteristic of many artists, whether they deal with a pictorial world or a verbal one, but Yeats's later work, because of such narrowing, can seem thin to a reader ignorant of the converging and compressing of symbolic themes. The detail of life has been pared away from the poetic skeleton. Though this may make for good poetry, it often makes for bad drama, and the limitations of Yeats's theory of creation appear most inescapably in the late plays.

The final portion of Yeats's analysis of the Fifteenth Phase is beautiful but obscure. It scrupulously refuses to subside into easy total analogies with love or death, but borrows some elements from each, as Yeats gives a symbolic view of the aesthetic process. The analogy of love and sexual intercourse to the creation of images has appeared before in the poetry, notably in "Solomon and the Witch." The symbol is sexual intercourse; the aim, perfect union; the result, failure; and the last line, cried out by Sheba, is "O! Solomon! let us try again." The attempt is made "under the wild moon" (which locates the poem in, or near, Phase 15) and if it is successful, it will bring back Eden in eternity. But the attempt fails, precisely because imagination and reality fail to coincide:

> 'Maybe the bride-bed brings despair,
> For each an imagined image brings
> And finds a real image there;

> Yet the world ends when these two things,
> Though several, are a single light.'

Sheba replies that the world has not ended, and Solomon's explanation describes, if anything, artistic failure:

> 'Maybe an image is too strong
> Or maybe is not strong enough.' [47]

Since the perfect fusion of the imagined and the real has not been accomplished, "all that the brigand apple brought" is still with us; but the fact that the lovers will try again is the affirmation of the poem, and is as well an affirmation about poetic effort.

There is yet another perspective possible. If the perfect congruence between imagination and reality were to occur, and the world were to end, love would cease to exist — and for Yeats, that is an unthinkable conclusion. The notion of love implies two separate persons, and if Solomon and Sheba were not distinct, the dialogue, and therefore the poem, would be impossible. Therefore Yeats insists on the separation of reality and image in Phase 15, to show that creative activity exists only as an attempt to bridge the gap. "Now contemplation and desire, united into one, inhabit a world where every beloved image has bodily form, and every bodily form is loved. This love knows nothing of desire, for desire implies effort, and though there is still separation from the loved object, love accepts the separation as necessary to its own existence." [48] "The tragedy of sexual intercourse," said Yeats in a much-quoted remark, "is the perpetual virginity of the soul," [49] but in the Fifteenth Phase that perpetual virginity is accepted as necessary. (This is partially the point of "Leda and the Swan" as we shall see in Chapter V.) The poet, then, tries endlessly for the perfect fusion of reality and image, but at the same time sees their individual recalcitrance as the condition for creation and so accepts it.

Besides the image of intercourse, Yeats uses as a symbol

for the Fifteenth Phase the image of Paradise, somewhat oc-
cluded, but still unmistakable. As we might expect in *A Vision*,
the paradise has scholastic overtones, and the beatific vision
experienced in Phase 15 is an intellectual rather than a sensuous one. On the other hand, it differs from the traditional
heavenly vision in being directed inward rather than outward:
"All that the being has experienced as thought is visible to its
eyes as a whole, and in this way it perceives, not as they are
to others, but according to its own perception, all orders of
existence." Dante too saw, in the *Commedia*, all orders of
existence, but he saw them in a framework of scholastic realism, so that those orders appear to have an autonomous existence. For Yeats, images are impersonal, but at the same time
strongly individual. It is a "subjective" beatific vision which he
describes, and in fact the only justification for calling it a
"beatific" vision at all is for the useful connotation of total
comprehension which the phrase possesses. The beatific vision
of Phase 15 is, like its religious counterpart, at once simulta-
neous and whole: that is, in it all experience is integrated,
everything finds its place. But it has one startling difference
from the perfect joy of the traditional ecstasy. It involves
somehow a process of purgation, a "time of pain, a passage
through a vision, where evil reveals itself in its final meaning."
The hint becomes more explicit in Book III, when Yeats clarifies his ideas of purgation, but like the identification of death
and resurrection, the connection between perfect beauty and
a purgative process is a central theme in Yeats.

   In the phase of perfect beauty, not only are the warring
faculties of the soul at peace with each other, but the body
is transfigured as well, changed into "that body which the
soul will permanently inhabit, when all its phases have been
repeated." [50] This transfigured body presents one of the real
difficulties in the nonesoteric interpretation of *A Vision*, for
although aesthetic explanations spring to the mind easily
enough when Yeats is discussing immaterial "Faculties" (Will,

Mask, and so on), the Celestial Body is less easy to see symbolically. Although Yeats denied knowing anything about "The Four Principles" (irritatingly similar to the Four Faculties) when he wrote "The Great Wheel," and only defines them in Book II of *A Vision*, he evidently had the terms in mind somehow, since Celestial Body is one of the four. When he eventually arrives at defining it, it appears that the Celestial Body is nothing other than "the Divine Ideas in their unity," "all other Daimons," and "intellectual necessity." It is the last because it is no longer subject to intellectual contingencies of the phenomenal world — time and space, cause and effect; it is the two former because through it the spirit participates in the life of other spirits, other Daimons. Though in this life knowledge of others is only through the bodily senses, in the "supernatural" life of Phase 15, one Daimon knows another without the barriers of the mental categories. This is, in the last analysis, a way of saying that in poetic activity, during the moments of creation, the poet sees objects and relationships in a less cluttered way; they are stripped down to essentials, the archetypes disclose themselves, the universals emerge. Moreover, the poet becomes what he contemplates: "what the *Spirit* knows becomes a part of itself." [51] Hopkins would say that the spirit was feeling the instress of inscape; Yeats chooses to say that one Daimon knows another, and for a moment shares its being.

4

It is striking to see, beneath the elaborateness of Book I, a rather simple plan, in which Phase 15 is evidently the keystone. The book is pyramid-shaped, with everything before Phase 15 leading up to that illumination, and everything after it declining from it. Just as measurement of the waxing and waning of the moon can only be determined by reference to the moon at the full, so the other phases are determined by their approximation to Phase 15, the standard of perfection. Yeats's classification becomes nearly a new morality, with a sinless prototype and varying degrees of approach to that prototype, as we are shown a whole and perfect being surrounded by a group of incomplete and imperfect aspirants to his perfection. The wording of the descriptions of the early phases leaves no doubt that those phases are stages in progress toward Phase 15, and that subjectivity and personality are the great goals. However, there are hindrances. Of Phase 11, for instance, Yeats writes:

> While Phase 9 was kept from its subjectivity by personal relations, by sensuality, by various kinds of grossness, and Phase 10 by associations of men for practical purposes . . . Phase 11 is impeded by the excitement of conviction, by the contagion of organized belief, or by its interest in organization for its own sake.[52]

"Kept from," "impeded" — the vocabulary shows the direction of the thought. Everything which keeps us from Phase 15 is an obstacle, whether it is the "dangerous narcotic or intoxicant" of facts at Phase 12, or the "intoxication or narcotic" of the Body of Fate at Phase 14. The obstacles, in Yeats's terms, blunt the sensibility, the intellect, and the perception, which must be at their most acute to achieve the final union of objectivity and subjectivity at the Fifteenth Phase.

In the same way, the descriptions of the phases after Phase 15 show a steady decline, and the vocabulary is usually pejorative: the man of Phase 16 has "an aimless illusionary inner excitement"; the Daimonic man of Phase 17 has a will which is in fragments; the man of Phase 18 is distracted by action; and so on. By the accretion of recurrent descriptive phrases the "lost unity of Being" grows to something far greater than merely one of twenty-eight phases, and begins to take on the quality of a lost Paradise. It is inevitably described in nostalgic terms. From the original unity, Faculties begin to separate, remain "neighbors and kin" for some time, and finally are entirely diverse, until a code of personal conduct or the "arrogance of belief" takes complete command, all other faculties having been exhausted.

If, as we have said above, Phase 15 is the phase of Art, all artists, one would think, should be of this phase. This is not so — in fact, the being of Phase 15 is not a human incarnation. Phase 15 is, in life, a transitory state experienced by the artist in the moment of illumination and creation (and by the lover and saint in sexual and religious ecstasy). From this momentary joy and knowledge in Phase 15, the artist must return to the ordinary world, for "In all great poetical styles there is saint or hero, but when it is all over Dante can return to his chambering and Shakespeare to his 'pottle pot.' They sought no impossible perfection but when they handled paper or parchment." The moment of seeking impossible perfection, the moment of Phase 15, is the only moment worth living for, in Yeats's scheme of life. It is the source of the joy which gives the "new earth and new heaven" of Coleridge, and it must always be the final desire of poets. "I think," says Yeats, "that we who are poets and artists, not being permitted to shoot beyond the tangible, must go from desire to weariness and so to desire again, and live but for the moment when vision comes to our weariness like terrible lightning." [53] In this sentence from *Per Amica Silentia Lunae* Yeats gives his four central ideas concerning poetic inspiration. First, it takes place essentially in a heightened moment; second, the moment is a period in a cyclical process; third, it is a moment of illumination, when the poet is struck by an insight so clarifying that it appears as a bolt of lightning, or as a flooding of the whole being with light; and fourth, the vision comes from outside the poet, the thunderbolt from the hand of Jove. These are, needless to say, ideas and images common in Yeats's masters, Blake and Shelley, and are standard enough romantic equipment. Only Yeats's use of them in his "system" is distinctive.

The outside agent of ecstasy can be, Yeats says, any one of many things — but when he is constrained to give an example, only poetry will serve, since it is at once the cause and effect of the intensest joy and knowledge. "At certain moments I become happy," he writes, and goes on to admit,

"most commonly when at hazard I have opened some book of
verse . . . Perhaps I am sitting in some crowded restaurant,
the open book beside me, or closed, my excitement having
overbrimmed the page . . . It seems as if the vehicle had suddenly grown pure and far extended and . . . luminous." [54]
The same experience, with the same open book as the cause,
yielded the fourth section of "Vacillation":

> While on the shop and street I gazed
> My body of a sudden blazed;
> And twenty minutes more or less
> It seemed, so great my happiness,
> That I was blessèd and could bless.[55]

Poetry and Phase 15, then, are intimately related in Yeats's
mind, so much so that Phase 15 was his major symbol for the
creative moment. For him, *A Vision* was principally the poet's
vision, and although he pays token tribute to the lover, the
saint, and the hero, their ecstasy is usually described to illustrate the heightened apprehension of the poet. This was the
vision Yeats knew from his own experience and the one he
could write about with most authority.

This point raises the central issue: what, in effect, *A Vision*
is all about. As a hypothesis, I would say that, like a good number of the plays, it is primarily about poetry, about the nature
and value of symbolism in poetry, about what poetry should
include, about the relationship between the poet and his Muse,
about how the Muse operates, and finally about literary history. It is not on the surface a book about poetry, and Yeats
never said that it was: the references to poetry in it are often
brought forward almost apologetically, while references to
mysticism and esoterica are paraded in every chapter. But
there are indications that the mysticism and esoterica are the
means of expression, rather than the end of *A Vision*, one
proof of this being the names cited in Book I to exemplify the
twenty-eight phases. About two thirds of all the examples
Yeats chooses to give are literary men; of these, about two

thirds are poets. The twenty-eight phases become virtually, in the course of the book, a scheme of literary history, bizarre perhaps, but literary history all the same — and most especially, poetic literary history.

If Book I is poetic literary history, Book II (with its pages on Daimons, antinomies, states of light, and the reworking of images) is essentially concerned with the process of poetic creation; and Book V, "Dove or Swan," is about the Muse of the arts. Book IV presents, in its concept of the Magnus Annus, the necessary world view for the imaginative shaping of history, and Book III, in its discussion of the Purgatorial State, is an elaborate analysis of poetic activity, developing hints from Book I. There are many other things in these books of *A Vision*, but the central spindle of each book seems to be a poetic one, around which Yeats winds endless relevant and irrelevant threads. "We have come to give you metaphors for poetry," said Yeats's instructors, and their statement is generally interpreted to mean that *A Vision* contained metaphors (such as gyres) that could be used in a poetic way. A truer interpretation might be to say that all of *A Vision* is a series of metaphorical statements about poetry, that *A Vision* is the poet's vision in a metaphorical disguise.

5

The scheme of literary history in *A Vision* demands our first attention. It is eclectic and obstinate, but it suggests Yeats's submerged literary affinities and prejudices. No names are given as examples of the first five phases, and we may assume, given Yeats's encyclopedic tendencies at this stage in his writing, that there are no names because he could not think of any. What is both curious and interesting about the descriptions of these five phases (with the exception, of course, of Phase 1, for which there is no human incarnation) is the fact that Yeats substituted for the concrete example a view of the phase as seen by a poet; that is, he explained what the phase means as a poetic image, what poetical purpose it can serve. What happens, in each case, is that the figure representing the phase seen as a Mask by a poet of the opposite phase. In Phase 2, the incarnation of the phase is "a personification or summing up of all natural life" — a Bacchic figure.

> Seen by those lyrical poets who draw their *Masks* from early phases, the man of Phase 2 is transfigured. Weary of an energy that defines and judges, weary of intellectual self-expression, they desire some "concealment," some transcendent intoxication. The bodily instincts, subjectively perceived, become the cup wreathed in ivy.[56]

It is hardly necessary to point out that Yeats is one of the "lyrical poets who draw their Masks from early phases" (since he placed himself in Phase 17, his Mask is at Phase 3), and that his own search for Dionysus is revealed in this description. The process continues in the analysis of Phase 3, the pastoral phase of "perfect bodily sanity":

> Seen by lyrical poets, of whom so many have belonged to the fantastic Phase 17, the man of this phase becomes an Image where simplicity and intensity are united, he seems to move among yellowing corn or under overhanging grapes. He gave to Landor his shepherds and hamadryads, to Shelley his wandering lovers and sages, and to Theocritus all his flocks and pastures; and of what else did Bembo think when he cried, "Would that I were a shepherd that I might look daily down upon Urbino"? [57]

Phase 4, whose incarnation embodies "the wisdom in instinct" becomes an "image of peace" to Browning (who presumably was "worn out by a wisdom held with labour and uncertainty"). As for the figure of Phase 5, embodying the mastery of nature, "seen by a poet of the opposite phase, by a man hiding fading emotion under broken emphasis, he is Byron's Don Juan or his Giaour." [58]

So far, then, *A Vision* seems to be a classification of poetic archetypes, including the Satyr, the Shepherd, the Rural Sage, and the Don Juan — all available personae for the poets who cluster around the charmed Phase 17. It should be noticed, too, that the relation of each phase to the lyrical poet is made at the close of the description of the phase, in the climax of each analysis. This is anything but accidental. The description exists only as a vehicle, really, for the final poetic statement.

Once we arrive at Phase 6, we hear no more about how lyrical poets see the phase. From now on, we find writers exemplifying the phases, and so each phase can be discussed in itself, not as an object of vision. Phases 6 through 12 are in general an uninteresting part of *A Vision*: they have neither the appeal to Yeats of being his own Mask (or close to it) nor the attractiveness of being phases adjoining his own Phase 17. He gets over them cursorily, pausing from time to time for some literary invective.

Walt Whitman, the example of Phase 6, "created an Image of vague, half-civilised man, all his thought and impulse a product of democratic bonhomie, of schools, of colleges, of public discussion." Antipathetic as the embracing of multitudes was to Yeats, it was a lesser literary offense than Carlyle's "vast popular rhetoric" which Yeats condemned as what we would today call overcompensation for sexual impotence. Yeats reserves his most bitter gibe for the last sentence on Carlyle: "Sexual impotence had doubtless . . . strengthened the False *Mask*, yet one doubts if any mere plaster of ant's eggs could have helped where there was so great insincerity." [59] Phases 8 and 9 are simply fillers without examples (though Yeats, abandoning the world of men, tentatively cites Dostoevsky's Idiot for Phase 8) to get us on to Phase 10. This is the phase of the Iconoclast, for which Parnell is the historical example and Faustus the literary one. The alliance of Parnell with Faustus is not so startling as it might appear when we recall certain nationalist Irish views — Maud Gonne's, for instance — of Parnell's unsuccessful struggle for parliamentary Home Rule, and his subsequent tragic death.

With Phases 11 and 12, we come to what could be called

poètes manqués, the "half-solitaries who cannot or will not abandon the world for the isolation of the creative life." We have seen already how Yeats speaks of the men of these phases as being "impeded" from subjectivity by one or the other factor, whether in Phase 11 (Spinoza) by "the contagion of organised belief . . . some bundle of mathematical formulae" [60] or in Phase 12 (Nietzsche is named but not introduced into the description) by a tendency to self-exaggeration. In both cases the equilibrium between inner and outer world is disturbed.

Finally, in Phase 13, Yeats arrives at personalities more amenable to his scheme, and from Phases 13 through 25, we are treated to a display of Yeats's opinions on literary men in general and Irish writers in particular, beginning with Baudelaire and Ernest Dowson, and ending with Cardinal Newman and A.E. What saves this portion of *A Vision* from being merely a collection of spiteful, witty, and sometimes profound personal observations is Yeats's constant attention to poetic creation. The personal asides are usually there to help shape the theory, not as ends in themselves.

According to Yeats, perfect imaginative experience (Phase 15) can be approached in one of two ways, either hyperaesthetically or coldly. The "aesthetes" in his scheme precede the full of the moon, and the sterner "cold" poets follow it. Yeats had views on some poets, Baudelaire and Keats for instance, that seem to us mistaken: he saw them more as "feminine" geniuses than as spirits capable of "strong lines," and he groups them with men like Beardsley and Dowson who, to us, appear to be of a lesser kind altogether. But we see from Yeats's comments something perhaps more interesting than a fair estimate — we see what Yeats perceived in those artists. In Baudelaire, for instance, he saw (through his bad French) only those qualities which Baudelaire's English imitators had seized on — the dandyism, the morbidity, the sensational images — ignoring the gulfs of sensibility which separate Baudelaire from Dowson. Yeats's portrait of Keats outside the sweet-shop window is almost too well known, but our indignation on reading "in Keats . . . intellectual curiosity is at its weakest" [61] is mitigated when we recall that literary parricide is a common enough occurrence. Yeats had worked hard and long to shake off the Keatsian sweetness.

Once we grant Yeats his literary prejudices, *A Vision* appears as the literary dramatization of the choice he felt called upon to make in shaping his poetry — the choice, in fact, which the 1890's forced upon English poetry — whether to follow the Romantic sensibility into more and more morbid bypaths or to take an entirely new approach to poetic language:

> Shakespearean fish swam the sea, far away from land;
> Romantic fish swam in nets coming to the hand;
> What are all those fish that lie gasping on the strand? [62]

It was not enough to be one of "the last romantics," and Yeats placed himself on the further side of the full moon, leaving behind the enthusiasms of his early days. But in spite of his final disaffection, his comments on the decadents are acute ones. Having known Lionel Johnson, Beardsley, and Dowson, whose divided personalities took refuge alternately in drink and theology, in prostitutes and Catholicism, he realizes that the Mask of the Sensuous Man is located "at the phase of the Saint, a virginal purity of emotion." As usual, though the classification is general, the references are specifically to poetic activity. "There is almost always," Yeats writes of the decadents, "a preoccupation with those metaphors and symbols and mythological images through which we define whatever seems most strange or most morbid." Phase 13 is also the phase of *l'art pour l'art* (anglicized by Yeats into "expression for expression's sake") [63] which corresponds in the antithetical life, says Yeats, to sanctity in the primary. In such phrases, affection for the early springs of his poetry shows itself in a certain regret that the naïveté of his predecessors is no longer possible.

Phase 14, like Phase 13, embodies a too precious approach to art; but it demands special attention, because in it the two strands of *A Vision* finally converge: the first is the poetic Archetype or Image, the second is the figure of the Poet. In Phase 14 we have both at once — Helen of Troy and Keats. It is hardly necessary to say that for Yeats Helen represents perfect human beauty (the best source of the poetic archetype); and in spite of what we may think a slighting of Keats, it is no small tribute to him that he, with William Blake at Phase 16, guards the portals of the Fifteenth Phase. The "essential honey" of things pervades Phase 14, and the images chosen by its poets seem studied for their own sake. For the first time, the symbol of the dance appears in *A Vision*, linking this phase with all those lyric and dramatic works of Yeats in which a dance is the prelude to the enlightenment symbolized by the Fifteenth Phase. The images "float as in serene air, or lie hidden in some valley, and if they move it is to music that returns always to the same note, or in a dance that so returns into itself that they seem immortal." The images are powerful because traditional: Yeats remarks of Keats that "there is scarcely an image, where his poetry is at its best, whose subjectivity has not been heightened by its use in many great poets, painters, sculptors, artificers." The soul's preoccupation with itself as subject is clearly an aspect of the phase, since "the being has almost reached the end of that elaboration of itself . . . All is reverie." [64] Wordsworth, as well as Keats, is of this phase, and the shell of *The Prelude* is pre-eminently the symbol of the self-absorbed poetry natural to a phase of increased subjectivity. "Poetry is the subject of the poem" says Wallace Stevens, in the logical extension of the Wordsworthian attitude. That is, of course, why the dance appears in this description. It, more than any other art, is its own subject, at least in its purest state when we cannot tell the dancer from the dance. "It was the dream itself enchanted me," says Yeats, as the images, and not their referents, become the true subject of the poem.

If we pass for a moment from the Poet to the Image, we may see (what will be made even more evident in the plays) how a beautiful woman is for Yeats the most satisfactory symbol of all images of desire. Yeats's Helen does not seem to be the ultimately desirable woman: she is not accessible, responsive, human, but rather remote, aloof, without desire, self-sufficient. It is true enough in one sense to say that Yeats is simply describing Maud Gonne (or rather his idea of Maud Gonne, because she comes alive quite differently in the pages of her autobiography) but we must, all through *A Vision*, go beyond biography (and even beyond the nineties' conception of the *femme fatale*) to relate the images of the system to the images of the poetry. It is remarkable the way the two blend into each other. For instance, the words Yeats uses to describe the images of desire sought during the Fourteenth Phase could equally be used of one of the Women of the Sidhe, of Helen, or of the Dancer in the poems: "They float as in serene air, or lie hidden in some valley, and if they move it is to music that returns always to the same note, or in a dance that so returns into itself that they seem immortal." [65] This description of the poetic image shows how closely woman and the poetic image are identified and share each other's qualities, becoming, like woman and Daimon, reciprocal symbols. This is as good a place as any to examine Yeats's idea of the image, and in what follows, I borrow freely from terms which Yeats applies to Helen of Troy, since she incarnates the image in its perfection.

The image has a double life: the life drawn from the thing it represents and the life drawn from its poetic context (which includes its psychological, personal, and mythical qualities as well as its strictly literary ones). It is, to use Yeats's terminol-

ogy, both primary and antithetical, and represents, when perfect, the fusion of both aspects into one. Since the image is
a concrete thing, it cannot inhabit Phase 15 ("a supernatural
condition") but it does come closest of all concrete things
to that "condition of fire." In Phases 14 and 16, and especially
in the symbol of Helen, the image is described in metaphorical
terms: "Helen was of the phase; and she comes before the
mind's eye elaborating a delicate personal discipline, as though
she would make her whole life an image of a unified *antithetical* energy. While seeming an image of softness and quiet,
she draws perpetually upon glass with a diamond." The image,
while seeming transitory and mute, like the physical world,
nevertheless in a mysterious way masters creation and becomes, like the words upon the windowpane etched in diamond, an immortal thing. Over and over Yeats stresses the
self-containment of his symbol, which "understands nothing
yet seems to understand everything; already serves nothing,
while alone seeming of service." The paradoxical nature of
the completed image which, "expressionless, expresses God"
comes from its apparent uselessness, the superfluous quality
of all art. Of Helen, Yeats says, "the Fool's *Mask* is her chosen
motley," and of the Fool we read, "His thoughts are an aimless reverie; his acts are aimless like his thoughts; and it is in
this aimlessness that he finds his joy." This is the aimlessness
of art, and we find the idea continued in some sense in Phase
15, where the reverie of creation is directed to no end, but is
"sufficient of itself." [66]

The cruel and absorbing nature of the image, its despotic
claim on the poet, are symbolized in the image of Helen and
of women like her. The image demands the immolation of
personal experience, and once the sacrifice is made, seems
unconscious of what devotion it has demanded. Yeats's description of the Image-Muse, though phrased in the terminology of *A Vision*, has its origin in his early speculations about
the Irish fairy Muse, the Lianhaun shee, of whom he wrote in

one of the headnotes for *Irish Fairy and Folk Tales*: "The Lianhaun shee lives upon the vitals of its chosen, and they waste and die. She is of the dreadful solitary fairies. To her have belonged the greatest of the Irish poets, from Oisin down to the last century." We can assume that Yeats thought of himself as belonging to this Vampire-Muse, and she colors all his subsequent writing about the relation of poet to Muse. Even in a milder mood, the Muse or Image remains indifferent to adoration. Yeats offers the "Eternal Idol" of Rodin as an example — "that kneeling man with hands clasped behind his back in humble adoration, kissing a young girl a little below the breast, while she gazes down, without comprehending, under her half-closed eyelids." Her business is to be engaged in never ending contemplation of herself, the *"antithetical* self-absorbing dream."⁶⁷

The women of Phase 16, on the further side of the full moon, resemble Helen in their sovereignty, and there is a side glance in Yeats's description of them toward the Virgilian and Spenserian "O dea certe": "They walk like queens, and seem to carry upon their backs a quiver of arrows, but they are gentle only to those whom they have chosen or subdued." The "radiant intensity" of image and Muse fuse in these descriptions. Helen is at once the inspirer of epic and the image celebrated in the epic; the Muse is at once the initiator of the poem and the incarnation which, Phoenix-like, renews itself in the image. Yeats's final remark about these Muse-like women is particularly relevant to some of the plays (especially *The Player Queen, The King of the Great Clock Tower, A Full Moon in March,* and *The Herne's Egg*): "Boundless in generosity, and in illusion, they will give themselves to a beggar because he resembles a religious picture and be faithful all their lives, or if they take another turn and choose a dozen lovers, die convinced that none but the first or last has ever touched their lips, for they are of those whose 'virginity renews itself like the moon.' "⁶⁸ We are reminded of Attracta's assertions of virginity in *The Herne's Egg*, and of the Queen in the dance plays who gives herself to a Stroller or a Swineherd. Capricious and yet generous, but in the end consuming those who have loved them, these are not so much human women as allegorical figures. What use Yeats made of them poetically will be seen later.

Phases 16 through 25 present to us the second possible approach to poetic activity, different from the approach of Dowson, Baudelaire, and Keats. The waning of the moon represents, we must recall, the approach to objectivity, to a public rather than a private morality, and to violence. Hate and rage appear on the scene as possible poetic emotions, and we realize that we are nearing Yeats's own position on the Wheel. He is preceded by his master, Blake, the Positive Man, whose Creative Mind (accurately stated to be Vehemence) reacts against the "still trance" of Phase 15 by creating as untrancelike a state as possible, surrounding itself by a proliferation of myth, a "scattering," a "rushing out into the disordered and unbounded." Yeats's opposition to the intense fineness of concentration practiced by the aesthetes is reflected in his praise of Blake and other writers of this phase, and some of his remarks about them are applicable to his own work: "There is always an element of frenzy, and almost always a delight in certain glowing or shining images of concentrated force: in the smith's forge; in the heart; . . . in some symbolical representation of the sexual organs; for the being must brag of its triumph over its own incoherence." [69] We recall the golden smithies of the Emperor as well as Los's forge, and the Songs from "The Three Bushes" as well as Blake's world of Beulah.

Yeats seems, at first, to belong far more to Phase 16 than to the following phase (where he has for company the unlikely trio of Dante, Shelley, and Landor), but when we call to mind Yeats's wayward views of those three poets (especial-

ly of Dante) we realize that Yeats is putting himself where he
would like to be rather than where we might incline to place
him. Landor as Daimonic Man is simply funny, until we remember biographical anecdotes of his violence of action, and
realize how this attracted the dreamy Yeats, forced into action by his passion for Maud Gonne. Shelley presented to
Yeats an even more congenial self-image, and if we substitute
lectures on a national literature for pamphlets on Godwinism
there is a tolerable biographical parallel, especially if we recall
as well Shelley's ill-fated attempts to convert the Dublin Irish
to atheism. Dante presents a more difficult problem. If we try
to reconstruct the personal affinities Yeats felt for Dante, we
suspect that the primary one was caused by the figure of Beatrice, whom Yeats allied with Helen of Troy (and Maud
Gonne) as a symbol of the poetic Image. "Guardami ben:
ben son, ben son Beatrice" [70] — the line represents the most
famous confrontation of poet and image of desire in all Western literature. Such an event belonged in Yeats's mental history and so, regardless of literary similarities, he put it there.
He liked to think of his system as analogous to Dante's, but if
he had not invented the similarity it is unlikely that critics
would have thought of it.

It is in the description of Phase 17, however odd its examples
may seem to us, that we find Yeats's analysis of his own artistic activity, and for that reason the phase is interesting. The
poet, Yeats says in words which have become famous, assumes
a mask (a *persona* or attitude) and seeks an Image — "Shelley's Venus Urania, Dante's Beatrice, or even the Great Yellow Rose of the *Paradiso*." Any attempt at purely intellectual
synthesis at this phase is doomed to fail, because synthesis can
come about only through images, not through ideas. This
statement in itself should have warned off the critics who are
disappointed in *A Vision* as intellectual synthesis.

In these antithetical phases, Yeats continues, the intellect is
better described as the imagination [71] — and he continues, in

a passage which is absorbing once we get through the barbaric terminology, to show how the modern poet copes with
his situation. The Body of Fate, or situation in which the
poet finds himself, is one of Loss (or tragedy), but out of
it he must find "the shaping joy" which only the imagination
can confer. He must realize, in fact, that loss is somehow gain.
He does this by substituting for the Image that has been
snatched away, another Image — once again, we see the
Phoenix perpetually renewing itself. The point Yeats is making is that the compensatory imagination descends to work
its healing power upon the occasion of loss, so that the creative
moment of greatest joy coincides with the moment of depriva-
tion. (The nearest analogies outside of Yeats are Wordsworth's passage on the Simplon Pass in the sixth book of *The
Prelude*, and Wallace Stevens' descriptions of the Northern
Lights in "The Auroras of Autumn.") [72]

Curiously, Yeats chooses at this point to bring in a phrase
we do not associate characteristically with him: "the Vision
of Evil." [73] He reproves Shelley for lacking it, praises it in
Dante, and admits a qualified version of it in Landor; we are
left to draw our own conclusions about its presence or ab-
sence in himself. Certainly, if we accept his definition of the
Vision of Evil — to "conceive of the world as a continual
conflict" [74] — it is present in his own verse; but that is hardly
what is usually conveyed by the phrase. Of human bonds to
the earth as well as to the heavens Yeats was well aware, but
the Infernos of both Dante and Blake formed no part of his
cosmology.

There are moments of skepticism in which the critic of *A
Vision* decides that the only reason Yeats had for assigning
any person to any phase was pure caprice, and that Alice's
Wonderland was a paradise of sense compared with the world
of the gyres. From Phases 18 through 25 we find, scattered in
no reasonable order, artists from Shakespeare to Synge, from

Goethe to Dostoevsky. Why, we are tempted to ask in despair, should Flaubert, Herbert Spencer, Swedenborg, Dostoevsky, and Darwin inhabit all together one of these heavenly mansions? Such a grotesque menagerie almost defeats the imagination, and it is not my intention to pursue the vagaries of Yeats's intellect to their ultimate conclusions. Nevertheless, simply to defend Yeats against accusations of charlatanism, it must be said that his arrangements are not quite so lunatic as they appear on the surface. They are not defensible as anything beyond "stylistic arrangements of experience," but as that, they are often quite remarkable.

In Matthew Arnold, for instance, Yeats saw a poet who had succumbed to the fatal temptation of action, who in fact found self-definition possible only by action, not by "the dialogue of the mind with itself." Sentimentality in social action (a danger Arnold did not escape); the substitution of learning for desire; and finally, the tragic choice to "love what disillusionment gave" rather than what the ideal had promised — all of these marked in Arnold's life a poetic path which Yeats chose not to follow. When we consider all the fruitless and perishable work of Arnold's later years, all the Biblical readings ending only in equivocation and palliation, we find ourselves agreeing with Yeats that Arnold was a nightingale who refused to be impaled upon the thorn.[75] Still, the fact that Arnold is placed next to Yeats on the further side of the full moon represents Yeats's admiration for Arnold's sense of the dilemma of the modern poet. What Arnold tried to find by using the legends of Sohrab and Rustum, Tristan, and Baldur — some exterior center of gravity for his poetry — Yeats was to attempt by means of Irish myths. Any effort to avoid the faintness of aestheticism won Yeats's approval, and therefore Byron and Browning, with their various types of energy, appear as well on the "cold" side of the moon. Oscar Wilde's deliberate gaiety and insolence win him a place with Byron, not so strange a coupling as it might seem considering the double-sidedness of both men, the assuming in each of an extremely artificial Mask.

Special mention should be made of the two dramatists whom Yeats chooses as examples of these later phases, Shakespeare and Synge. One represents to Yeats the peak of Western drama, the other points the path that modern drama should follow, we are told, in order to regain its artistic nobility. Shakespeare is what Yeats chooses to call the Concrete Man, who saves himself from the fragmentation of experience by the unity of the creative act:

> He no longer seeks to unify what is broken through conviction, by imposing those very convictions upon himself and others, but by projecting a dramatisation or many dramatisations. He can create, just in that degree in which he can see these dramatisations as separate from himself, and yet as an epitome of his whole nature.[76]

It is by preserving the delicate balance between creative intuition and factual reality that drama exists at all. While it provides a more objective means than the lyric for the expression of the poet's nature, it at the same time serves as a receptacle for his disturbing awareness of the multiplicity of creation. To write drama is to master the world by incorporating it, through the act of creative domination, into one's intuitions, and the act is most useful when it is no longer possible to master the world by a belief. Things in themselves can lose their alien quality only by one of those two means, and by inviting the entire concrete world to enter into the world of vision, the dramatist transforms the one into the other. At Phase 20, the phase of Shakespeare, we enter the imaginary world "and become a portion of it; we study it, we amass historical evidence, and, that we may dominate it the more, drive out myth and symbol, and compel it to seem the real world where our lives are lived." [77] Looked at from Yeats's perspective, Shakespeare's history plays, for instance, take on new life and dimensions.

Shakespeare's method (literally, holding the mirror up

to nature) is no longer possible, as Yeats so often remarked regretfully; and we must turn to the description of Synge to discover the avenue Yeats thought was open to the modern dramatist. It is, we find, to be "receptive." Synge is characterized as the Receptive Man, and what this seems to mean to Yeats is that the modern writer of plays, unlike Shakespeare, cannot bind all things into a unity but must stand by and accept the fragmentation of life which he encounters in the world. "He must kill all thought that would systematise the world," Yeats announces sternly, and adds that "to others he may seem to care for the immoral and inhuman only, for he will be hostile, or indifferent to moral as to intellectual summaries." [78] Contemplating the fragmented world, the artist reacts with pity; this may be perverted to self-pity (and again we think of the aesthetes) but in a true artist will be transformed by an effort of the will.

Yeats revered Synge beyond any other colleague chiefly because of Synge's self-transformation in leaving Paris for the Aran Islands: "In Synge's early unpublished work, written before he found the dialects of Aran and of Wicklow, there is brooding melancholy and morbid self-pity. He had to undergo an aesthetic transformation, analogous to religious conversion, before he became the audacious, joyous, ironical man we know." The "aesthetic transformation" is the assuming of the Mask, and it becomes the way out of a dilemma for the artist to whom religious conversion, the adoption of a belief, is not possible. Yeats, of course, wanted to have it both ways, and the fact that to some extent he succeeded may help to explain an amplitude and depth in his final success which we do not find in Synge, admirable though some of Synge's plays are. Synge "looks on and claps his hands" and turns "the violent objectivity of the self or *Will* into a delight in all that breathes and moves." Yeats's late attempts at the drama may have sprung from a conscious effort to transform himself in the same way as Synge; but self-discovery for Yeats inevitably came when he, like Shelley, "first created a passionate image which made him forgetful of himself." [79] This is a partial explanation, at least, for some of the opposing pulls in the plays, since the tendency to create passionate images works in most cases against the tendency to dramatize.

After we pass the phases of Synge, Lady Gregory, and A.E., we approach the dark of the moon. Like the initial phases of the Great Wheel, the final phases function chiefly as poetic images, not as human exemplars. It is true that Yeats gives examples of the Saint (Socrates and Pascal), but Hunchback and Fool are without human reference, and the Saint is so much a part of their company that we may regard the trio as outside the scheme of literary history which we have been examining.

In the case of these Figures from the end of the cycle, we must, as Yeats admitted, "create the type from its symbols without the help of experience." Hunchback, Saint, and Fool form a Triad "that is occupied with the relations of the soul;" [80] when we ask what the soul meant to Yeats, we find a convenient definition in a letter to Olivia Shakespear: "You can define soul as 'that which has value in itself,' or you can say of it 'it [is] that which we can only know through analogies.' " [81] These are traditional attributes of God, and Yeats comes close to equating God and soul in "The Four Ages of Man": the line "At stroke of midnight God shall win" [82] represented, he said, the triumph of soul.[83] Both are linked to Yeats's definition of the spiritual in the section on the Hunchback — "a reality known by analogy alone." The insistence on analogy appears peculiar until we realize that any outright triumph of "spirituality" in Yeats's sense would mean the disappearance of analogical knowledge, if we are to believe that "now we see through a glass, darkly; but then face to face." Any poet will prefer the dark glass, his realm of symbolic meaning, to the "gaze, blank and pitiless as the sun" which these waning lunar crescents announce. We saw above that an image is the fusion of the concrete thing with the subjective inference about it, that it is at once both primary and antithetical. If the subjective reverie dissociates itself from the concrete world, as it does in these late phases, the fusion cannot be accomplished. Self-absorbed "spirituality" unrelated to the visible, tangible world is always a fatal danger to the poet:

The Solar circle represents all that comes from outside the man and is therefore the Bride, the Enemy, the Spiritual Life, the Physical World, though it is only through the *Faculties*, separated form, that he apprehends it . . . The condition of truth is that neither world separate from the other and become "abstract." [84]

The entire movement of the waning of the moon represents for Yeats the separation of antithetical from primary, until at the end of the cycle there seems no relation at all possible between the two. The separation is symbolized by "deformity of body and of mind" [85] and we recall the crippling effects attributed to such deformity in any system with neo-Platonic overtones.

The figures of the last phase cannot tolerate conflicting attitudes within themselves: "A Roman Caesar is held down / Under this hump," says the Hunchback to the Saint,[86] and the Saint replies that he too harbors a Caesar within himself, but drives him daily from his flesh. Imaginative images are rejected, one way or another, by the crooked Figures of the later phases: "There is no deformity / But saves us from a dream," as Robartes says.[87] The Hunchback is bitter at the loss of dream, the Saint rejoices in it, and the Fool, engaged in aimless reverie, does not know that he has lost anything at all. "God" has won, and the light of the moon is eclipsed in the solar ascendancy.

All three Figures of the last crescents are inimical, then, to the shaping spirit of imagination. Self-realization, renunciation and oblivion are their Masks, and they have no desire to create a new self by quarreling with the old. They are all passive, at the mercy of exterior reality which they are unable to relate to their inner selves. One however, the Fool, occupies a special place. He is the last incarnation before a new cycle begins, and it is through him that a revelation can appear or the voice of the new era can speak. What Yeats needed in his system, and found in the Fool, was an image that could represent the psychological truth of inspiration. At the Fifteenth Phase there is conscious mental activity on the part of the poet; the Daimon speaks, it is true, but he has been defined as the artist's inner self. One recognizes one's own Daimon; but there is another variety of inspiration, more accurately called revelation, which arises unconsciously as a perceived truth, not self-shaped like the truths elaborated at Phase 15. "At his best," the Fool "would know all wisdom if he could know anything," [88] and Yeats's inspired Fools (Crazy Jane and Tom the Lunatic among them) are examples of the Fool at his best, acting as the medium through which a new truth is made known. The Fool lives in the most dualistic of all worlds, and in spite of his own inability to relate the two halves of his life, he is, by this experience of the duality, a witness to both in a special sense. "Things" and "God" are his two poles, and until he is inspired, the two remain isolated, but in the moment of revelation, he can announce "All things remain in God" and assure us by his words, uttered at the dark of the moon, that the cycle will continue.

The Hunchback and the Saint have no such prophetic function, and they exist, like the Fool when he is uninspired, in "contact with supersensual life," a transcendence in which they wish to submerge individual forms. (The poetic danger of such a submersion becomes more clear if we call to mind the emphasis nineteenth-century poets put upon individual forms; Hopkins' inscape is a case in point.) The Hunchback is the particular enemy of metaphor, since he cannot see

things and actions in relation to each other, but only as radically separate entities. The Saint, even worse, abjures the
senses: "He will, if it be possible, not even touch or taste or
see." [89] Because desire, the energy impelling all creation,
is stifled, art is dried up at its source. The Image has no meaning at this phase, and poetry is at its dead-low water.

6

There are two dangers involved in trying to explain *A
Vision*: one is the risk of being swamped by detail, in an effort toward fidelity; the other is the temptation to ignore important details in order to make some schematization work.
The only solution is to try to steer between the two hazards,
and admit that all solutions are partial. It seems to me, even
so, that certain clear lines emerge. First, we may conclude
that *A Vision* is not to be taken literally, but as an arrangement of experience; second, that it is open to interpretation
from psychology, biography, and poetry, but far less from
scholarly history or from esoterica; third, that its five books
all bear principally on poetry and the poetic process; fourth,
that it is truly a conscious production on Yeats's part (in spite
of all the automatic writing); and fifth, that because it refers
so often to artistic creation, it stands in the closest possible
relation to the poetry and plays which Yeats wrote during
its period of composition and revision.

Throughout the analysis of individual phases, Book I is
concerned almost transparently with Poet and Image more
than with the world at large. The first phases represent literary archetypes attractive to the poet; the last phases, archetypes opposed to aesthetic activity; and the intermediate
phases propose a scheme of literary history, centering around
Phase 15. The poets who precede this dividing line represent a poetic method rejected by Yeats as effete; the poets
who follow the Fifteenth Phase represent desirable examples
of poetic detachment and energy. Finally, in Phase 15 itself,

Yeats devised a symbol for the moment of creative inspiration toward which both groups of poets converge, and by allying Phase 15 with the image of the full moon, made it a workable poetic metaphor. It seems, in the end, that the phases of the moon making up the Great Wheel were invented largely for the sake of the moon at the full, since the other crescents are very rarely of use poetically. The remaining books of *A Vision* can be judged by the same general principles applied here to the Great Wheel, and usually the relations between Yeats's "dry symbolic bones" and the poetry make the trek through his schemes worthwhile.

Chapter II

The Completed Symbol

A MARKED change in subject occurs as we pass from Book I to the succeeding books of *A Vision*. Books II and III are concerned, not with the "human history" of the Great Wheel, but with what Yeats chose to call "the life after death," the state of artistic creation. Although the Four Principles (the subject of Book II) have apparently an existence in "history," they are not important in that existence: "I shall write little of the *Principles*," Yeats concludes, "except when writing of the life after death." [1] For all practical purposes, then, Books II and III compose a unit, the most difficult by far of the three main divisions of Yeats's book.

In the broadest sense, Books II and III are about what Blake named "Mental Travel," the wanderings of the imagination within its own realms. I choose Blake's golden string to lead us through the Yeatsian maze for two reasons: first, Yeats cites four times [2] Blake's poem "The Mental Traveller" as symbolic of his lunar circuit (the circuit of the imagination); and second, if truth be told, Yeats probably derived part of his system from the poem. In *A Vision*, Yeats conjectures that Blake and "the unknown instructors" drew upon some common historical source. [3] We can smile at the happy coincidence, and turn to Blake's poem.

The Mental Traveller, ostensibly a spectator, is actually describing his own experience in some mental world. He is born an infant, is led by "The Female" to suffering and old age, and then, reversing the process, "is beguiled" by her into infancy once again. During his double lifetime, he is both Victim and Tyrant: crucified and eviscerated by the Female in his infancy, he binds her down in turn in his sexual maturity. In the course of his suffering — or rather because of his suffering — he produces jewels, "gems and gold," which oddly enough nourish him and others too:

> And these are the gems of the Human Soul,
> The rubies & pearls of a lovesick eye,
> The countless gold of the akeing heart,
> The martyr's groan & the lover's sigh.

> They are his meat, they are his drink;
> He feeds the Beggar & the Poor
> And the wayfaring Traveller:
> For ever open is his door.

> His grief is their eternal joy;
> They make the roofs & walls to ring;
> Till from the fire on the hearth
> A little Female Babe does spring.[4]

To produce riches and plenty from suffering, to give others eternal joy from one's own grief — these are common enough metaphors for artistic activity, and I do not think there is any doubt that "The Mental Traveller" may be read as a poem about the imagination. Yeats saw it as symbolizing any system of conflict,[5] and its violent antinomies made the poem peculiarly congenial. Grief in the Traveller engenders joy in those whom he nourishes; he sows the seeds of his own future torment by his delight in conceiving the Female (who, like his art, is "all of solid fire/ And gems & gold"); and he is led by her power through the realms of both innocence and experience.

In the Traveller's old age, he claims a Maiden (the Babe grown up) "to allay his freezing age," but the union brings about a cosmic change, as the world of innocence gives way to the world of experience:

> The Cottage fades before his sight,
> The Garden & its lovely Charms.
>
> The Guests are scatter'd thro' the land,
> For the Eye altering alters all;
> The Senses roll themselves in fear,
> And the flat Earth becomes a Ball;
>
> The stars, sun, Moon, all shrink away,
> A desart vast without a bound,
> And nothing left to eat or drink,
> And a dark desart all around.[6]

"For the Eye altering alters all": into the symbolic landscape Blake projects the subjective imagination, explaining the metamorphoses in the poem. The changes from innocence to experience and back to innocence represent of course changes in the Traveller's point of view, imaginative stance, or "vision." Abandoned in the desert, the Traveller finds food from an unexpected source, in "the honey of her Infant lips,/ The bread & wine of her sweet smile." He allows the Female to beguile him to "Labyrinths of wayward Love" and in the process grows younger as the Female grows older. The landscape undergoes a reversal of its former metamorphosis, and regains its innocence:

> The Sun & Stars are nearer roll'd.
>
> The trees bring forth sweet Extacy
> To all who in the desert roam;
> Till many a City there is Built,
> And many a pleasant Shepherd's home.[7]

Once again, the Traveller's embracing of his opposite nourishes the world — by civilization and fruitfulness this time, as by jewels and gold in his first attempt. From the second union, another child is born, but this time it is the Traveller reborn as an infant, "the frowning Babe" who, as the wheel comes full circle, is once again nailed to the rock by the Female grown old, while the pleasant landscape grows blasted and withered.

The theme of "The Mental Traveller" seems to be the trans-
mutation and immolation of experience. In the act of conquering the objects of desire and transforming them into riches
and fruit, man is himself consumed and martyred. We need
go no further than this poem to find the source of Yeats's
identification of Daimon and female, and the poem reminds
us as well of Yeats's view of the Muse as tyrant:

> The *Leanhaun Shee* (fairy mistress) seeks the love of mortals . . .
> The fairy lives on their life, and they waste away . . . She is the
> Gaelic muse, for she gives inspiration to those she persecutes . . . She
> is of the dreadful solitary fairies. To her have belonged the greatest
> of the Irish poets, from Oisin down to the last century.[8]

If we ask for further relationships between Woman and the
terms of *A Vision*, Yeats gives them to us in saying, again with
reference to Blake: "*Mask* and *Body of Fate* are symbolic
woman, *Will* and *Creative Mind* symbolic man; the man and
woman of Blake's *Mental Traveller*." [9] Woman is at once the
object of free desire and inescapable destiny. In her, Chance
and Choice can momentarily become one, and she is the
most complex of all images representing the goal of the will.
Besides relating Woman to the Faculties in the passage just
quoted, Yeats relates her to the Four Principles which we are
about to see in operation, but the quotation can best be kept
until after the Principles are defined.

2

The definitions of the Principles are scattered through many
pages, and are divided into two classes: first, the Principles
are defined in themselves; and second, they are defined in
relation to the Daimons. In the first group of definitions we
learn that the Principles, like the Faculties, are four in number,
and are called Husk, Passionate Body, Spirit, and Celestial
Body. Although Yeats includes in this Book complicated,
ingenious, and dizzying diagrams of the interaction, through
various phases, of Faculties and Principles, they are of no

help at all, so far as I can see. For all practical purposes, Yeats keeps the Faculties and Principles separate. The innate Principles are lodged in the mind (not, like the voluntary and acquired Faculties, in the Will [10]) and are the forms through which imaginative activity proceeds. Husk (symbolically the human body) includes the images and impulses of the senses, while the objects of the senses are collectively called the Passionate Body, which is subject to time and space, cause and effect, and the other attritionary forces of the physical world. These two Principles prevail during "life," and therefore are of less interest for us than the two Principles, called Spirit and Celestial Body, that prevail "in the period between lives" [11] (the period of creation). Spirit and Celestial Body are the two most unhappily named qualities in *A Vision*, and require some explanation to be understood.

Spirit (or Mind) is, according to Yeats, Coleridge's "Reason" or Kant's *Vernunft*: [12] it is the quality in the mind which perceives the universal beneath the particular, the eternal beneath the transitory, the necessary beneath the contingent. Its proper object, "the Divine Ideas in their Unity," is named the Celestial Body (where once again "Body" may have a collective sense, as in "a body of opinion"). The Celestial Body has affinities with the Platonic world of Forms and represents the Timeless.[13] It also has a cross link, saving it from antiseptic sterility, with the Passionate Body, the objects of sense: "The *Passionate Body* exists that it may 'save the *Celestial Body* from solitude.' " [14]

We may translate this by saying that the poetic consciousness is being constantly assailed by the objects of the world, and it perceives them via these two Principles as doubled, participating in "heaven" (the Celestial Body) and "earth" (the Passionate Body). It assimilates them from primary impressions into poetic images by a delicately preserved equilibrium between sense perception and "ideal form," but this balance may be disturbed, and one principle grow at the expense of the other. "The *Celestial Body* is said to age as the *Passionate Body* grows young," and vice versa. Age implies weakness, youth implies strength, and Yeats is saying that when the mind is being assailed by sense impressions, when experience is undergone, there is only a scanty place for reflection and creation; imaginative activity at such times is weak. On the other hand, when life is to all intents and purposes quiet (whether in a lull between experiences or in old age) the imagination is active. "The intellect of man is forced to choose/Perfection of the life, or of the work." [15]

The inverse proportion between bodily vigor and imagination is a recurrent theme in Yeats:

> What shall I do with this absurdity —
> O heart, O troubled heart — this caricature,
> Decrepit age that has been tied to me
> As to a dog's tail?
>   Never had I more
> Excited, passionate, fantastical
> Imagination.[16]

In writing "The Tower," Yeats may have recalled a letter of Blake's which he had quoted years earlier: [17] "I have been very near the Gates of Death & have returned very weak & an Old Man feeble & tottering, but not in Spirit & Life, not in The Real Man The Imagination which Liveth for Ever. In that I am stronger & stronger as this Foolish Body decays." [18] Blake's image of old age was summoned up once more by Yeats; when he received the Nobel Prize in 1925, he reflected upon the medal which showed a young man listening to the Muse: "I was good-looking once like that young man, but my unpractised verse was full of infirmity, my Muse old as it were; and now I am old and rheumatic, and nothing to look at, but my Muse is young. I am even persuaded that she is like those Angels in Swedenborg's vision, and moves perpetually 'towards the day-spring of her youth.' " [19]

The reciprocal relation of inverse strength which *A Vision* describes as existing between the Celestial Body and the Passionate Body is, then, nothing new. What is important is keeping somehow the balance between the two principles. There is always the danger that as the honey of earth "comes and goes at once" [20] the relation of sense impression to image will deteriorate, for "sometimes the *Celestial Body* is a prisoner in a tower rescued by the *Spirit*." There is the converse danger that the poet will lose all touch with the primary sense of the physical world, and then the Celestial Body, grown old and abstract, "becomes the personification of evil." [21]

To explain these alternate paths open to the poetic mind, Yeats refers us once again to "The Mental Traveller." When the man and woman are young, and the senses predominate over the spirit, the Traveller is vigorous and the scene is a garden:

> He plants himself in all her Nerves,
> Just as a Husbandman his mould;
> And she becomes his dwelling place
> And Garden fruitful seventy fold.

On the other hand, when the Female becomes old and dominates, the landscape is a desert, momentarily fertile when the allegorical union takes place, but soon reduced to a wilderness again when the "frowning Babe" is born:

> For who dare touch the frowning form,
> His arm is wither'd to its root;
> Lions, Boars, Wolves, all howling flee,
> And every Tree does shed its fruit.
>
> And none can touch that frowning form,
> Except it be a Woman Old;
> She nails him down upon the Rock,
> And all is done as I have told.[22]

The imagination, grown abstract, becomes the personification of evil as "it pursues, persecutes, and imprisons the *Daimons*." [23] This sentence, enigmatic enough, becomes more

so as we contemplate Yeats's choice of verbs; such violence
scarcely belongs to the Platonic world, even in its evil aspect.
But the reference to "The Mental Traveller" which Yeats
makes at this point clarifies the sentence, indicating that we
are to equate the evil Celestial Body with the female in her
destructive role. When we recall that symbolically the Celestial Body stands as well for the objects of philosophy (the
universal, the eternal, the necessary, as we have said above),
another of Yeats's peculiar linkages appears. Woman, though
in some cases in league with the Daimon, is at other times
bound to the service of the "cold philosophy" at whose
touch all charms fly:

> Philosophy will clip an Angel's wings,
> Conquer all mysteries by rule and line,
> Empty the haunted air, and gnomed mine —
> Unweave a rainbow.[24]

Whether she clips an Angel's wings or nails the Poet to a
Rock, the Woman Old is the abstract threat. Yeats usually
tended to make woman closer to the Muse than to the Harpy,
but Maud Gonne's unswervably pragmatic mind may have
given Yeats reason to cling to certain pejorative fragments of
Blake's symbolism.

3

The Daimons, or spirits of inspiration, preside over the
creative activity "between lives," as we might expect, and
the definitions of the Four Principles in relation to the Daimons
both clarify and obscure their function. Essentially, says
Yeats, the Principles exist in order that the Daimons may
communicate with each other. This bizarre statement seems
to embody Yeats's theory of the place of tradition in literary
creation. Previously, we have seen the Daimon only as that
spirit of selfhood in the poet which speaks to him as a voice
from elsewhere, and yet is still his own. At this stage in his
argument, wishing to convey his attitude toward tradition,

Yeats reveals to us that all things, including "nations, cultures, schools of thought," have Daimons — and "behind the *Husk* (or sense) is the *Daimon's* hunger to make apparent to itself certain *Daimons* . . . The *Passionate Body* is the sum of those *Daimons*." [25] The idea of the selfhood of all inanimate things is probably most familiar to us in Hopkins:

> As kingfishers catch fire, dragonflies draw flame;
> As tumbled over rim in roundy wells
> Stones ring; like each tucked string tells, each hung bell's
> Bow swung finds tongue to fling out broad its name;
> Each mortal thing does one thing and the same:
> Deals out that being indoors each one dwells;
> Selves — goes itself; *myself* it speaks and spells;
> Crying *What I do is me: for that I came.*[26]

"That being indoors each one dwells" is the best definition of the Daimon-in-things, but Yeats goes even further than Hopkins by devising a double Daimon for each thing: beyond the Daimon known by the Husk through the sense organs, there is the Daimon known by the Spirit (and all these spiritual Daimons taken together compose the Celestial Body). Yeats as usual is having his cake and eating it too: the old debate concerning the principle of individuation (is it in the body? is it in the soul?) is solved by doubling the *haecceitas*.

The appetite of the poetic selfhood to unite itself to the selfhood of other things is not taken care of in the scheme of the Faculties: Yeats invented the Principles to explain the moment when, in Wallace Stevens' terms,

> . . . the central poem became the world,
> And the world the central poem, each one the mate
> Of the other, as if summer was a spouse,
> Espoused each morning.[27]

This moment occurs in the life "between lives" and that is one reason why the central phase of that life is called "The Marriage." The Daimon unites itself in a succession of mar-

riages to all that the poet has known, and holds it all simul-
taneously present; but because such an idea is beyond our
comprehension, Yeats's condescending instructors announced
that they would substitute for it the idea of a Record, "where
the images of all past events remain forever 'thinking the
thought and doing the deed.' " This is not the Memory of
popular definition but rather Mnemosyne, the Mother of the
Muses, whom we may call Tradition. It is a memory perpetually alive, in which events remain always available poetically because time does not wither them nor custom stale their
variety. The Daimon who holds these memories we have
already identified with Mnemosyne. Yeats goes even further
and identifies it with the Holy Ghost [28] who, by way of
Milton, has an honorable place as representative of the Muse.
In his use of the word Record, Yeats also identifies the discarnate Daimons with the *Anima Mundi*, or so it seems to me.
Seeing the spirit of inspiration as the subconscious is, no
doubt, the step the modern poetic mind has taken beyond
Milton in finding a name for the Muse.

The relation of the Daimon in the self to the Daimon in
things is a precondition of poetry, not exactly a step in the
process of creation itself. As we have said, the voluntary
craft of poetry, the willed adoption of the Mask, lies within
the province of the Faculties; the Principles are invoked to
take care of the promptings of tradition and of the subconscious before the actual moment of creation. The process
of creation takes place *after* the visitation by the Daimon:
Passionate Body and Celestial Body give way to willed crafts-
manship or Mask, and "we dwell in aesthetic process, so much
skill in bronze or paint, or on some symbol that rouses emotion for emotion's sake." [29] This is the activity which follows
ideally upon apprehension by the senses. When the process
is abused, and Mask gives way to the random knowledge of
sense objects, the product is "spurious art"; when Mask gives
way to Will, we get "commercial art"; and (worst offense in

Yeats's casebook) when Mask gives way to exterior concerns, the result is "common realism." Mask is the artistic faculty *par excellence*, but it is the conscious shaping spirit of the imagination, not the deeper springs of the image. Yeats could not deny a concern for these, and they are more fully treated in Book III; but before describing that "life between lives" in which the Daimons are active and the Principles preside, he turns to some presages of the last two books, the "historical" essays of *A Vision*.

4

Yeats always publishes the most grandiose aspect of his plans at the beginning of an essay, and in this instance it is the Magnus Annus:

> And then did all the Muses sing
> Of Magnus Annus at the spring.[30]

Although Yeats makes less frequent use of the Magnus Annus than he does of the phases of the moon, it stands implicit behind all the cyclical themes as the guarantee that after multiple revolutions the Wheel finally completes its orbit, the constellations return to their ancient places. The Great Year comprises six "Great Wheels" of two thousand years (and twenty-eight incarnations) each,[31] and each of these Great Wheels is what we are accustomed to call a civilization. Each of these cycles, Yeats continues, can be thought of as a symbolic year, in which the months are assigned to phases of the moon, but this is purely a pretext on Yeats's part to associate seasonal metaphors with the archetypes already established in Book I. The only months whose symbolic value becomes important are March, June, September, and December — representing Phases 15, 22, 1, and 8 respectively.

It is hardly surprising, after what we have seen of the central position of Phase 15 in "The Great Wheel," that from the arbitrary assignment of March to Phase 15 all the other symbolic associations of months and phases are determined. It is no more surprising to find that Yeats's year, like the ancient calendar, begins in March, in the spring, at the time of the vernal equinox. The Great Wheel's nadir is Winter, its zenith is Spring, and it declines through Summer into Autumn.[32] March is both the month in which Christ was conceived, and, according to Yeats, the month of the Resurrection; in each case, it is the month of revelation. On the other hand, the system as it has been developed so far requires that Christ be symbolically represented not only by March and Phase 15, but also by Phase 1, where any civilization, the Christian one included, must originate. Finally, Christ should appear also at Phase 8, since that is the phase representing December, the month of his birth. It is to the credit of Yeats's ingenuity, if nothing else, that he dovetailed his various cycles into each other so as to make it possible for the figure of Christ to appear at three different phases. Some explanations and diagrams will make the scheme intelligible, if not simple.

The first thing that must be said is that Yeats is radically inconsistent in his historical schemata. As far as I can see, there are two opposing arrangements of history at work in *A Vision*, the first an early and more spontaneous one, included in the original "Dove or Swan" of 1925, reprinted in 1939; the second, a neater and more rational schema occurring in certain poems, and prompted by some second thoughts about the original conjectures.

The first arrangement might be called a Heraclitean one, since it shows two civilizations "living each other's death, dying each other's life." Essentially, it concerns only the decline of classicism and the rise of Christianity, and is represented in the complicated conic diagram prefacing Book V. In this diagram, the classical civilization declines as Christianity gathers strength to achieve Byzantium, and Yeats emphasizes in his description of the first millennium of the Christian era

the tension caused by the coexistence of the two societies, antithetical and primary. We may represent the classical era by
the following diagram.[33]

TOTAL CLASSICAL ERA [34]

Phase 1	Phase 8	Phase 15	Phase 22	Phase 28
First Millennium			Second Millennium	

1000 B.C.	500 B.C.	A.D. 1	A.D. 1	A.D. 500	A.D. 1000
Homer	Phidias	Christ	Christ	Fall of Rome	Breakup
Phase 1	Phase 15	Phase 28	Phase 1	Phase 15	Phase 28

And the Christian era, in turn, may be similarly represented.

TOTAL CHRISTIAN ERA

Phase 1	Phase 8	Phase 15	Phase 22	Phase 28
First Millennium			Second Millennium	

A.D. 1	A.D. 500	A.D. 1000	A.D. 1000	A.D. 1500	A.D. 2000
Christ	Byzantium	Breakup	Romances	Renaissance	Breakup
Phase 1	Phase 15	Phase 28	Phase 1	Phase 15	Phase 28

The second millennium of Christianity is rather ignored in
favor of the first, which may be shown overlapping with the
classical era, combining the dying phases of classical life with
the rise of Christianity.

1000 B.C.	500 B.C.	A.D. 1	A.D. 500	A.D. 1000	A.D. 1500	A.D. 2000
Homer	Phidias	Christ	Byzantium Fall of Rome	End of Classical Era	Renaissance	End of Christian-ity

In this arrangement, Byzantium is the magic place; A.D. 500,
the magic date of intersection. Everything is held for a moment in unstable equilibrium as the two civilizations meet on
the stair of history, one ascending, one descending. It is this
scheme which we should keep in mind as we read such poems
as "Sailing to Byzantium" and "Byzantium."

However, there is another arrangement of history latent
in Yeats's mind, one which sees civilizations not as overlapping
but as discontinuous. The reason why Yeats needed this
second system is open to conjecture, but my own guess is

that he was troubled by a lack of analogy between the classical and Christian eras in his first scheme. He dates the Christian era there from the birth of Christ — but the classical era begins 1000 years after the birth of Helen. Such a discrepancy badly upsets the idea of parallel times and parallel divinities: Leda and the Swan *must* be made completely analogous to Mary and the Holy Ghost. And both must foreshadow the birth of the divinity who will usher in the next cycle — the Rough Beast who slouches toward Bethlehem to be born. These incarnations, each beginning a Great Wheel, are separated by about two thousand years. Yeats places Leda at 2000 B.C.[35] and, as we know from "The Second Coming," expects the Rough Beast momentarily.

BIRTHS OF "DIVINITIES"

2000 B.C.	A.D. I	A.D. 2000
Leda	Christ	Rough Beast

We might think that Yeats would have put the classical era in the two thousand years preceding the birth of Christ, but that would be too much at variance with history even for the author of *A Vision*. Recalcitrant fact demands that the civilization lag behind the annunciation by a millennium, and that the classical civilization be bisected by the birth of Christ. The logical conclusion to be drawn is that the Christian era must lag by a millennium behind the birth of Christ, and be bisected by the birth of the Rough Beast. This presents us with a Christian era beginning in the year 1000 (*not* at the birth of Christ, as in the preceding scheme) and continuing to the year 3000, when it will be succeeded by another cycle.

TOTAL CHRISTIAN ERA

Phase 1	Phase 8	Phase 15		Phase 22	Phase 28
First Millennium			Second Millennium		
A.D 1000	A.D. 1500	A.D. 2000	A.D. 2000	A.D. 2500	A.D. 3000
Charlemagne	Renaissance	Rough Beast	Rough Beast		
Phase 1	Phase 15	Phase 28	Phase 1	Phase 15	Phase 28

The Rough Beast ("a supernatural incarnation") comes at Phase 15 of the total Christian era, as Christ came at Phase 15 of the total classical era, and that much we had expected. Even more interesting results appear when we draw the diagram of the total cycle, including both antithetical and primary, both classical and Christian:

TOTAL CLASSICAL-CHRISTIAN CYCLE

1000 B.C.	A.D. 1	A.D. 1000	A.D. 2000	A.D. 3000
Homer	Christ	Charlemagne	Rough Beast	
Phase 1	*Phase 8*	*Phase 15*	*Phase 22*	*Phase 28*

Here, surprisingly enough, we find Christ at Phase 8, corresponding to December, the month of his birth. And even more surprisingly, we see Charlemagne as the "supernatural incarnation" of the Fifteenth Phase, the pivotal figure for the entire cycle.

Are we to conceive of Charlemagne as one of the "worldrestorers" of whom Yeats writes in Book IV? [36] They include the Messiah, the Spirit that moved upon the Waters, and Noah on Mount Ararat; we hesitate to place Charlemagne in such company. But one of the poems confirms our suspicion that we are to do just that: it is the obscure *"Whence Had They Come?"* published in *Supernatural Songs* in 1935. The mysterious "They" of the title are the divinities (like Jove or the Holy Ghost) who suddenly thrust themselves into human history — or into the history of the individual soul. No poem demonstrates better Yeats's conviction that things are "doubled in history, world history, personal history." [37] The divinities speak as much through the passionate lover, the inspired poet, and the religious flagellant as they do through their "historical" impregnations. In the poem, Yeats chooses to call the divinities "Dramatis Personae" but they are easily recognizable as kin to the swan that caught up Leda:

Eternity is passion, girl or boy
Cry at the onset of their sexual joy
'For ever and for ever'; then awake
Ignorant what Dramatis Personae spake;
A passion-driven exultant man sings out
Sentences that he has never thought;
The Flagellant lashes those submissive loins
Ignorant what that dramatist enjoins,
What master made the lash. Whence had they come,
The hand and lash that beat down frigid Rome?
What sacred drama through her body heaved
When world-transforming Charlemagne was conceived? [38]

The analogy that Yeats draws between Charlemagne's conception and the conception of Christ cannot be missed, and
the adjective "world-transforming" leaves us no choice but
to ally Charlemagne with the Messiah and the other "worldrestorers."

These two patterns of civilization, the overlapping and the
discontinuous, whatever we may think of their historical
accuracy, provide for both conflict and similarity, each necessary to Yeats's poetic constructions. The contraries in the
overlapping scheme permit Yeats to view Byzantium, for
instance, as at once a glory of Christian civilization and a
manifestation of dying classicism. Other phases may lack
the prestige of Byzantium, but they all have a multiple significance from the double or triple cycles in which they participate. Poetically, this means that a perpetual contradiction
is set up each time they are evoked — a phenomenon which
explains, for instance, why the imagery of the poem "Byzantium" is concerned not only with golden smithies, but with
death, and why in "The Magi" we find an uncontrollable
mystery on a bestial floor. The discontinuous pattern of
history, on the other hand, allows for perpetual recurrence,
so that Christ may be compared, unlikely as it may seem, to
Helen, Achilles, Charlemagne, and the Rough Beast, as Yeats
declares that "all civilisations [are] equal at their best; every

phase returns, therefore in some sense every civilisation." [39]

After his digression into the symbolic months, Yeats begins to consider astrological conjunctions. If the reader is not already out of patience (and Book II is of all the Books the most exasperating) this invitation to consider astrological symbols (as well as lunar and seasonal ones) is enough to wear out the last shreds of tolerance. It is all the more annoying because the symbolism hardly appears in the poetry — only in two cryptic couplets, really:

> If Jupiter and Saturn meet,
> What a crop of mummy wheat!
>
> The sword's a cross; thereon He died:
> On breast of Mars the goddess sighed. [40]

As a poem, this fails abysmally, because it makes no sense without the system. On the other hand, the poem is tangentially interesting because it relates immediately to the Fifteenth Phase, and almost anything which casts light on that phase takes on a borrowed luster. We are told that "These two conjunctions [of Mars with Venus, and Jupiter with Saturn] . . . stand, so to speak, like heraldic supporters guarding the mystery of the fifteenth phase." In the phases immediately preceding Phase 15, Creative Mind is under the conjunction of Jupiter and Saturn, standing for "introspective knowledge of the mind's self-begotten unity," while after Phase 15, Creative Mind is under the conjunction of Mars and Venus, standing for "love and its lure." [41] This is another version of Yeats's old distinction between the hyperaesthetic poets before Phase 15 and the poets conscious of the "outside world" after Phase 15. The astrological discussion occurs only to confirm the single persuasive fact that Yeats is attempting to establish: that somehow the Fifteenth Phase partakes both of the nature of Jupiter and Saturn and of the nature of Mars and Venus — meditation and desire, knowledge and love. "Love" is not only the sexual act, at least not in the

couplets above — while Mars embraces Venus, his sword
becomes the cross where Christ died, and sexual and nonsexual
love join in contrast to the Sphinx-like intellect.

Before leaving the discussion of astrological conjunctions,
Yeats slips in one final analogy, which in view of all the diagrams of interlocking gyres, he hardly needed to state: "All
these symbols can be thought of as the symbols of the relations of men and women and of the birth of children."
The Wheel, he adds, is "an expression of alternations of
passion" [42] as power veers from man to woman. In "The
Gift of Harun Al-Rashid" he again allies the symbols of *A
Vision* with sexuality:

> The signs and shapes;
> All those abstractions that you fancied were
> From the great Treatise of Parmenides;
> All, all those gyres and cubes and midnight things
> Are but a new expression of her body
> Drunk with the bitter sweetness of her youth.[43]

Given this *carte blanche*, Freudian interpreters can allegorize
the entire *Vision* in terms of libido, and not be wrong in any
absolute sense; but often enough the sexual meaning is itself
symbolic, and interpretation which stops at sexual union
misses other facets of the later poetry and plays.

The last symbol that Yeats introduces in Book II is the
mysterious "Thirteenth Cycle," "Thirteenth Cone," or "Thirteenth Sphere." The words he uses to describe it in Book II
and Book III are confusing: at times, it seems like a governor,
because it can command, summon, permit, teach, consent;
at other times it seems like a place, because Teaching Spirits
live within it; at still other times, it seems like a thing, because
it is called a sphere. And to confuse us still further, the
Thirteenth Cone is one thing as seen in itself and another as
seen by man. Yeats's remarks about the Thirteenth Cone are
scattered, but for intelligibility they must be brought together,

and my quotations here will come from Book III as well as Book II.

Within the Thirteenth Cone "live all souls that have been set free and every *Daimon* and *Ghostly Self*," and it is therefore of special interest in regard to the moments when "We are laid asleep in body, and become a living soul" — those "discarnate" moments to be anatomized in Book III. For the moment, in Book II, Yeats tells us only that the Thirteenth Cycle represents all that contrasts with material life as we know it: it represents the "spiritual objective." How then does it differ from the Mask? In one sense, hardly at all, except that the Mask is a singular and personal objective, fluctuating from person to person. We can think of the Thirteenth Cone as the locus of all Masks, if we like, "the antithesis to our thesis," [44] as Yeats calls it. As a spiritual objective, it can as well be described as the ideal, in the best sense a figment of our imagination. The Thirteenth Cone, it must be remembered, lies somewhere in the mental realm, not in the physical world. It is not made, or created, or incarnated — it is a goal, not a product.

The resemblances between Phase 15 and the Thirteenth Cone are obvious, but strictly speaking, the correspondence is not between the Phase and the *Cone*, since when the Cone is seen as it is in itself, not from the vantage point of man, it is called the Phaseless Sphere.[45] Just as Phase 15 is not a human incarnation, but rather an extrapolation from the incarnations we know, so the Phaseless Sphere is an extrapolation from certain mental experiences, chiefly the experience of aesthetic creation. This statement must be taken on faith for the moment, until it is explained in Chapter III. The descriptions of the Phaseless Sphere, as we might expect, are analogous to the descriptions of Phase 15. Richard Ellmann quotes unpublished notes which Yeats made for *A Vision* in which the language reminds us strongly of the language of Book I concerning the phase of the full moon:

At first we are subject to Destiny . . . but the point in the Zodiac where the whirl becomes a sphere once reached, we may escape from the constraint of our nature and from that of external things, entering upon a state where all fuel has become flame, where there is nothing but the state itself, nothing to constrain it or end it. We attain it always in the creation or enjoyment of a work of art, but that moment though eternal in the Daimon passes from us because it is not an attainment of our whole being.

In another passage from the same notes, Yeats comes even closer to his description of the Fifteenth Phase:

All whirling [is] at an end, and unity of being perfectly attained. There are all happiness, all beauty, all thought, their images come to view taking fullness, to such a multiplicity of form that they are to our eyes without form. They do what they please, all [struggle] at an end, daimons and men reconciled.[46]

In some ways, we can regret that Yeats identified the fusion of thought and image by two different symbols, Phase 15 and the Phaseless Sphere, but the seemingly needless duplication was inevitable because he had already split his system in two, into "incarnate life" and "discarnate life," into Faculties and Principles, and therefore he required a symbol of perfection for each half of the system. What the Fifteenth Phase is to created art — the embodiment, *in a form*, of thought fused with image — the Phaseless Sphere is to creation — the fusing of thought and image *in the mind*. This in itself warns us, when we are interpreting a poem like "Chosen," that when Yeats speaks of lovers

> Adrift on the miraculous stream
> Where — wrote a learned astrologer —
> The Zodiac is changed into a sphere,[47]

he is referring more to the discarnate life, the life of the mind, than to the phasal incarnate life of the body. Yeats was conscious of the difficulties inherent in the multiplication of similar images "of which the greater number, precisely because they tell always the same story, may seem unnecessary." [48] But, to quote Robert Graves, "There is one story, and one story only." [49] Yeats agreed: "Every symbol . . . has evoked for me some form of human destiny, and that form, once evoked, has appeared everywhere, as if there were but one destiny, as my own form might appear in a room full of mirrors. [50]

To evoke by symbols the universal and human forms that are visible everywhere in life is a good definition of the principle behind all poetic activity, and in tracing the course of Mental Travel via the Principles, the Daimons, and the Thirteenth Cone, Yeats does "give us back the image of our mind" strangely but accurately. Book II is partial and fragmentary, and is intruded upon by the first hints of the cycles of civilization which belong more coherently to Books IV and V; nevertheless, in giving us further information about the relation of sense and image, individuality and tradition, the Book does, as it promised, complete the symbol. In the following section Yeats can use freely the symbols established in Book II to discuss the mental process "between lives" — the process of creation.

Chapter III

The Soul in Judgment

THE image of a singing girl has a poetic power all out of proportion to its overt content. Wordsworth first fixed the image in the modern consciousness, incarnating it in "The Solitary Reaper":

> Will no one tell me what she sings? —
> Perhaps the plaintive numbers flow
> For old, unhappy, far-off things,
> And battles long ago . . .
> Whate'er the theme, the Maiden sang
> As if her song could have no ending;
> I saw her singing at her work,
> And o'er the sickle bending.

Coleridge gave the singer a more exotic setting, fixed her as the central point of a vision in "Kubla Khan":

> A damsel with a dulcimer
> In a vision once I saw:
> It was an Abyssinian maid,
> And on her dulcimer she played,
> Singing of Mount Abora.

In the twentieth century, Wallace Stevens has celebrated "the one of fictive music" in poem after poem, and in the most famous, "The Idea of Order at Key West," the singer becomes "the single artificer of the world":

> . . . There never was a world for her
> Except the one she sang and, singing, made.

Yeats uses the same image (and uses it almost irrelevantly, as it first seems) to introduce the third book of *A Vision*. As he remembers Iseult Gonne, he writes:

My imagination goes some years backward, and I remember a beautiful young girl singing at the edge of the sea in Normandy words and music of her own composition. She thought herself alone, stood barefooted between sea and sand; sang with lifted head of the civilisations that there had come and gone, ending every verse with the cry: "O Lord, let something remain." [1]

One reason for the attraction exerted by the image is that the girl represents the Muse; but these poets knew other available symbols for the Muse — Nature for Wordsworth, Joy for Coleridge, the swan for Yeats, the pianist for Stevens. It is the distinctiveness of the singer, her persistence in tradition, that catches our interest. The image appeals principally because only the singer is at once poet and Muse, whereas in other situations, the Muse becomes a Jovian animal or bird, a pantheistic Wisdom and Spirit of the Universe, an *Anima Mundi*, or some other force separate from the inspired poet. Though Yeats preferred a dualistic view of inspiration, at least for poetic purposes, a double symbol would not have been appropriate at all for the third book of his system. The book is essentially concerned with the aesthetic process as it occurs in the creating mind, or with the intimacy of relation between poet and Muse, together with their final identification in the created object. In its original inception, this was the book of the Daimon, as the first edition betrays, and the singer is a human version of that symbolic figure. [2]

The Singer, being a double symbol, is always represented as a bridge between two worlds. Wordsworth's Solitary Reaper unites the exotic material of her song with the familiar scene; Stevens' mysterious figure unites the ocean with the human self; Yeats's singing girl, standing between sea and land, remembers and gives present life to civilizations long past. It is the alliance with nature, never explicitly insisted on, which makes the bridging possible: Yeats's girl is barefoot, Stevens' girl is almost indistinguishable from the sea, and Wordsworth's girl stands single in the field of grain. Of course the pastoral convention of the rural singer is being invoked, but there is something more implied — the grounding of the song in the sand and tides and vegetable life of the earth. Emerson's comparison of the poet to a lightning rod applies to these Singers, whose songs reach from a footing in earth to abstractions distilled.

It is just this process of distillation which Yeats proposes to consider in Book III of *A Vision*, and his symbol for the peculiar timeless world inhabited by the Singer is the world "between lives," or the world of dreams. (He postulates a state of "dreamless sleep" too, but that Nirvana-like condition does not lend itself to description.) In the world of dreams "there are no carts, horses, roads, but [man] makes them for himself." The analogy between poetic creation and dream is not new, but some of the bypaths pursued by Yeats are unfrequented ones. One of the most interesting proposals is that the imagination serves to restore the integrity of impoverished reality: "in dreams we finish what we began awake or what the waking suggest." The converse — that the imagination would be itself poor without reality — is also true, and Yeats symbolizes it by the requests of the dead for material aid from the living: "Once an old woman came to Coole Park, when I was there, to tell Lady Gregory that Sir William Gregory's ghost had a tattered sleeve and that a coat must be given to some beggar in his name." [3] The normal process of poetic imagination stems from disappointment, and creation is to some extent compensation; [4] but the creation becomes "a new knowledge of reality," [5] and the poet returns to the place "where all the ladders start." The classic instance of the progression is in the sixth book of *The Prelude*, where the poet first experiences disappointment in the real, as he learns that he has crossed the Alps without knowing it — no striking

barrier, no topmost pinnacle, has marked the dividing line.
Then, at the moment of disappointment, Imagination rises and
envelops him, revealing to his later meditation that reality is
inherently unable to satisfy the mind:

> Whether we be young or old,
> Our destiny, our being's heart and home
> Is with infinitude, and only there;
> With hope it is, hope that can never die,
> Effort, and expectation, and desire,
> And something evermore about to be.

The perception of infinity that Imagination has brought with
it then returns upon reality, and as the poet describes his
descent of the gorge, he sees infinity in the natural scenery,
imagination embodied in the real:

> Tumult and peace, the darkness and the light —
> Were all like workings of one mind, the features
> Of the same face, blossoms upon one tree;
> Characters of the great Apocalypse,
> The types and symbols of Eternity,
> Of first, and last, and midst, and without end.[6]

This circular progress — from the meager real to the full
imagined to the fuller real — is the normal trajectory of
poetry, and must be kept in mind while Book III of *A Vision*
is being considered. The whole purpose of the state between
lives is to accomplish with the events of life what "this brief
tragedy of flesh" did not provide enough time for. It is
humanly impossible to burn always with a hard gemlike flame
and to taste each moment to the full. It is even more impossible
to understand as well as to taste; and to weigh choices would
ask two lifetimes at least. In a strange way, *A Vision* is one
answer to Walter Pater. The Conclusion to *The Renaissance*
had laid an enormous burden on the poets of the nineties,
and many of them exhausted themselves and their art in trying
to "maintain that ecstasy" of constant awareness. Yeats had

sense enough to provide a multiplicity of lives (metaphorically speaking) for the accomplishing of understanding. Creation, for Yeats as well as for Wordsworth, springs from
emotion recollected in tranquillity. The purgatorial state of
suspension in which emotion is relived and contemplated is
called in *A Vision* "the period between death and birth" or
"the period between lives," and though Yeats speaks about
it in terms of knowledge, we are to realize that his essay is
the conceptualizing of a chaotic and for the most part unconscious experience: he is "reasoning about these things with
a later reason."

The period "between lives" is divided into six states,[7] of
which the second, the *Meditation*, is of especial interest for
the plays. For the sake of completeness, and because the
principal state is best understood in context, the six states will
be dealt with here in order.[8] Although these symbolic states
may have many parallels with "real" life, I will discuss only
their application to poetic activity, the aspect where the symbolism seems to me most understandable and most coherent.

The first state, *The Vision of the Blood Kindred*, is sum-
marily described and dismissed. As the threshold to the other
states, it is "a synthesis, before *disappearance*, of all the impulses and images which constitute the *Husk*,"[9] and it corresponds to Orpheus' last look at the world before the descent
into Hades, a last glance at things in their "real" rather than
imaginative relations. We are to leave behind "all complexities of mire and blood" in the process of purgation, and the
Blood Kindred are the first to be abandoned.

The second state, called the *Meditation*, is described by Yeats
in paragraphs full of confusion and misleading statements. It
is in a way falsification to impose an artificial clarity on this
section of Book III because one of the impressions the book
exists to convey is the sense of mystery attendant upon the
workings of the imagination; on the other hand, Yeats was not
above making deliberate gestures of mystification whenever

he thought of himself as a Magus. With all due respect to the seriousness of *A Vision*, we are still obliged to make what we can of his interwoven description of the second state. Just as Phase 15 is the nucleus for the construction of the Great Wheel, so the *Meditation* is the kernel of Book III. The other states are preludes and codas to the central experience. Depending on how one looks at it, the state either has three names or contains three stages — Yeats uses both terms.[10] It is simpler to consider it as having three stages, and although Yeats names these in italics, I will use roman type in order to avoid confusion with the six states.

The first stage is the Dreaming Back, in which the Spirit is engaged in ridding itself of the Passionate Body and finding the Celestial Body. The closer the union in life between the Spirit and the Passionate Body, the more painful and long is the Dreaming Back: a woman may cling to her beauty, a man killed violently may cling to his former life.[11] Events that have troubled the spirit exert in the Dreaming Back an obsessive power upon the soul, and Yeats knew very well that haunting power which he evokes symbolically in this stage.

> Did that play of mine send out
> Certain men the English shot?
> Did words of mine put too great strain
> On that woman's reeling brain?
> Could my spoken words have checked
> That whereby a house lay wrecked? [12]

"In the *Dreaming Back*," says Yeats, "the *Spirit* is compelled to live over and over again the events that had most moved it; there can be nothing new, but the old events stand forth in a light which is dim or bright according to the intensity of the passion that accompanied them." [13] The most passionately experienced events appear most clearly illuminated in the strong light of this stage, and in each successive reliving of the event, the pain or joy associated with it becomes less, as a gradual process of detachment takes place.

> But body gone he sleeps no more,
> And till his intellect grows sure
> That all's arranged in one clear view,
> Pursues the thoughts that I pursue,
> Then stands in judgment on his soul,
> And, all work done, dismisses all
> Out of intellect and sight
> And sinks at last into the night.[14]

This stage is, in fact, the progress to that tranquillity which must be achieved before recollected emotion becomes amenable to poetic treatment.

Detachment is not the only prerequisite to creation. There must be knowledge as well, and this knowledge, in the Yeatsian scheme, comes in the second stage of the *Meditation*, the Return. In the Dreaming Back, the spirit had lived through events in the order of their intensity; in the Return, the spirit lives through past events in the order of their occurrence, compelled "to trace every passionate event to its cause until all are related and understood, turned into knowledge, made a part of itself." Past life becomes the object of poetic contemplation until the spirit can "see life steadily and see it whole," realizing that from a godlike perspective the entire panorama can be seen as a unity and not as a random succession of disparate events. In one of the most obscure passages of this section, Yeats makes another of his curious links between imagination and reality, saying that in the Return, the "dead" are in some sense dependent upon the "living" — dependent not for the concrete events which the dead are reliving, but for the language in which the drama must be expressed. It would seem that expression is indissoluble from life, and that the reliving is not actually accomplished until it is expressed in "the names and words of the drama." [15] This may mean simply that the poet is dependent on the language of his time, and that for the writer, the only knowledge that matters is expressible knowledge; it probably means as well that without the store of images, connotations, and associations resident in the *Anima Mundi* (or tradition) the poet would be helpless.

Detachment and knowledge are interrelated, since each fosters the other, and "the more complete the *Dreaming Back* the more complete the *Return* and the more happy or fortunate the next incarnation." [16] That next incarnation is the new state of awareness attendant upon the revelation which creation brings, but speculation upon what any given experience may bring is unwise. Yeats asks, without really expecting an answer,

> O Rocky Voice,
> Shall we in that great night rejoice?

He replies to his own question in a statement of the limited knowledge possible even to a poet:

> What do we know but that we face
> One another in this place? [17]

The confrontation of experience in its causes and consequences is more important than its eventual outcome.

The third stage of the *Meditation*, which completes the Dreaming Back and the Return, is called by Yeats the Phantasmagoria. The Dreaming Back exhausted pain and pleasure; the Return exhausted the relations of natural experience; the Phantasmagoria will exhaust emotion. Emotion differs from the pain and pleasure associated with the Dreaming Back, and though Yeats nowhere defines it, emotion, linked in this passage with the moral and imaginative life, seems to be a composite word representing the moral and imaginative bent of the person during life. The Phantasmagoria completes life: "if the life was evil, then the *Phantasmagoria* is evil, the criminal completes his crime." Just what this means in relation to the creative act is cloudy, but it certainly involves facing, like the criminal, the logical consequences of unachieved desire; this act, like the reliving of past events, is a way to self-knowledge. Therefore, Yeats goes on to say that the Phantasmagoria "completes not only life but imagination." [18] In this stage, interior desires and apprehensions receive their appropriate exterior images, the congruence between idea and image is established:

> I think of a girl in a Japanese play whose ghost tells a priest of a slight sin, if indeed it was sin, which seems great because of her exaggerated conscience. She is surrounded by flames, and though the priest explains that if she but ceased to believe in those flames they would cease to exist, believe she must, and the play ends in an elaborate dance, the dance of her agony. [19]

In this typical passage, Yeats finds a congenial symbol to link the Phantasmagoria to the artistic process, and the passage in fact has an embarrassment of riches, including as it does several favorite Yeatsian themes. Simply by virtue of being a ghost, the girl belongs to the world of artistic creation, and can be called an artist; by being a character in a play, she represents as well the created image. [20] Like the singer evoked at the beginning of Book III, she is a double symbol, and even a triple one: since the dancer *is* her own Muse (unlike the poet and musician, who have symbolically exterior Muses) this girl is at once Muse, Artist, and Art. Her "exaggerated conscience" resembles the acute sensibility of the poet, which, like her sense of sin, demands visible manifestations, in spite of the dismissal of those manifestations by unsympathetic witnesses. Imagination demands an embodiment in concrete form for its intangible apprehensions (which, to return for a moment to Wordsworth, is why, after each imaginative intuition, a natural scene arises to confirm the revelation). For Yeats, the Phantasmagoria does what Wordsworth coerced nature into doing: it provides all that emotion can imagine.

But in the Phantasmagoria the spirit does not work unaided. It is assisted by the Teaching Spirits of the Thirteenth Cone, who, Yeats warns us, are not like conventional angels, since they have none of the "pure benevolence our exhausted Plato-

nism and Christianity attribute to an angelical being." The
Teaching Spirits have a suspicious resemblance to the Muse;
they come from the Thirteenth Cone, they conduct the spirit
through its past acts, and they "substitute for *Husk* and
Passionate Body supersensual emotion and imagery." What
this last seems to say is that they make possible the transition
from events to images, from body to spirit, which is the core
of the experience "between lives." But the Teaching Spirits
do not act disinterestedly. They are in some sense vampires
like the Leanhaun Shee, feeding upon the actions they trans-
mute: "Our actions, lived in life, or remembered in death,
are the food and drink of the *Spirits* of the *Thirteenth Cone*,
that which gives them separation and solidity." [21] The Teaching Spirits are in fact the djinns which are smoke in the bottle
and only take on substance when they are fulfilling a wish: the
Muse exists only insofar as she operates. If we ask ourselves
why Yeats bothered to invent the Teaching Spirits at all, we
have only to recall the long tradition of the guide through the
wilderness. In the *selva oscura* of past experience (or, in Yeatsian terms, in Purgatory) a guide through the labyrinth, a ferry-
man across the Styx, seems a poetic and moral necessity.

So much for the first two states of "Purgatory." The soul
has freed itself from the concrete, and has come to knowledge of its past life and desires. In the third stage, called the
Shiftings, the soul comes to know the other half of experience:
"his nature is reversed until that knowledge is obtained." [22]
If the man has not known evil, he learns about it; if he has
not known good, he learns about it. This is a purely intellectual experience, not physical, because no new raw material
can be amassed "between lives." In this way, the soul comes
to a tranquil contemplation of good and evil, regarding both
impassively; it is no longer obsessed, as it was in the Dreaming
Back, or caught in the treadmill of repetition, as it was in the
Return. The description of the *Shiftings* in the 1937 *Vision*
is unfortunately elliptical. The 1925 edition is far more com-

plete, and I give the essence of the description here because of its relevance to the poetry:

> At the end of the *Return* . . . the *Spirit* is freed from pleasure and pain and is ready to enter the *Shiftings* where it is freed from Good and Evil, and in this state which is a state of intellect, it lives through a life which is said to be in all things opposite to that lived through in the world, and dreamed through in the *Return* . . . This is brought about by no external law but by a craving in the *Principles* to know what life has hidden, that the *Daimon* who knows intellect but not good and evil, may be satisfied . . . Evil is that which opposes Unity of Being and . . . a relationship of sex displays good and evil in their most subtle and overpowering form. Therefore it is said that in the *Shiftings* men and women relive their loves, and not as in the *Dreaming Back* to exhaust pleasure and pain, but that they may separate that which belongs to their true *primary* or true *antithetical* from that which seems to, and therefore exhaust good and evil themselves. The man would know the woman utterly and so he must relive his love in all things whereof he was ignorant . . . Whether she be there or not there, the dream will be but the same, for he can see nothing but his dream. All now is intellect and he is all Daimon, and tragic and happy circumstance alike offer an intellectual ecstasy at the revelation of truth, and the most horrible tragedy in the end can but seem a figure in a dance.[23]

The theme is again the transformation of life into art, tragedy into a dance, by means of "dream." "It was the dream itself enchanted me" — the line might serve as epigraph to the description of the *Shiftings*. In the equilibrium of creation, the balance that is achieved perhaps falsifies the original experience, precisely because the balance has become more interesting than the original disturbance. The Daimon is not "living" in this state as the man "lived" the opposing experiences; one does not react with intellectual ecstasy to the primary experience of tragedy, only to the contemplation of it. A play in which a character reacts to tragedy with "intellectual ecstasy" is not a play about tragedy but about the contemplation of tragedy, as we shall see later. In this attitude of contemplation, the seeds of creation are laid down, but nothing is actually produced, since the Janus-faced attitude of the soul during the *Shiftings* is one of learning, not expounding. The announced purpose of the *Shiftings* is to bring the soul "to quiescence." [24] After the violent activity of the first two states, the soul gathers together its inner faculties and waits for revelation, for in every Yeatsian system, there comes a time when effort is exhausted and outside intervention is necessary.

That intervention comes in the fourth state, called the *Marriage* or the *Beatitude*, where remorse yields to harmony. This is the state of perfect definition of form: "In life, seeing that the *Four Faculties* and the *Husk* and *Passionate Body* constrain all, we are in accident and passion; but now *Spirit* and *Celestial Body* constrain all, the one calling up all concrete universal quality and idea, and the other closing it in the unique image." Yeats's language describing the *Beatitude* lacks all coherence. It "is said to pass in unconsciousness, or in a moment of consciousness" and it is useless to ask which; like all indescribable states, it is both at once. Yeats has recourse to the terminology of religion and mystical experience in order to recount the moment of union between idea and image, but the Beatific Vision is described only metaphorically, in Christian terms: "The *Celestial Body* is the Divine Cloak lent to all, it falls away at the consummation and Christ is revealed." [25]

We are back to the imagery of the Fifteenth Phase, and it is no accident that the *Marriage* is so briefly described in this section of *A Vision*. For one thing, Yeats had said all he could about it in Books I and II; for another, there is very little that can be said about the ineffable.[26] Outside *A Vision*, on the other hand, there are several interesting comments on the point of rest represented by the *Beatitude*, and these comments emphasize what *A Vision* for the most part omits — the state of "innocence" regained by the soul after it has relived, in various ways, its past life. In the *Autobiographies*,

Yeats writes: "When we are dead, according to my belief, we live our lives backward for a certain number of years, treading the paths that we have trodden, growing young again, even childish again, till some attain an innocence that is no longer a mere accident of nature, but the human intellect's crowning achievement." Or, as he put it in "A Prayer for My Daughter":

> . . . All hatred driven hence,
> The soul recovers radical innocence
> And learns at last that it is self-delighting,
> Self-appeasing, self-affrighting,
> And that its own sweet will is Heaven's will.[27]

The discovery of the oneness of Heaven and the self means in poetic terms that "the kingdom of heaven is within you," and though Yeats sometimes uses Christian terms in his symbolism, more often than not he will turn elsewhere, as in this passage where he clothes his discovery in Shelleyan imagery combined with Irish myth:

> Sometimes the soul is a boat, and in this boat Asia sails against the current from age to youth, from youth to infancy, and so to the pre-natal condition "peopled by shapes too bright to see." In the fourth act [of *Prometheus Unbound*] this condition, man's first happiness and his last, sings its ecstatic song: and yet although the first and last it is always near at hand, "Tir n'an og is not far from any of you," as a countrywoman said to me.[28]

The discovery of Tir n'an og comes in the achieving of "radical innocence," since it is in the moment of perfect detachment from the contrary impulses of past experience that Paradise momentarily exists. "Poetry concerns itself with the creation of Paradises," Yeats's father had written in a letter of 1914 [29] and like so many of his opinions, it had been incorporated by Yeats into his own system of thought. The connection of Paradise with Purgatory is only momentary, and not permanent, as Yeats tells us later in Book III,[30] but

that is rather because of the limitations of the human mind
than because of lack of affinity between the two states.

It might seem that the *Marriage* would be the terminal state
in Purgatory, but that is not the case; it is followed by two
more states, called the *Purification* and the *Foreknowledge*,
where the Spirit "is in the presence of all those activities
whose *Complementary Dream* is in our art, or music or literature," according to the 1925 *Vision*. The term "Complementary Dream" (which Yeats later abandoned) suggests
strongly the reciprocal relation between human art and the
"life" of "the dead" in Book III. The "dead" dream about
human life, reliving it; the living, when they produce art, are
incarnating a dream about the life in the world of the dead.
"We can know nothing of the *Daimon* except by the *Complementary Dream*," [31] says Yeats unequivocally; what he tells
us in Book III, then, he presumably learned from art.

The first of these two states, the *Purification*, is familiar to
us from "Byzantium," in which the soul breaks "bitter furies
of complexity": " 'We have no power,' said an inhabitant
of the state, 'except to purify our intention,' and when I asked
of what, replied: 'Of complexity.' " [32] The old *Husk* and
Passionate Body are replaced by new ones, in Yeats's parallel
to the Christian doctrine of the glorified body, in which the
senses operate in a way mysteriously transfigured. There is
no denying that in the creative act the senses are involved,
but the daffodils flash upon the inward eye, not upon the outward one. Those inward senses, as acute and as responsible
to the outside world as their organic counterparts, compose
the new *Husk* of this state, which exists, as Yeats says, sub-
ordinate to the *Celestial Body*, to the inscapes or Daimons
of the world. In the *Purification*, the Spirit is freed of its
obsessive concern with its past actions, and can begin to look
forward to "its own particular aim." It is in control, not
possessed: "It becomes self-shaping, self-moving, plastic to
itself." [33] We are, at this point, not surprised to hear that the

aim toward which the Spirit works is a form of perfection, and more specifically, "those forms copied in the Arts and Sciences." [34] What the Spirit knows is Ideal Form, the *haecceitas* grasped by intuition, and this is what it seeks to imitate, by itself becoming one of these forms. Yeats makes, as he almost inevitably does, an analogy with lyric poetry: "The creative power of the lyric poet depends upon his accepting some one of a few traditional attitudes, lover, sage, hero, scorner of life. They bring us back to the spiritual norm." [35]

This is a most peculiar doctrine, and needs some justifying. The whole idea of the *persona* seems artificial at first glance, a product of the morbid self-consciousness of modern poetry. The striking of "attitudes" has overtones of the *Yellow Book*, and in Yeats an attitude is often confused with a pose. Nevertheless, the attitude has a nobler intent: it is not only a mask through which the poet can project feelings; it is also a tap root sent down to sources of art. It has not been said often enough that the mask is adopted in order to free creative power, that it is a condition of penetration to the *Anima Mundi*. What matters to Yeats is that most lyric poetry has been written by "the lunatic, the lover, and the poet" who are "of imagination all compact"; add the sage and the hero and the disillusioned man, and you have Yeats's group. The doctrine of the mask is one more way in which Yeats emphasizes the usefulness of tradition to the poet. He insists that the traditional attitudes are "spiritual norms" and that there is no point in trying to avoid them; discounting them leads only to impoverishment. In the *Purification*, then, what we think of as "creation" proper begins. Adopting an attitude, the Spirit can begin its proper work; and freed of distraction, in touch with the *Anima Mundi*, purified of "complexities of mire and blood," it can see before it an aim of perfection.

Again, we might have expected this to be the terminus of the creative act, but Yeats adds another stage, the *Foreknowledge* (which we would call the Acceptance), probably derived from Plato's myth of Er in the tenth book of *The Republic*.[36] Yeats's state of foreknowledge precedes reincarnation because "the *Spirit* cannot be reborn until the vision of that life [of the next incarnation] is completed and accepted." The "next life" is one which incorporates the new awareness resulting from creative expression, and to refuse to accept the new life would be for the poet to deny his poem, since each new poem in some way is an advance over its predecessor. "During its sleep in the womb," says Yeats, "the *Spirit* accepts its future life, declares it just." [37] That future life, in terms of the growth of the poet's mind, includes three stages: a new equilibrium after the catharsis of creation; the inevitable unbalancing of that equilibrium by the assaults of experience; and presumably, the desire to re-establish the equilibrium by another term of purgation. But more than this, the future life must be lived in the knowledge gained by past existence, incorporating the always painful advances in wisdom. The temptation to deny experience is always present in the state of the *Foreknowledge*, where lassitude or fear or both together may deter the soul from "rebirth." But if the choice of acceptance is made, the soul is freed from Purgatory, "reincarnation" takes place, the creative act is completed, and the renewed spirit stands open once again to the invasions of life.

Certain questions arise from the descriptions of Purgatory, and Yeats's answers to them are equivocal, as they had to be. What form does the Spirit have in Purgatory, he asks himself, and answers that its forms are multiple:

In the *Meditation* it wears the form it had immediately before death; in the *Dreaming Back* and the *Phantasmagoria*, should it appear to the living, it has the form of the dream, in the *Return* the form worn during the event explored, in the *Shiftings* whatever form was most familiar to others during its life; in the *Purification* whatever form it fancies, for it is now the Shape-changer of legend.[38]

There is clearly a progression in this description from physical to imaginative form, with dream as an intermediate stage; and there is a passage from a determined to an autonomous form. This change tallies with the description so far given of the mental states during the process of creation. The mind in creation receives the unrefined and determined sense impression, transforms it to an image, reduces it to its essence by deleting irrelevant details, and at last confers on it its final imaginative shape.

This passage describing the metamorphoses of form is the apogee of Book III, and in fact Yeats prepared for it twenty-two pages earlier in *A Vision*, when at the end of Book II he announced that "one discovers . . . at a certain moment between life and death, what ancient legends have called the Shape-Changers." In making this discovery, "one illustrates a moment of European history, of every mind that passes from premise to judgment, of every love that runs its whole course." [39] Things are tripled: in the world, in the mind, in the heart, the same process occurs, and the Shape-Changers are its genii. "The Soul in Judgment" is an attempt to discover the paradigm that lies beneath these similar processes, to discover, in fact, the map of mental travel. "It is not too extravagant," says Wallace Stevens in *The Necessary Angel*, "to think of resemblances and of the repetitions of resemblances as a source of the ideal," [40] and this type of metaphorical thinking, underlying Yeats's parallels between universal history and interior activity, accounts for his efforts to make the resemblances as close as possible, even to the point of falsifying history. It is this wish to connect the mental process with those things which resemble it, while being outside it, that makes Yeats lead into a discussion of universal history in the book which follows "The Soul in Judgment."

Yeats asks himself two more questions about the sojourn in Purgatory: is the spirit alone there? and is Purgatory a species of Paradise? [41] To each he answers yes and no. In the first instance, sometimes the spirits are alone, and sometimes they are accompanied by those they have known during life, by their own opposites, or by those whom they choose to summon. We recall the vision in "Byzantium":

> A mouth that has no moisture and no breath
> Breathless mouths may summon;
> I hail the superhuman;
> I call it death-in-life and life-in-death.[42]

The Spirit is most likely to meet in Purgatory those people with whom it has had in life a passionate relationship, and this again stands to reason by analogy with the creative process: "The child of one life [becomes] the husband, wife, brother or sister of the next. Sometimes, however, a single relationship will repeat itself, turning its revolving wheel again and again, especially . . . where there has been strong sexual passion." [43] Although Yeats speaks here in terms of successive lives, and not of the period between lives, he makes it clear in the following paragraphs that what is lived in life must be "expiated" in Purgatory, till the Spirit is freed of its passionate attachment to these few people.[44] Sometimes the Spirit remains eternally bound (and in Yeats's case the eternal bond seems to have been to the image of Maud Gonne, who appears as child, woman, wife, Muse, and Fury in different poems).

Purgatory, in spite of its brief moment of Beatitude, "should not be considered as a reward or paradise. Neither between death and birth nor between birth and death can the soul find more than momentary happiness; its object is to pass rapidly round its circle and find freedom from that circle." [45] The *Beatitude* is a foretaste of the freedom of the Thirteenth Cone, but is not itself that stasis of perfect creation. It must be recalled that in Book III Yeats is speaking of the activity, not the product, of creation; only the product is free from the depredations of "devouring time," since the engendering intuition is brief and passing, and the happiness it brings is momentary.

> Beauty is momentary in the mind —
> The fitful tracing of a portal;
> But in the flesh it is immortal.[46]

In the object and in the poem the incarnate beauty is to be found, but in the mind, it is transitory. When Yeats comes in Book III to talk about the Thirteenth Cone, which is the mental equivalent of the Fifteenth Phase, he calls it not a cone but a sphere: it is, then, the mental world to which purgatorial activity theoretically, but only in the ideal realm, would lead.

> The *Thirteenth Cone* is a sphere because sufficient to itself; but as seen by Man it is a cone. It becomes even conscious of itself as so seen, like some great dancer, the perfect flower of modern culture, dancing some primitive dance and conscious of his or her own life and of the dance.[47]

We are at once reminded of several of the late poems, where something is seen at the same time under two aspects, temporal and eternal. The dancer, in the act of creating the dance, is at once primitive and modern, and by combining the two qualities, ageless or eternal. It is only man's perspective, we are led to think, which bestows a niche in time on the creation of art; seen properly, all creation is contemporaneous; or better, time is irrelevant to it.

Yeats apparently felt obliged to provide an explanation of how entrance to the Thirteenth Cone becomes possible, but in the course of the explanation he entangled himself almost hopelessly in the many meanings of his symbols. If we recall that the Daimon can represent the poet's ideal selfhood, his subjectivity, his inspiration, his antithesis, and his beloved (all of these being somehow opposite to his natural self), we will not be surprised that in pursuing one of these meanings rather than another Yeats will come to peculiar conclusions. It seems to me that in writing about the escape into the Thirteenth Cone Yeats had in mind the Daimon as beloved, and in fact he makes the analogy explicit here, as will be seen shortly. Yeats says that to enter the Thirteenth Cone one's Daimon must unite with a Spirit of the Thirteenth Cone, and that this entrance represents "the deliverance from birth and death." We have already said that in such a mental state Muse and poetic mind would be in perpetual conjunction — desirable, perhaps, but obviously impossible. Yeats names as the two things that make this union possible, "cruelty" and "ignorance," which, according to Yeats's "instructors," constitute evil.

It is hard to see how this odd type of evil could be the conditions for entrance into a species of paradise: Yeats's metaphysics seems to have gone too far. But when we recall that for him, the cruelty of the beloved and the ignorance of the lover (themes which recur so often in the plays) were the two essential ingredients for a tenacious passion, the passage becomes less obscure. Otherwise, he would scarcely have said that those two conditions are necessary, not only for entrance into the Thirteenth Cone, but also for the union of the Daimons of man and woman.[48] The human fact suggested the analogy, which seems strained at first reading. There are elements of truth in it, however, which I hope will appear in the discussion of *A Full Moon in March* and *The King of the Great Clock Tower*. Blake's "Mental Traveller" comes once again to mind, and gives us another clue to Yeats's meaning. Being overmastered, cruelly subdued, nailed down upon the rock, is one way to describe the artist's feelings under the weight of "inspiration": he who, by virtue of his special sensibility, had triumphed over reality, is in turn victim and reduced to helplessness by the despotism of the Muse. It may be only his ignorance of the price exacted that keeps him from renouncing art.

The union of a Daimon and a Spirit of the Thirteenth Cone can be frustrated, and art in consequence prevented. This frustration results "from the prevention or refusal of experience itself" which is for Yeats a cardinal sin. "Not the fruit of experience, but experience itself, is the end," said Walter Pater; [49] and Yeats, while diverging from Pater to explore "the rag-and-bone shop of the heart" [50] nevertheless believed in his prime axiom. The refusal of experience may spring, says Yeats, "from pride, from the fear of injuring another or oneself, from something which we call asceticism; it may have any cause, but the *Spirit of the Thirteenth Cone* is starved." [51] The "Ghostly Self" becomes a victim in this species of artistic cowardice, where the Muse is starved in order that some other Deity may be propitiated. [52] Pater had warned against this too: "The theory or idea or system which requires of us the sacrifice of any part of this experience, in consideration of some interest into which we cannot enter, or some abstract theory we have not identified with ourselves, or of what is only conventional, has no real claim upon us." [53]

Reversing the theory of sublimation, Yeats would have it that ascetic experience is a lower form of the true divine communion which is attainable only through the material world. For Yeats the two are easily reciprocal:

So closely do all the bonds resemble each other that in the most ascetic schools of India the novice tortured by his passion will pray to the God to come to him as a woman and have with him sexual intercourse; nor is the symbol subjective, for in the morning his pillow will be saturated with temple incense, his breast yellow with the saffron dust of some temple offering. Such experience is said, however, to wear itself out swiftly giving place to the supernatural union. [54]

That "supernatural union" is the true union with a spirit of the Thirteenth Cone. The ascetic progresses from carnal experience to "mental travel," but even this may have its carnal side: "Sometimes the God may select some living symbol of himself. If the ascetic is a woman, some wandering priest perhaps, if a man, some wandering priestess, but such loves are brief." [55] We will encounter the figure of the priestess in *The Herne's Egg*, Yeats's longest dramatic exposition of the "supernatural union"; till then it is enough to notice that the idea of an ascetic finding supernatural communion in sexual intercourse includes several of Yeats's favorite antinomies reconciled. "Sex and the Dead," Yeats is reported to have said, "are the only things that can interest a serious mind," and outrageous as the statement is, it sums up Book III.[56]

Yeats ends Book III with a variant on one of the closing statements of Book II, quoted earlier: "Only one symbol exists, though the reflecting mirrors make many appear and all different"; or, as Yeats says in "The Statues," "Mirror on mirror mirrored is all the show." [57] In Book I, the *Vision* is seen from the vantage point of an exterior observer who can watch, without being involved, the turning of the wheel; in Book II, the mechanism is turned inside out, so to speak, and we see the inner works of the great system; in Book III, the works are wound up and we observe their progress, as the soul moves from "death" to "life." Book IV brings us to an elaborately metaphorical view, couched in terms of history, of what we have so far seen in terms of archetype and image.

Chapter IV

The Great Year of
the Ancients

I N Book IV of *A Vision*, Yeats returns once more to
the experience of the Fifteenth Phase, but he considers it
under a new system of metaphors, a hodgepodge of astronomical and historical terms. Book IV, the most incoherent
section of *A Vision*, is neither so geometrical as Book II nor
so ghostly as Book III, and it seems at times only "Vague
memories, nothing but memories" of Yeats's intellectual rag-
and-bone shop. In it, however, two broad areas emerge spot-
lighted, of which the first is the antithesis between Christ
and Caesar, and the second, the idea of the Great Year. The
two areas are united in the central theme of the book: that in
the Great Year the warring images are absorbed in a larger
pattern. "My instructors," Yeats writes, "offer for a symbol
[of the Great Year] the lesser unities that combine into a
work of art and leave no remainder." [1]

The analogy between the Great Year and the unity of art
can work both ways; if art tells us something of the Great
Year, so may the Great Year tell us something of the nature
of art. The "system" is, after all, a "stylistic arrangement of
experience," and we may therefore decode the Great Year in
human terms. The fruitlessness of a quasi-scientific treatment
of the Great Year must have been apparent even to Yeats.
Indeed, this is suggested by his comment that scholars, at-

tempting to determine the duration of the world by Plato's Golden Number in the *Republic*, had arrived at fourteen different solutions.[2] If we look at the Great Year as a historical symbol of the Fifteenth Phase, or as a temporal symbol for poetic unity, we may progress beyond the fourteen answers to the conundrum. Even Yeats admitted that the ancient world accepted the idea of the Great Year "not for its astronomical but for its moral value." [3]

The scholarly refinements of the Great Year held no charm for Yeats, who was interested in it only insofar as it was a visible symbol. "It grew more complicated with the spread of Greek astronomy," he admits, "but it is always the simpler, more symbolic form, with its conflict of light and dark, heat and cold, that concerns me most." [4] The Year, then, is not so much a progress of successive states as an oscillation from antithesis to antithesis. Time is measured qualitatively rather than quantitatively, a fact that the King of the Great Clock Tower, for one, fails to understand.

The central problem is the relation of the parts of the Great Year (the oscillations, the antitheses) to the Year itself. Are they simply its component parts? Is the whole equal to the sum of its parts? If it is greater than the sum of its parts, what sort of totality does it finally exhibit? Does it resemble its component parts or wholly surpass them? The questions, which may seem esoteric when predicated of a dubious astrological phenomenon, become much more to the point when we apply them to those "lesser unities that combine into a work of art" which the Year represents. Yeats is concerned with the problem of conflicting symbols, and the conflicting realities that the symbols represent. Is the unity imposed by the work of art an arithmetical sum? Does one symbol plus one symbol equal only two symbols or something more? Is there any real relation between the order generated by formal composition and a natural order in things? Can one discover an order, not impose one? Wallace Stevens makes the distinction:

                              To impose is not
        To discover. To discover an order as of
        A season, to discover summer and know it,

        To discover winter and know it well, to find,
        Not to impose, not to have reasoned at all,
        Out of nothing to have come on major weather,

        It is possible, possible, possible. It must
        Be possible.[5]

Stevens' desperate protestations put Yeats's difficulties in
their most acute form. If the order of the Great Year is indeed
"discovered," then the generic work of art which it resembles
is not a contrived collection of unrelated fragments but a
mirror of integrity.

Though there is a temporal succession (in a poem as well
as in the Great Year) there is no discontinuity, and Yeats
sums up the relations between the parts and the whole in one
of the most far-reaching statements in *A Vision*: "development is indeed a temporal image of that which remains in
itself." [6] To say that succession is symbolic of stasis seems
paradoxical, but we remember Crazy Jane's affirmation of
the same thesis; all her perceptions of God come from succession and change.

            That lover of a night
            Came when he would,
            Went in the dawning light
            Whether I would or no;
            Men come, men go,
            All things remain in God.[7]

This is not, I think, a case of stating a contrary as compensation. It is not because Crazy Jane is repelled by her body
("like a road that men pass over") that she sings her refrain
about stability; she is not turning in disgust from the endless
changing traffic of her life. By no means: she perceives in the
succession of men, in the reverses of civilization even, the
guarantee of a permanence beyond flux. Poetic composition

can be seen as the fragmenting of a psychological experience into a succession of words and images, so that what originated as an instantaneous and integral vision has somehow to be displayed in component parts. The Great Year "proves" that the parts, given time to work themselves out, indeed reproduce the pattern of the original experience, at which point "the Great Year begins anew." The movement, oddly enough, *is* the pattern, instead of being a falsification of it.

The aspect of the Great Year that interested Yeats was, as we might expect, the month of March, when the world "was restored, where Love began to prevail over Discord, Day over Night." In that month, according to tradition, the world was created, re-established after the flood, and finally redeemed. The presiding spirits of the month of March are the "world restorers" — the Spirit that moved upon the Waters, Noah on Mount Ararat, and the Messiah. Yeats invokes two "heresies" to support his views, declaring that "the creation itself had been but a restoration" and that the Resurrection was only one of many periodical revolutions — as of course it is, symbolically viewed.[8]

The Great Year meant to Yeats, then, "the freshness of an early world," and represented the possibility of perpetual genesis, of inexhaustible creation. The point needs no laboring in respect to poetry; the Year is the guarantee that poetic springs will not fail. It is characteristic of Yeats to add a reference to the Phoenix by quoting Francis Thompson's line "Love unconsumed shall chant in his own funeral pyre," since Yeats associated the Phoenix with the life peculiar to the poetic image, as we can see in *Per Amica Silentia Lunae*. The Phoenix represents the quintessential element of the mental image, the element which the image possesses beyond earth ("one's own life"), water (the element where the images are "mirrored"), air ("the images themselves"), and fire ("certain aims and governing loves"). The obscure passage which I have been summarizing implies that the image in the poet's mind is certainly grounded in both psychological fact and the physical object which it mirrors; further, it has a separate existence of its own and participates in certain overriding concerns which go beyond the single emotion that gave it rise; but, beyond these four "elements," it has an autonomy (raising it, presumably, from the simple level of self-expression to the level of art). Born of the four elements, it is yet unique, like the Phoenix, "a bird born out of the fire." [9]

We have already seen that the Great Wheel and the doctrine of reincarnation are for Yeats symbolic ways of affirming the truth of poetic creation and renewal, and we may conclude from the references to the Phoenix that the Great Year too is a symbol for the same truths. In Book IV Yeats is again assuring himself that "for all this, nature is never spent." He tries, in fact, to impose Books I and II on Book IV, with disastrous results from the point of view of logic. In one place, for instance, he assumes a lunar zodiac as well as a solar one, and has the Faculties moving in one, the Principles in the other. This is mainly an exercise in ingenuity, and one of many sporadic efforts Yeats made to imply a consistency in *A Vision* which simply does not exist; I mention it only to show that Yeats was aware that the phenomena he chooses to discuss in one book of *A Vision* are fundamentally the same as the phenomena appearing in any other.

One of the difficulties in the symbol of the Great Year is that the return of the constellations to their original places implies, as Yeats points out, "civilisation perpetually returning to the same point." And, by extension into the poetic realm, it implies that nothing has been learned by each venture into creation; but this is the last thing that Yeats would want to assert. And so, in addition to summoning up the metaphysical Great Year, Yeats must invoke history, where it is evident that although cycles resemble each other, they are by no means duplications of each other. Yeats says rather defensively:

An historical symbolism which covers too great a period of time for imagination to grasp or experience to explain may seem too theoretical, too arbitrary, to serve any practical purpose; it is, however, necessary to the myth if we are not to suggest, as Vico did, civilisation perpetually returning to the same point.[10]

Consequently, in this book, as I have said above, Yeats has recourse to Christ and Caesar as well as to the symbolism of the astronomical Great Year. I pass over the explanation of the detailed historical interactions (as shown in the diagram preceding Book V) both because the fantastic scheme as it is worked out has few, if any, implications for the line of interpretation I have chosen, and because Yeats's prose is so tangled in explaining it that the space required to expound it would be all out of proportion to its importance. Yeats's inferences about history are sometimes naïvely charming: "I consider," he disarmingly admits, "that a conflict between religious and secular thought, because it governs all that is most interior and spiritual in myself, must be the projector of the era." [11] For him, macrocosm and microcosm are one, and all the remarks about history are indeed remarks about his own "interior and spiritual" states.

Christ and Caesar, East and West, primary and antithetical, form the antinomies of the historical discussion. Yeats's lists of the opposing qualities are well known, but they must be quoted again here. "A *primary* dispensation looking beyond itself towards a transcendent power is dogmatic, levelling, unifying, feminine, humane, peace its means and end; an *antithetical* dispensation obeys imminent power, is expressive, hierarchical, multiple, masculine, harsh, surgical." [12] We cannot doubt that the antithetical qualities, supposedly those of the civilization that we are approaching, are in reality the poetic qualities toward which Yeats had consciously directed his writing in his later work. Yeats was fully aware of the originality of his poetry: "You say that poetry cannot be changed but all my life I have tried to change it," he wrote to

Edmund Dulac in 1937.[13] In pursuing untried directions, the destination is always problematic; or, historically speaking, we can never say what the new Incarnation will be.

What else it must be no man can say, for always at the critical moment the *Thirteenth Cone*, the sphere, the unique intervenes.

> Somewhere in sands of the desert
> A shape with lion body and the head of a man,
> A gaze blank and pitiless as the sun,
> Is moving its slow thighs, while all about it
> Reel shadows of the indignant desert birds.[14]

It has not been generally recognized, I think, that Yeats, for all his fascinated horror, *approves* intellectually, if not emotionally, of the Second Coming. "When I was a boy," Yeats writes in *Wheels and Butterflies*, "everybody talked about progress, and rebellion against my elders took the form of aversion to that myth. I took satisfaction in certain public disasters, felt a sort of ecstasy at the contemplation of ruin . . . I began to imagine . . . a brazen winged beast that I associated with laughing, ecstatic destruction." [15] The destruction of the known is always a terrifying experience; and the clutching of the familiar is the greatest deterrent to new knowledge. "The Second Coming" is a poem of intellectual acceptance and emotional retreat; the two attitudes produce the curious conflict in tone. The terror of the unique outdoes, finally, the horror of the original anarchy, simply because anarchy is known, historically and personally, and has been coped with before, while the Beast forebodes an entirely new experience. The Deluge is a familiar symbol, and so is disintegration:

> Things fall apart; the centre cannot hold;
> Mere anarchy is loosed upon the world,
> The blood-dimmed tide is loosed, and everywhere
> The ceremony of innocence is drowned.[16]

The original Deluge, we recall, did not drown "the ceremony of innocence," but rather came to cleanse corruption, and this is the characteristic function of mythical cataclysms. Yeats's world, however, is not being destroyed out of wrath, but out of necessity.[17] There is no agency at work, no God repaying with vengeance. The ceremony of innocence is drowned by a tide of anarchy which, though evil and murderous in itself, is nevertheless historically innocent, acting as an agent of inevitable historical necessity. Yeats makes this clear in "A Prayer for My Daughter," written close in time to "The Second Coming" and immediately following it in the *Collected Poems*. Yeats paces in his tower,

> Imagining in excited reverie
> That the future years had come,
> Dancing to a frenzied drum,
> Out of the murderous innocence of the sea.

Innocence is opposed to innocence: the purging innocence of blind matter in the sea yet destroys the evolved "innocence" of civilization, which is a very sophisticated thing, the delight of the soul in itself:

> . . . All hatred driven hence,
> The soul recovers radical innocence,
> And learns at last that it is self-delighting,
> Self-appeasing, self-affrighting,
> And that its own sweet will is Heaven's will . . .
>
> How but in custom and in ceremony
> Are innocence and beauty born? [18]

It is a piece of consummate trickery on Yeats's part, in one sense, to give destroyer and destroyed the identical name of "Innocence." We should not forget that for him the word has overtones from Blake. In the *Songs of Innocence*, the word has several reaches of meaning, the first being the obvious one of a state unviolated by experience, but the others having to do with a state beyond experience (as, for example, in "The Little Girl Lost," "Night," "The Little Black Boy"). So, in Yeats, the Rough Beast represents one variety of innocence, a blind, primitive sort. He symbolizes, literally, a new birth, a passing to another level, leaving behind all that has been developed and refined in the old state. The Beast is a world-restorer, like the Spirit that moved upon the Waters, like Noah on Mount Ararat, and like the Messiah; but while the biblical and classical accounts of world renewal celebrated the beauty of the fresh world, Yeats has nothing to say of a Golden Age. The fertility of the Fourth Eclogue, the rainbow of Genesis, the gifts of the Magi, have no part in the Yeatsian comment on the renewal of experience; his *Parousia* takes place in a desert, whose attributes ("a gaze blank and pitiless as the sun") are transferred to the Beast. There is likewise no place for the ideal beauty which is often a corollary of renewal. Christ, traditionally, was ideally formed according to artistic canons of harmony, and Virgil's "parve puer," smiling at his mother, lies in a cradle full of flowers. Yeats's Beast, however, is a monstrous slouching combination of lion and man, enigmatic as the Sphinx, but without the monumental grandeur of statuary.

If, as we have said, the Great Year is Yeats's guarantee that poetic springs will not fail, then the Second Coming, being one of the manifestations of the several recurrences that make up the Magnus Annus, must be a symbol to us of the nature of Yeatsian inspiration. The Beast is no conventional Muse, certainly, and we may momentarily be as indignant as the desert birds at its sudden hulking appearance. However, the poem is in every sense the narrating of a vision which reveals new knowledge:

> A vast image out of *Spiritus Mundi*
> Troubles my sight . . .
> The darkness drops again; but now I know
> That twenty centuries of stony sleep
> Were vexed to nightmare by a rocking cradle.[19]

For twenty centuries (during the primary Christian civilization) the antithetical Beast has slept like a granite sphinx; now somewhere the cradle has been set rocking for it and its

sleep, turned to nightmare, has been broken. Translated out
of the historical symbolism, the images would seem to mean
that some event has triggered one variety of imagination from
its dormant state into sudden and violent activity, as the
poem begins its struggle to be born. If this seems a farfetched
interpretation, we have only to look at Yeats's comment on
coming revelation: "Why should we believe that religion can
never bring round its antithesis? Is it true that our air is disturbed, as Mallarmé said, by 'the trembling of the veil of the
Temple', or 'that our whole age is seeking to bring forth a
sacred book'?" [20] To bring forth not a Savior, not a Restorer,
in any personal sense, but "a sacred book." It does not matter
that we can be amused at Yeats's credulity in thinking *Louis
Lambert* and *Seraphita* the sacred books he had been waiting
for. What is revealing is that for Yeats the Second Coming
is on one level at least a literary phenomenon.

I have spent so much time on "The Second Coming" because it illustrates very well the poetic use to which Yeats
put materials from *A Vision*, and moreover, it is a poem which
has been given, in most commentaries, an exclusively historical
or esoteric interpretation rather than a psychological one.[21]
It seems to me not so much a poem about Fascism, or about
war, as about mental experience, and while the First World
War may have provided symbols, it hardly provided the
core.

"The Second Coming" is a case in point of the interlocking
of the two main concerns of Book IV of *A Vision*: the Great
Year (recurrence) and Christ versus Caesar (antithesis). We
have seen what the Great Year meant to Yeats; we must now
decide what divinity symbolizes. F. A. C. Wilson, in his
exposition of Yeats's symbolic links between Christ, Caesar,
Dionysus, and St. John the Baptist shows that Christ and
Caesar are messianic opposites, Christ being primary, Caesar
antithetical. Yeats's intention, Wilson says, "is to suggest that
the fact of Caesar's death at the Ides of March, and of his

subsequent apotheosis, led a large part of the Roman empire to regard him as the Messiah prophesied in the Sibylline books." Dionysus and Christ "are to be associated in that they stand for two opposite types of saviour, Dionysus the victim-god mankind can imagine in a subjective, pagan period, and Christ the redeemer in an objective, self-obliterating cycle." Finally, Wilson remarks that an essay on John the Baptist by Coventry Patmore gave Yeats grounds for finding St. John, like Dionysus, a symbol of natural love — "the precursor and necessary antithesis of Christ." [22]

But Mr. Wilson neglects to say that divinity for Yeats is associated with the moon and its phases. In *A Vision*, Yeats explicitly associates the two:

> Before "Ides" lost its first meaning, the ceremony [of the discovery of the body of Attis] needed a full moon or the fifteenth day of a lunar March. Even Easter, which the rest of Christendom commemorated on the first full moon after the Vernal Equinox, would sometimes be commemorated by Christians living under the influence of the Julian Year upon the day before the fifteenth day of the solar March.[23]

We can hardly ignore so clear an indication that Christ and Caesar have something to do with the imaginative efflorescence which takes place at Phase 15. Caesar, like the Rough Beast, Dionysus, and St. John, belongs to the antithetical group, and he was not the expected Messiah because it was time for a primary revelation when Christ was born. Although Yeats clearly prefers antithetical revelation to primary, he does not deny imaginative power to the primary. Christianity is born at the full of the moon just as much as the classical civilization or the new antithetical civilization which, according to the system, we are now about to witness. Yeats never denies the intrinsic imaginative stimulus attached to the Christian symbols; he simply denies their present validity, at least for himself. Wallace Stevens' meditative woman asks in "Sunday Morning,"

> What is divinity if it can come
> Only in silent shadows and in dreams? . . .
> Divinity must live within herself.[24]

This is Yeats's stand too, and for Yeats, the most convenient images for that interior divinity were all the gods outside Christianity, whether Attis, Dionysus, Caesar, or the Rough Beast. The plurality of Yeats's divinities is an indication of their psychological origin. Yeats is not erecting a counter-system to Christianity, as most commentators seem to assume, but rather abolishing imaginative monotheism in favor of a plurality of worship, since it is the single-minded devotion demanded by Christianity which is natively repugnant to Yeats's imagination. The only divinity the imagination can acknowledge is Proteus, and the most distinguishing character-istic of the antithetical view is its multiplicity, by which it satisfies the desires of the imagination. "*Antithetical* revela-tion," says Yeats in the conclusion to Book IV, "is an intel-lectual influx neither from beyond mankind nor born of a virgin, but begotten from our spirit and history." [25] If we understand that the Second Coming is to be "begotten from our spirit" we can guess, at least, that its primary interest to Yeats is its origin in the imagination. In Book V of *A Vision*, Yeats will describe the passage of the imagination from its "classical" antithetical phase to its single-minded "Christian" phase; the transformations of imaginative response will give him, he hopes, some clue to the impending change toward a new source of poetry.

Chapter V

Dove or Swan

Dove or Swan? asks Yeats, and decides for the Swan, in this most metaphorical of all the books of *A Vision*. The issue is between Christianity, the Holy Ghost as the Dove of procreative Divinity, the primary revelation; and the Classical, the Swan as Jove the impregnator, the antithetical revelation. Book V is distinguished by having as its epigraph one of Yeats's finest poems, "Leda and the Swan," here called simply "Leda." In a sense, the whole of Book V is an enigmatic commentary on that enigmatic poem, so it seems worthwhile to consider the issues suggested by Yeats's extraordinary sonnet before going on to the prose.

The poem is a disturbing one: the form itself is enough to cause vague uneasiness in us without our knowing why. When we "reason about these things with a later reason" we realize how completely the poem is at war with the sonnet form as we know it, even as it has been transformed by Hopkins and later poets. Contemporary poets (Auden is a good example) have altered the diction of the sonnet, but not its movement; if one of their sonnets ends with a question, more likely than not it is a purely rhetorical one, not affecting at all the neat unity achieved in the sestet. In reading both traditional and modern sonnets we are generally left exalted or depressed, either foreseeing "new styles in architecture, a change of heart," or hearing "thoughts against thoughts in groans grind."

Yeats changes all this, and with design, in "Leda and the Swan." The question at the end is not a rhetorical one at all, and I mean by that that Yeats himself did not know a final answer to it. The poem is about a transference of power; the question is whether knowledge was transferred as well.[1] If we examine the poem to see just what sort of power is meant, we are likely to think at first that merely physical power is implied:

> A sudden blow: the great wings beating still
> Above the staggering girl.

This is rape, after all, or seems to be; the power is an impregnating one, and violent; but it has a peculiar (if inhuman) tenderness, for Leda feels

> . . . her thighs caressed
> By the dark webs . . .
> And how can body, laid in that white rush,
> But feel the strange heart beating where it lies?

Eternity is in love with the productions of time, said Blake, and the truth of his aphorism appears in Jove's assault. Leda, although she attempts a helpless resistance, finally is stirred by the presence of the "feathered glory," and the shudder in the loins is hers as well as the swan's. We sense this, I think, in Yeats's language; Leda's thighs are "loosening," not "loosened"; she may be terrified, but she finds the swan glorious (as I show below, we see the poem through her eyes); she is not numbed, but alive to the strange heartbeat.[2]

The power, then, although in itself Olympian and "indifferent," is something that can move the heart as well as master the body. Leda in the octave is "caught," but in the sestet she is "caught up"; there lies all the difference between captivity and rapture. Something has happened to Leda, but what? She has become a channel for cataclysmic change, it is true:

> A shudder in the loins engenders there
> The broken wall, the burning roof and tower
> And Agamemnon dead.[3]

If Yeats were interested only in historical revolution, the poem would end there, and if the poem were a conventional sonnet, this would be the conclusion. The final three lines make it perfectly clear that it is Leda's interior change, and that alone, to which the poem has been directing itself. What is the result, the poem asks, of being violently assaulted, mastered, and impregnated by an alien thing: does one become simply the unknowing host of a new birth, the mindless vessel of parturition; or is the momentary ecstatic cooperation in the assault continued beyond the climactic moment into a new knowledge?

Like "The Second Coming," "Leda and the Swan" may be interpreted as a poem about mental experience; but unlike "The Second Coming," it is not recounted by a detached spectator, in spite of the third-person narration. The poet identifies himself with Leda; everything is seen with her eyes, felt with her body. The poem was not "right" until this total identification had been accomplished; Ellmann's transcripts of the early drafts [4] show Yeats working away from an impersonal description of the incident toward an impressionistic beginning meant to convey Leda's terror and resistance. We are to assume, I think, that Leda's experience is similar to that of the poet, and it follows that the central concern of the poem is not, as Ellmann says, "whether power and knowledge can ever be united in life," [5] but rather whether a special knowledge attaches to the conferred power of artistic creation. What Yeats hoped had happened to Leda, according to one of the early drafts, was that she had had a vision:

> Being so caught up,
> Did nothing pass before her in the air? [6]

It is a wish, rather than a question, an ironic desire for a compensatory visionary splendor to offset the devastation of Troy. What I have said in the preceding chapter about the terror and destruction attendant upon the Second Coming applies to "Leda and the Swan": another large tract of the familiar and even the beautiful has been laid waste and vitiated by a "violent annunciation" which requires that the mind reorganize its entire landscape, and the bruised consciousness, after the assault, demands to know what it has gained.

Yeats's answer is an equivocal one. Leda has been changed (to feel the heart of a phantom beating is an experience that challenges sanity, as the Greek's reaction to the Resurrection shows), but she has not become equal to Jove, since she remains finite and mortal. The "perpetual virginity of the soul" prevents her from putting on all of Jove's knowledge; it is certain, however, that she has had a glimpse of divinity entirely outside ordinary human experience.

We are now in a position to say that for Yeats historical change is often a symbol for mental and artistic cataclysms. He confirms this in his note to "Leda and the Swan," when he tells us that although it indeed had a political genesis, the poem itself is anything but political. He says:

I wrote Leda and the Swan because the editor of a political review asked me for a poem. I thought 'After the individualistic, demagogic movement, founded by Hobbes and popularised by the Encyclo-paedists and the French Revolution, we have a soil so exhausted that it cannot grow that crop again for centuries.' Then I thought 'Nothing is now possible but some movement, or birth from above, preceded by some violent annunciation.' My fancy began to play with Leda and the Swan for metaphor, and I began this poem, but as I wrote, bird and lady took such possession of the scene that all politics went out of it.[7]

Luckily for us, the bird and lady had more appeal for Yeats as symbols than as political personages, and the same may be said for the other "historical" images in Book V. Who will say that Yeats's Byzantium is a historical city? I would not

labor the point so much if both Yeats and his critics had not
taken his historical chapters so seriously. As history, these
chapters amount to nonsense at worst and wildly intuitive
guesses at best, but as symbolic commentaries on experience
they are at least revelations about one of the best poetic minds
of the twentieth century.[8]

Any essay that attempts to scan the years from 2000 B.C.
to A.D. 2000 in thirty pages must be sketchy, to say the least,
and it is clear to anyone leafing through Book V of *A Vision*
that Yeats is interested only in hitting the high spots of these
4000 years. This means he is concerned with Phase 1 and Phase
15, the phase of inception or revelation and the phase of perfection or glory. By the same sort of ingenuity which made
Christ an inhabitant of Phase 1, Phase 8, and Phase 15, Yeats
juggles his eras to permit a multiplicity of phases at the same
point in time. I repeat for clarity and convenience some
material from Chapter II.

We have first the Great Era, 4000 years long, which comprises both the classical and Christian civilizations:

2000 B.C	A.D. 1	A.D. 2000
Leda	Christ	Rough Beast
	Salome	
Phase 1	*Phase 15*	*Phase 28*

Next we have the two Sub-Eras, Classical and Christian:

2000 B.C	1000 B.C.	A.D. 1
Leda	Homer	Christ
Phase 1	*Phase 15*	*Phase 28*

A.D. 1	A.D. 1000	A.D. 2000
Christ	Charlemagne	Rough Beast
Phase 1	*Phase 15*	*Phase 28*

Finally, we have four Half-Eras, two classical and two
Christian, each a complete cycle in itself:

2000 B.C Leda Phase 1	1500 B.C. Phase 15	1000 B.C. Phase 28

1000 B.C. Homer Phase 1	500 B.C. Phidias Phase 15	A.D. 1 Christ Phase 28

A.D. 1 Christ Phase 1	A.D. 500 Byzantium Fall of Rome Phase 15	A.D. 1000 Phase 28

A.D. 1000 Phase 1	A.D. 1500 Renaissance Phase 15	A.D. 2000 Rough Beast Phase 28

The schemes are infinitely extendable in all directions (up to the Great Year, one presumes). It is evident that every Phase 1 is also a Phase 15: Christ is in one sense an inception, and in another a perfection; so too, we might add, is the Rough Beast. It all depends on the angle of vision. If we look at the world in A.D. 500 we can see it either as disintegration (the Fall of Rome) or as glory (Byzantium). If we look at it in A.D. 1500 the same is true: "Things fall apart, the center cannot hold," as Christianity, according to Yeats, begins its dissolution, but at the same time the Renaissance announces a new glory. As Yeats puts it, "Aphrodite rises from a stormy sea . . . Helen could not be Helen but for beleaguered Troy." Salome from one point of view seems decadent, but at the same time her decadence is "the exaltation of the muscular flesh and of civilisation perfectly achieved." [9]

Yeats's schemes, then, far from being a tiresome successive record of birth, maturity, and death, affirm the simultaneity of these events. This is why Yeats mentions so often the Heraclitean reciprocal relationship in which two nations "die each other's life, live each other's death":

Each age unwinds the thread another age had wound, and it amuses one to remember that before Phidias, and his westward-moving art, Persia fell, and that when full moon came round again, amid eastward-moving thought, and brought Byzantine glory, Rome fell; and that at the outset of our westward-moving Renaissance Byzantium fell; all things dying each other's life, living each other's death.[10]

The thought in this passage is another version of "si le grain ne meurt," and Yeats gets most of his best poetic effects from his reciprocal symbols of birth and death. Always he insists that one is symbolic of the other, that the two are not only concomitant but identical. This is the substance of some of the plays, as we will see later, but it is as well the substance of both "Sailing to Byzantium" and "Byzantium." In one, decrepitude is the condition for rebirth as a golden nightingale, and in the other, Yeats hails his vehicle of enlightenment as "death-in-life and life-in-death."

The intertwining of mental death with mental life was, we may suppose, primarily a psychological discovery on Yeats's part; it became very rapidly a literary principle; and finally he hunted at random through all phases of civilization for confirmatory evidence. He preferred literary evidence, of course, since he was on firm ground in writing about his own art. However, he was uncomfortably handicapped, and comically so, by his lack of languages, and the four thousand years he chose to range over had literary records so sparse in some cases, so difficult in others, and so overabundant in still others, that he was diverted into different channels. His next recourse, as we would expect, remembering his training under his father, was to the plastic and graphic arts. When he concerns himself with the modern period (1450–1925) he writes almost exclusively in literary terms to describe the stages of culture, but except for Dante and Homer he knew almost nothing about literature before Chaucer's time. We may, if we like, regard his remarks on the other arts as genuine illustrations of his literary theories.

The ancient civilizations are represented in Yeats's mind by statuary, and "The Statues" should be regarded as a poem analogous to "The Second Coming" and "Leda and the Swan" if it is to be properly understood. It represents a condensation of several pages of scattered commentary in Book V, in which Yeats is arguing that art creates civilization, rather than the reverse. We should expect this view from him, of course, given the symbol of the Mask, for art always creates the images which teach desire what to long for: "Phidias / Gave women dreams and dreams their looking-glass." On the other hand, only human involvement gives art its final being: we kiss those images of desire once we have been instructed by them. There is an intimation in the first stanza that the statues constructed in accordance with Pythagorean principles are brought to life, given "character," by a living kiss:

> Pythagoras planned it. Why did the people stare?
> His numbers, though they moved or seemed to move
> In marble or in bronze, lacked character.
> But boys and girls, pale from the imagined love
> Of solitary beds, knew what they were,
> That passion could bring character enough,
> And pressed at midnight in some public place
> Live lips upon a plummet-measured face.[11]

After two more stanzas celebrating the power of art to incarnate cultures,[12] we find Yeats imitating those "boys and girls." He speaks of "we Irish," but Yeats is not, and never was, a spokesman for the common people. It is himself he means:

> We Irish, born into that ancient sect
> But thrown upon this filthy modern tide
> And by its formless spawning fury wrecked,
> Climb to our proper dark, that we may trace
> The lineaments of a plummet-measured face.[13]

This, like "Byzantium" is a "midnight" poem, where mid-

night is a time in the first stanza, but a place in the last, a state
of the solitary soul. The intense devotional attitude in the
last two lines is not primarily historical nor political; it is
artistic. The poem is not one of revelation or vision, but of
search, an example of the deliberate exclusion of the world
which Yeats found so necessary to his art. We are left not
with the heroic image of Pearse summoning Cuchulain to his
side but with the peculiarly desolate tracing of an unseen
image in the isolating dark. The creation of the proper mask,
or image, or artistic ideal, is for Yeats a solitary commitment,
requiring an aloof and almost inhuman aspiration.

The poem is a good example of Yeats's use of material
from *A Vision* in a nonrevelatory mode; a mitigated hope is
all he permits himself in "The Statues." Like "Sailing to
Byzantium," "The Statues" expresses a longing rather than
a prophecy, and so does most of Book V of *A Vision*, at
least whenever Yeats is speaking of the ideal. A curiously
tentative and wistful tone pervades the famous description
of Byzantium:

> I think if I could be given a month of Antiquity and leave to spend
> it where I chose, I would spend it in Byzantium . . . I think I could
> find in some little wine-shop some philosophical worker in mosaic
> who could answer all my questions . . .
> I think that in early Byzantium, maybe never before or since in
> recorded history, religious, aesthetic and practical life were one, that
> architect and artificers . . . spoke to the multitude and the few alike.
> The painter, the mosaic worker, the worker in gold and silver, the
> illuminator of sacred books, were almost impersonal, almost per-
> haps without the consciousness of individual design, absorbed in their
> subject-matter and that the vision of a whole people; . . . and this
> vision, this proclamation of their invisible master, had the Greek
> nobility . . . To me it seems that [Christ] had in His assent to a full
> Divinity made possible this sinking-in upon a supernatural splendour,
> these walls with their little glimmering cubes of blue and green and
> gold.[14]

Yeats wanted to identify Phase 15 with Byzantium;[15] by this identification Christ becomes the artist who, in choosing "perfection of the work" makes possible the glories of Hagia Sophia. The full moon of Byzantium makes a Christ of stern majesty whose "Byzantine eyes of drilled ivory staring upon a vision" [16] show affinities to the plummet-measured face of the statues. Remote and harsh, ascetic and hieratic, the image of Byzantium is the one transcendent glimpse in *A Vision*, and deservedly the most famous of Yeats's mythical symbols. In *A Vision*, Yeats permits himself the tone of wonder and repose in his descriptions of the sacred city, but in the poems, he is wrenched from his contemplation by the importunities of the body. The tattered coat upon a stick acts as a counterpoise to the sages standing in God's holy fire, and "Byzantium" is a poem tortured by the antitheses it confronts, where "the fury and the mire of human veins" always inundate the marbles of the dancing floor.

Because "Byzantium" is Yeats's most authoritative poetic word on Phase 15, I do not want to bypass the poem without comment. It is, I think, Yeats's greatest single triumph; in it, that sense of agonizing balance between opposites which was his primary poetic intuition receives its most acute rendering. "Byzantium" is a poem about the images in a poet's mind, and this in itself implies that perhaps *A Vision* may be about images too, at least in part. Images are the raw material of poetry, and Yeats divides them into two varieties, purged and unpurged. The unpurged are those belonging to the daytime, to the random mass of heterogeneous experience, and they contain

> All that man is,
> All mere complexities,
> The fury and the mire of human veins.[17]

The purged images are those of night. Yeats calls one of them, paraphrasing Dante's address to Virgil,[18] "shade more than man, more image than a shade," and we conclude that these images do not have even the shadowy humanity of the spirits of Hades, but rather are dehumanized "bobbins" without moisture or breath. As superhuman beings, they have affinities with the Jove who visited Leda, or with any other visitants from supernatural regions. Any image, once arisen, can bring others in its train:

> A mouth that has no moisture and no breath
> Breathless mouths may summon.

Images have this in common with the mask: they are opposites of the poet who invokes them, they are the creations of his desire. Will and mask exist always in the Heraclitean relationship, "living each other's death, dying each other's life," and therefore Yeats addresses his image in a conscious recollection of Coleridge:

> I hail the superhuman;
> I call it death-in-life and life-in-death.

The purged images of night are associated with the holy city of Byzantium, and when the gong strikes, "the unpurged images of day recede," while the starlit or moonlit dome disdains the complexities it banishes. The dome may be starlit (at Phase 1) or moonlit (at Phase 15); the perfect objective and the perfect subjective are alike independent of "the fury and the mire of human veins." The golden bird (who is probably the golden nightingale of "Sailing to Byzantium") scorns aloud the "common bird or petal / And all complexities of mire or blood." Like the floating superhuman image, the golden nightingale is refined almost beyond recognition; just as the image was "Shade more than man, more image than a shade," so the nightingale is "More miracle than bird or handiwork."

Once Yeats has set up his oppositions between images, seemingly irreconcilable ones, he shifts his ground. What do the unpurged images of day have to do with the purged images of night, he has asked; and for a moment he leaves us unsatisfied, as he breaks off to describe the flames of Byzantium. Their relation to the city is not immediately clear, but it seems to me that they are the flames of the golden smithies of the Emperor: they are the refiner's fire, with all the associations that image commands. The refiner's fire is a "purging" medium, driving out the dross of "mire and blood"; however, it is a shaping force as well, since metal is malleable only in the fire. By passing into the flame, the unpurged images of day become the purged images of night:

> At midnight on the Emperor's pavement flit
> Flames that no faggot feeds, nor steel has lit,
> Nor storm disturbs, flames begotten of flame,
> Where blood-begotten spirits come
> And all complexities of fury leave,
> Dying into a dance,
> An agony of trance,
> An agony of flame that cannot singe a sleeve.

That stanza, with its suggestions of almost indescribable activity, its intolerably high-pitched apprehensions, and its intricate syntax, exists in a shuddering poise of energy. As a description of the mind in its highest-keyed state of transforming and creating power, beyond interruption and beyond destruction, it forms the fulcrum of the poem. Yeats's intensity implies a racked perfection that strains human capacities to the breaking point.

Yeats did not stop at this description of Phase 15. As always, he must return "where all the ladders start." When *A Vision* is reproached for its inhuman remoteness, the reproach is partly deserved; on the other hand, I think we must remember that for Yeats, all symbols in *A Vision* had immediate human relevance, since *he* knew from which section of the rag-and-bone shop he had resurrected them, although their origin is sometimes obscure to us. *A Vision* is not a frigid document when it is successful in hinting at its inception in "the fury and mire of human veins." I do not think it is illegitimate to read back into the prose certain intimations which we find in the poetry or the plays. "Byzantium," then, casts light on Book V by intimating why Yeats needed so much the symbol of the golden city.

In the final stanza of "Byzantium," the things so carefully separated begin to interact. No longer is the city an entity remotely disdaining the mire of day's unpurged images. The two are plunged into each other and submerged in each other as a wave of fire confronts a wave of mire and blood. The sacred dolphins, bearing the blood-begotten spirits, inhabit the unpurged medium; the flood sweeps against the fire of the smithies and is broken by them, but returns with renewed force. The marbles of the pavement shatter the "bitter furies of complexity" but no victory is final, as the violent clashes continue. Suddenly, in a dazzling syntactical victory, the resolution, so unforeseeable, is accomplished: the two kinds of images, purged and unpurged, are not hostile but symbiotic. The unpurged images *beget* the purged images; blood *begets* spirits. There is even a hint that the begetting is accomplished by the violent shock wave of flood and fire, at the moment of crisis.

> Astraddle on the dolphin's mire and blood,
> Spirit after spirit! The smithies break the flood,
> The golden smithies of the Emperor!
> Marbles of the dancing floor
> Break bitter furies of complexity,
> Those images that yet
> Fresh images beget,
> That dolphin-torn, that gong-tormented sea.

Grammatically, it is necessary to read the final sentence like this:

Marbles of the dancing floor break:
- bitter furies of complexity
- those images (that yet fresh images beget)
- that dolphin-torn, that gong-tormented sea.

Practically speaking, the governing force of the verb "break" is spent long before the end of the stanza is reached, and the last three lines stand syntactically as absolutes, two phrases which reconcile the conflicting systems which have been set up in earlier stanzas. Dolphins and gong are no longer enclosed within the protective wall of flame which surrounds Byzantium: it is a case of "la cathédrale engloutie" once again. The separations of the first stanzas are seen to be artificial, and the reality is the tormented connection between blood and spirit. "Out of the quarrel with ourselves, we make poetry," Yeats wrote, and "Byzantium" is a dramatization of that heightened struggle, beginning with the delusion of an inhumanly purified art, progressing to an almost hysterical account of the trance of creation, ending in a somber triumph of stormy and chaotic equilibrium.

I have spent so long on "Byzantium" because most of the traditional analyses of the poem seem to me fragmentary or tautological. Either critics have chosen to stay within Yeats's own system and say that this is a poem about the life after death [19] or they have gone to elaborate trouble in establishing neo-Platonic sources [20] without coming to grips with the poem's link with experience. Yeats, never a devout believer, could hardly have written dogmatically about a life after death as such, while there is every reason for a poet to use the ideas of purgation and immortality as symbols for certain events in creative experience. Richard Ellmann's brief and intelligent commentary on "Byzantium" in *The Identity of Yeats* [21] is a notable exception to the general critical uneasiness with the poem.

A true understanding of *A Vision* seems to me desirable for a proper approach to the poems and plays that share its symbolism, because we face in a poem like "Byzantium" a miniature problem which in *A Vision* takes on a massive form. Put quite simply, it is, "What is the relevance of all this to human experience?" Or, as the critic must ask it personally,

"To which of my experiences am I to relate this piece of writing?" None of us has any experience of the life after death. I can only wonder why so many critics have thought that Yeats was dogmatically describing it, and what point of personal relevance they could find and respond to, in a poem about an unimaginable state. Eliot's solution, taken up by Wilson, is that such poems teach us "what it feels like" to believe certain doctrines. I find this a help for a sociologist more than for a critic. *A Vision* arouses the same perplexities as do Blake's prophetical books, and not until Northrop Frye's brilliant *Fearful Symmetry* appeared had anyone successfully made a systematic link between Blake's mythological characters and the events of normal human experience. Systems like Blake's and Yeats's must be treated in their own terms up to a point, but at some time in his interpretation the critic must cross the symbolic border. Ellmann, though he does this on occasion with certain Vision poems like "Byzantium," had no space in his books on Yeats to do it for *A Vision* itself, and most of the other critics of Yeats seem to have no notion that it can be done at all.

Once the central intuition of Book V has been grasped — that the mind is renewed by a divine assault ("Leda") or by some world-restorer ("The Second Coming") — the "historical" illustrations of the thesis are easily enough followed, and are of only incidental interest. The literary illustrations are more rewarding, tracing, as they do, the influence upon literature of a coherent matrix of symbols derived from Christianity. If anyone doubts that there are literary concerns behind *A Vision* (and not only meditations on reincarnation or the life after death), he has only to read the pages in Book V detailing the contributions of a unified symbolic system to literary activity. The period from 1450 to 1500, Yeats says, corresponds to Phase 15; it does so because it "covers the principal activity of the Academy of Florence which formulated the reconciliation of Paganism and Christianity. This reconciliation . . . meant that Greek and Roman Antiquity were as sacred as that of Judea . . . that the human norm, discovered from the measurement of ancient statues, was God's first handiwork, that 'perfectly proportioned human body' which had seemed to Dante Unity of Being symbolised." [22]

But the syncretism that made Renaissance literature great was an unstable coalition of elements, and that perfect balance of "knowledge and power" so ardently hoped for in the Leda sonnet was not long maintained:

> Since the rebirth of the secular intellect in the eleventh century, faculty has been separating from faculty, poetry from music, the worshipper from the worshipped, but all have remained within a common fading circle — Christendom — and so within the human soul . . . Phase 15 past, these forms begin to jostle and fall into confusion . . . In the mind of the artist a desire for power succeeds to that for knowledge.[23]

It is useless, once the perfect moment has passed, to attempt a return to the former syncretism. Milton thought it possible, but Yeats found (with some justice) that in the "Hymn On the Morning of Christ's Nativity," "the two elements have fallen apart . . . the one is sacred, the other profane; his classical mythology is an artificial ornament." Later, dependence on the outworn symbols is replaced by reliance on "the solitary soul," and to Yeats such reliance "creates all that is most beautiful in modern English poetry from Blake to Arnold, all that is not a fading echo." [24]

What is frequently not taken into account is Yeats's detachment from his own position as one of the last romantics. His aloof irony in the later poems comes from the knowledge that he is working in a dying tradition, and paradoxically saves him from being of that tradition. Yeats has all the high romantic attitudes modified by speculative detachment: an odd classicism, bizarre certainly in its stance but still classicism, cools his passionate lines. The ironic detachment from his headlong impulses (to which nevertheless he gave free poetic rein) saved him from the alternative solution, which was indifference. "Our generation has witnessed a first weariness," he says at the close of *A Vision*; it seemed pointless, to many of Yeats's contemporaries, to affirm belief or preference. Such apathy led, as Yeats affirmed, to "synthesis for its own sake, organisation where there is no masterful director, books where the author has disappeared." [25] At all cost, Yeats would insist, the illusion of control must be preserved, and if we do not know what the next mythology will be, we must choose one, pretending it is the fated one.

> The prologues are over. It is a question, now
> Of final belief. So, say that final belief
> Must be in a fiction. It is time to choose.[26]

Yeats, like Stevens, has chosen to say that the world is what he makes it: in Stevens' words, "Thou art not August unless I make thee so." [27] In fact, the best text to set against *A Vision* is the Stevens essay "Two or Three Ideas," published in *Opus Posthumous*. "To see the gods dispelled in mid-air and dissolve like clouds is one of the great human experiences," says Stevens in his massive manner: [28] in Yeatsian terms, the experience produces "Lapis Lazuli." The "poets that are always gay" have seen

> All men have aimed at, found and lost;
> Black out; Heaven blazing into the head:
> Tragedy wrought to its uttermost.[29]

"It was their annihilation," Stevens goes on to say, "not ours, and yet it left us feeling that in a measure, we, too, had been annihilated." In an argument of sinuous complexity, Stevens proposes a reciprocity of being between the styles of different orders of experience: "Thus, it might be true that the style of a poem and the gods themselves are one; or that the style of the gods and the style of men are one; or that the style of a poem and the style of men are one." [30]

I would say that Yeats shared Stevens' premises, though Yeats might have put them in another way. Given the premises, there are two possible conclusions in creation, of which one is the Yeatsian path: to create, in the style of poetry, and with nothing but a poetic sanction, new "gods" and new heavenly mansions. Stevens was not immune to that temptation, and "To the One of Fictive Music" is precisely a poem creating a new divinity. But the path Stevens finally took was not evangelistic in the Yeatsian sense. He chose to preach a different gospel, announcing that "the indifferent experience of life is the unique experience, the item of ecstasy which we have been isolating and reserving for another time and place, loftier and more secluded." [31] Yeats is still sufficiently haunted by the Christian desire for an otherworld to ask the forbidden question:

> O Rocky Voice
> Shall we in that great night rejoice?

Immediately he turns on his momentary weakness, and answers his own question with another:

> What do we know but that we face
> One another in this place? [32]

That tone is not one that regards life as "the item of ecstasy," but rather it is the remnant of the Christian attitude viewing grieving man *in hac lacrimarum valle*. In Stevens, the mind is at last genuinely secular: although suffused by regret, tinged with the beauty of the images it has abandoned, the mind no longer feels obliged to create replicas of the forgotten systems, to think in systematic terms. Yeats, one feels, though he had no sympathy for the dogmatic content of the systems he rejected, never questioned at all the ultimate validity of system, and Stevens' shifting outlines could not have been his mode.

The diamond-sharp lines of Yeats's late poems require a

skeleton as rigid to support them. Stevens' divinities are half-seen, momentary apparitions:

> I am the angel of reality . . .
>
>   Am I not,
> Myself, only half of a figure of a sort,
>
> A figure half seen, or seen for a moment, a man
> Of the mind, an apparition apparelled in
>
> Apparels of such lightest look that a turn
> Of my shoulder and quickly, too quickly, I am gone? [33]

Yeats's stiff images — the Magi, the shade of death-in-life and life-in-death, the Rough Beast, the sages standing in God's holy fire — are made of different stuff. One cannot praise Yeats's cast of mind in his images and condemn it in his system: both are facets of the same stone. Although some may prefer Stevens' apprehension "that fluttering things have so distinct a shade," they cannot deny the strength of Yeats's very different kind of poetry and vision. Yeats's system is not an "answer," it is an attitude of mind in response to that threatened personal annihilation of which Stevens speaks. As such, it reflects on the late poems and more profoundly on the late plays, which I shall next consider.

Chapter VI

The Player Queen

"I BEGAN in, I think, 1907, a verse tragedy, but at that time the thought I have set forth in *Per Amica Silentia Lunae* was coming into my head, and I found examples of it everywhere. I wasted the best working months of several years in an attempt to write a poetical play where every character became an example of the finding or not finding of what I have called the Antithetical Self; and because passion and not thought makes tragedy, what I made had neither simplicity nor life . . . At last it came into my head all of a sudden that I could get rid of the play if I turned it into a farce." [1]

The germinal idea for *The Player Queen* was tragic, if we are to believe Yeats, and there is no reason why we should not. One aspect of its finale — the banishment of a poet from the kingdom — has something in common with *The King's Threshold*, which though conceived as a comedy,[2] was published as a tragedy. In the early scenarios of *The Player Queen*, the heroine, like Socrates, was forced to drink poison,[3] but in spite of this tragic ending, even the early drafts are full of wit and high spirits. As we now have the play, Yeats's irony plays perpetually over the potentially tragic surface, giving the play a charm that not even its confusions can entirely obscure. It is the irony of the poet foreseeing his own overthrow.

In spite of its appeal, *The Player Queen*, like most of Yeats's plays, is not really stageworthy.[4] Private, chaotic, allegorical in the bad sense, it has in spite of its faults a claim on our attention, if only because Yeats devoted so much time to it. As it stands, it is patched together, and shows it: the action is confused, the allegory is only sporadically remembered, and the issues are rarely clear.

However, some things are at once obvious. Like "The Second Coming" and "Leda and the Swan," *The Player Queen* takes place at the moment of revolution, as one dispensation ends, another begins. "Leda and the Swan" had asked whether a new species of power inevitably brings with itself a correlative knowledge, and we saw that the question was understandable primarily in respect to the aesthetic order. "The Second Coming" asked what shape the new dispensation would take; and *The Player Queen*, dealing with the flirtations of the Muse, asks, among other things, what stance the poet should adopt when he becomes obsolete.

The great obstacle in writing about *The Player Queen* is that the characters tend to melt into each other and into their allegorical types. Are both Septimus and the Beggar figures for the poet? Is Decima a Muse or an Oracle? What relation does the Unicorn have to Septimus and Decima? The action of the play is equally slippery, so much so that it is hard not to falsify the story in the retelling. Briefly put, Septimus the poet is deserted by his wife Decima because he has been unfaithful to her. She takes a new husband, the Prime Minister, and by her own arrogant confidence makes herself queen, banishing Septimus, his mistress Nona, and the troupe of players, whose play about Noah's Ark never takes place. The timid former Queen retires to a convent, and Decima and her commoner-husband inaugurate the new dispensation.

Decima, as the only link between old and new, is the center of the play, while Septimus and the Queen, the representatives of the old order, are her satellites. Nona, Septimus' mistress, is only a device; and the countrymen, citizens, and players are on stage simply to fill in bits of information and to make minor points. The Unicorn, on whom the play depends, never appears, and we infer his actions from the remarks of the other personages. Evidently the meaning of the play depends on Decima, and her apotheosis at the end, comic as it is, is constructed so as to resolve, if possible, the action. The resolution is not the banishment of Septimus; if it were, the play would be a tragedy. (As it stands, an undercurrent of possible tragedy can be glimpsed through the ripples of farce.) If the play were focused on Septimus, he would not exit expostulating and incredulous, but rather bereft and doomed. His last words in a tragedy would be in the tone of

> And what rough beast, his hour come round at last,
> Slouches towards Bethlehem to be born?

Instead, he is carried off to prison protesting obdurately that Decima still belongs to him: "She is my wife, she is my bad, flighty wife." [5]

I have said before that there is a certain approval of disaster and change implicit in "The Second Coming," but it is more an intellectual approval than a felt one. In *The Player Queen*, a gayer and more ironic manner of vision is trained on the prospect of cataclysm. Yeats is amused, in the first place, at the untoward nature of the expected destruction. It will not be a grievous second Deluge, but rather a commonplace reversal of fashion; the players may have pleased Kubla Khan in Xanadu, but their images do not suit here and now. Mental experience (once again, I do not believe that Yeats was writing politically [6]) never repeats itself: the new chaos does not resemble the old, and the new Queen in no way imitates her predecessor. Yeats is wryly appreciative (it is a joke on himself) at the way revelation is announced, coming by its own evangelist, a braying beggar. The beggar is a comic parody of Leda, and his speeches give a sardonic answer to the question posed by "Leda and the Swan" — the beggar puts on no knowledge with his power. "When I roll and bray," the beggar tells Decima, "I am asleep. I know nothing about it, and that is a great pity. I remember nothing but the itching in my back." This is the reduction to absurdity of poetic inspiration. Septimus the poet recognizes the affinities between himself and the beggar, giving us leave to do the same. The old beggar says to him, "Don't you know who I am — aren't you afraid? When something comes inside me, my back itches. Then I must lie down and roll, and then I bray and the crown changes." Septimus replies, "Ah! you are inspired. Then we are indeed brothers." [7] And so they are — Septimus drunk, the beggar tranced; oddly enough, the gaiety of the scene springs from their blowsy kinship. In some undefined way, the beggar's bray causes the Revolution by a poetical contingency, as a sunrise in poetry is contingent upon cockcrow. Septimus has "caused" the Revolution by his infidelity to Decima; together he and the beggar represent the contributory causes of the shift in power.

What we do not find in *The Player Queen* are images of horror and disintegration like those which pervade *A Vision* as well as "The Second Coming." Both may have been present in the germinal conception of the tragic *Player Queen*, but as it now stands, the play represents a gay shift of positions all down the line, with no tragic consequences at all.

Septimus begins and ends the play by complaining about Decima, and in his complaints the cranky relation between poet and Muse (for Decima is at least one possible incarnation of the Muse) is made immediately explicit. More interesting is the fact that Septimus defines himself in terms of Decima:

Third Old Man. Who are you? What do you want?
Septimus. I am Septimus. I have a bad wife. I want to come in and sleep.
Third Old Man. You are drunk.

Septimus. Drunk! So would you be if you had as bad a wife.[8]

Decima has proved too much for him; her flightiness exposes him to too much discomfort.

> *Septimus.* Bad wife — others have had bad wives, but others were not left to lie down in the open street under the stars, drenched with cold water, a whole jug of cold water, shivering in the pale light of the dawn, to be run over, to be trampled upon, to be eated by dogs, and all because their wives have hidden themselves.[9]

Septimus is not taken in by his own self-pity any more than he is later taken in by his own drunken oratory. Rhetoric is his natural mode, and he knows it. He has not the slightest intention of abandoning his romantic poses: "Robbed, so to speak; naked, so to speak — bleeding, so to speak — and they pass by on the other side of the street." [10] This is the last romantic, conscious of his romantic absurdity, a mode which Decima's brisk poetry is to make obsolete. In fact, the revolution of this play is posed in terms of fashion; it represents the light view of a serious phenomenon. Change is, after all, one of the attributes of the Supreme Fiction, and consequently has its cheerful as well as its terrifying aspects. *The Player Queen* is like a chapter from *A Vision* read with an eyebrow cocked.

Yeats pictures his revolution in terms of a change of religion. For Septimus, Christianity has become another cache of similes, useful for the grandiloquent gesture ("Bring me to a stable — my Saviour was content with a stable"), but when he declares his allegiance it is to "Venus and Adonis and the other planets of heaven." The countrymen have recourse to religion only to sanction their own clamor for violence ("The Bible says, Suffer not a witch to live. Last Candlemas twelvemonth I strangled a witch with my own hands" [11]) and the Queen's Christianity is indistinguishable from her apprehensiveness and furtive masochism. We have been given, then, enough examples of the irrelevance of the traditional religion to prepare us for the promulgation of a new one, and we are hardly surprised that it is Septimus who enunciates it, praising its symbol, the Unicorn.

> It is a most noble beast, a most religious beast. It has a milk-white skin and milk-white horn, and milk-white hooves, but a mild blue eye, and it dances in the sun. I will have no one speak against it, not while I am still upon the earth . . . For I will not have it said that there is a smirch, or a blot, upon the most milky whiteness of an heroic brute that bathes by the sound of tabors at the rising of the sun and the rising of the moon, and the rising of the Great Bear.[12]

This is the language of evangelism: superlatives, absolutes, cosmic rituals. It makes no difference that Septimus is drunk; Septimus has a stake in the Unicorn, insists that he is "no longer drunk, but inspired," and is affronted that his countrymen can be indifferent to his divine afflatus, "my breast-feathers thrust out and my white wings buoyed up with divinity." [13]

The only trouble with Septimus' view of the Unicorn is that it is a mistaken one. Conditioned by the existing tradition, Septimus cannot imagine the Unicorn as anything but chaste, and he insists that its chastity is as integral as its beauty. Decima, of course, knows better, but the reader has only Septimus' speeches to go on in the first scene of the play. For Yeats himself, the Unicorn was clearly a symbol for the daimon and therefore for artistic inspiration. Sturge Moore had done a bookplate for Yeats with a unicorn springing out of a broken tower, and Yeats refers to it as "that admirable faun or stag springing from the broken tower . . . That beast is the daemon." [14] Though Yeats's terms are vague, the "beast," in the reproduction of the bookplate on page 35 of the Yeats-Moore correspondence, is clearly a unicorn. One suspects that Yeats or his wife suggested the symbolism to Sturge Moore.

Yeats was courting danger in using religious imagery for his point about the Unicorn, but ever since Arnold, the aesthetic and the religious have been interchangeable, for literary purposes. Whenever art begins to speak of itself, as Northrop Frye has said, it uses religious terminology. In a sober context, the language no longer shocks at all, but in a comic context, we are somewhat at a loss to know what reaction to provide. The fact remains, uncomfortable as it sometimes is, that Yeats chose to use, in *A Vision* and in *The Player Queen*, religion as the only adequate symbol for art. Religion is the only symbol which can combine the revelatory and prescriptive elements which art possesses, but the connotations aroused by religious images tend to be so strong that the images draw all attention to themselves and cease to be windows to symbolic meaning. Politics possesses a similar type of prime force, and consequently the temptation to read Yeats as a prophet of religious or political disaster is still with us.

Warned that we must look beyond the religion of the Unicorn to what it symbolizes, we can proceed with the play. Just as Septimus wants some link between the Unicorn and the religion he knows, so do the townspeople, who like to think that the beggar who brays to announce the new regime is a reincarnation of the donkey that carried Christ to Jerusalem. Both are harking back to a former time, wishing things to be as they have always been, or as they were in the past. Septimus is similarly unwilling to accept a change in his relationship to his wife Decima, preferring to recall earlier days, when she was not the spirited creature she has now become: "All creatures are in need of protection at some time or other. Even my wife was once a frail child in need of milk, of smiles, of love, as if in the midst of a flood, in danger of drowning, so to speak." [15] This is the way Septimus would like Decima, obviously, but the Decima he now has is in no danger from a deluge; she, in fact, is the only person who will survive the coming one. The troupe of actors, with their play of Noah's Ark, are unfitted to deal with the flood they know only symbolically. Decima alone has an open mind, will not demand a unicorn or a cataclysm cut to order. The second scene of the play (to which the first is really only a curtain-raiser) belongs to her, and the rest of the personages are essentially her comic foils: the timid Queen, the sluttish Nona, the impatient Prime Minister, the evangelistic Septimus.

On the surface, Scene II joins a new theme to the cataclysm-revelation of Scene I: we see in the second half of the play the rivalry for Septimus between Nona, his mistress, and Decima, his wife. It is not the only time Yeats treated, with some wryness, the relation between poet, mistress, and lady. Always, in his musings on inspiration, we sense the uneasy relation between spirit and flesh. *The Player Queen* shows one solution: the wrong one. In the late poem "The Three Bushes" Yeats plays equivocally with what might be the right solution: deception into harmony. To the lady (who is the inspiration for all her lover's songs and is therefore a surrogate for the Muse) chastity is the essential virtue, and chastity for Yeats always denotes a certain final aloofness and self-possession, an almost inhuman independence. The lady, to keep her chastity, sends her maid in to her poet-lover; he is deceived and continues to write his love songs, all unsuspecting. Between them, lady and chambermaid stage the whole deception with a wryly compassionate indulgence for the poet's need and his innocence. Both women are vastly more sophisticated than the lover, and it is through the lady's three songs that the burden of the poem is made clear, as she passes from resentment of her maid to a metaphysical reconciliation of spirit and flesh. Her subjunctive wish has in fact the force of a decree.

> When you and my true lover meet
> And he plays tunes between your feet,
> Speak no evil of the soul,
> Nor think that body is the whole,
> For I that am his daylight lady
> Know worse evil of the body;
> But in honour split his love
> Till either neither have enough,
> That I may hear if we should kiss

> A contrapuntal serpent hiss,
> You, should hand explore a thigh,
> All the labouring heavens sigh.[16]

While the poem clearly has a purely human meaning as an expression of the soul's traffic with both ideal and real, it seems to me no accident that Yeats made the lover a singer and his sexual relation with the lady a necessary condition of his singing. The sexual act is the most accurate symbol for the "fine delight that fathers thought," that "strong spur, live and lancing like the blowpipe flame" which, according to Hopkins, engenders poetry, and most of Yeats's poems about sexual love can be read symbolically. With some, it is hardly necessary to press the point, but when Yeats writes specifically about a poet or singer (as in *The Player Queen*, *A Full Moon in March*, *The King of the Great Clock Tower*, and "The Three Bushes") it is logical to place in the foreground the application to the poetic act. In "The Three Bushes" it is up to the lady to straighten out the conflicting claims of spirit and flesh, and she does it by a fine poetic sleight of hand which begs a dozen questions. Invoking the principle of complexity in harmony, she finds a necessity for the "contrapuntal serpent," and her verbal audacity satisfies us as much as the concept it evokes. A contrapuntal serpent, if he existed, would be a creature of both worlds, spirit and flesh; and sighing heaven, the cosmos reduced to humanity, equally satisfies both terms of the relation. This is the artful peacemaking that the lady indulges in. Yeats provides a much simpler reconciliation in the ballad when he has the three rose trees on the graves of poet, lady, and chambermaid intertwine so that now

> . . . None living can,
> When they have plucked a rose there,
> Know where its roots began.[17]

Septimus, in *The Player Queen*, has grown resentful of his independent lady Decima, and has taken a mistress in her

stead. The situation of "The Three Bushes" is repeated; Septimus' poems still envision Decima, his "daylight lady," but they
are tapped out on Nona's shoulderblades. Nona senses that she
possesses the least important part of Septimus' soul; Septimus
knows that he is living in uneasy compromise; only Decima,
independent, can cast off the past and look for a new lover.
Noah's wife is not the part for her, so she will create a new
play of her own. In one early draft she recalls that she has
played the Queen of Sheba and Herodias; [18] the present version has her announcing "The only part in the world I can
play is a great queen's part . . . O, I would know how to put
all summer in a look and after that all winter in a voice." [19] It
is this play-acting quality in Decima which Septimus vaguely
mistrusts. Her chameleon transformations baffle and disturb
him, so that he utters the classic wish for the domestication of
the Muse: "Put off that mask of burning gold." The Muse
reminds him that it was the mask which engaged his mind,
not what lay behind it, and though he recognizes implicitly
the truth of her reply, he makes one more effort:

> 'But lest you are my enemy
> I must enquire.'
> 'O no, my dear, let all that be;
> What matter, so there is but fire
> In you, in me?' [20]

The more Decima torments him, the more aloof she remains, the more beautiful she appears in his eyes, and the
more powerful the poetry he writes to her becomes. The
Image must remain sovereign and demanding, as Decima scorn-
fully tells Nona when Nona accuses her of plotting to have
Septimus cast into prison:

Decima. Would they give him dry bread to eat?
Nona. They would.
Decima. And water to drink and nothing in the water?
Nona. They would.
Decima. And a straw bed?

Nona. They would, and only a little straw maybe.
Decima. And iron chains that clanked.
Nona. They would.
Decima. And keep him there for a whole week?
Nona. A month maybe.
Decima. And he would say to the turnkey, 'I am here because of my
 beautiful cruel wife, my beautiful flighty wife'?
Nona. He might not, he'd be sober.
Decima. But he'd think it, and every time he was hungry, every time
 he was thirsty, every time he felt the hardness of the stone floor,
 every time he heard the chains clank, he would think it, and every
 time he thought it I would become more beautiful in his eyes.
Nona. No, he would hate you.
Decima. Little do you know what the love of man is. If that Holy
 Image in the church where you put all those candles at Easter
 was pleasant and affable, why did you come home with the skin
 worn off your two knees? [21]

Lovers and poets (like nuns and mothers in another context) worship images, and images break hearts, as Yeats says
in "Among School Children." Decima belongs among those
images which Yeats apostrophizes as

> Presences
> That passion, piety or affection knows,
> And that all heavenly glory symbolise —
> O self-born mockers of man's enterprise.[22]

There is no denying some autobiographical reminiscence in
the treatment of Decima and Nona; it would be surprising if
Yeats's Muse did not bear traces of the features of Maud
Gonne. But by his fantastic allegory, Yeats has removed the
play from the purely human sphere, and by his transparent
allusions to poetry and plays, has made the transference to the
aesthetic realm unmistakable. The two are interwoven: Decima throws away a part and throws away a man in one and the
same gesture.

Once the rejection of Septimus is accomplished, Decima's
headstrong and willful choice of a new lover becomes the

motive force of the play, and Yeats's favorite symbol, the copulation of two worlds, begins to take shape. Though the players dance around Decima in their animal costumes, it is not among them that she will find her "beast or fowl." In fact, she suspects that any lover, human, bestial, or divine, is necessarily temporary.

> None has found, that found out love
> Single bird or brute enough;
> Any bird or brute may rest
> An empty head upon my breast.[23]

She regrets losing Septimus, but her metallic personality is untouched by the breaking of his marriage vow: anger, not sadness, is her reaction. Her function is to break hearts, not to have her own broken, and in her cool acceptance of the ineffectual Prime Minister at the end of the play we see the temporizing of the Muse until the time is ripe for her new master, the elusive Unicorn, to possess her. She sings her song of invitation:

> Shall I fancy beast or fowl?
> Queen Pasiphae chose a bull,
> While a passion for a swan
> Made Queen Leda stretch and yawn,
> Wherefore spin ye, whirl ye, dance ye,
> Till Queen Decima's found her fancy.[24]

Directly afterward, Septimus appears and announces "the end of the Christian Era, the coming of a New Dispensation, that of the New Adam, that of the Unicorn; but alas, he is chaste, he hesitates, he hesitates." Indeed the Unicorn hesitates, but not out of chastity. We sense that he is waiting for Septimus and the Players and the timid Queen to be gotten rid of before he takes possession of the kingdom through Decima. I think we are obliged to believe that Septimus' vision is accurate up to a point. After all, the old beggar's testimony corroborates his announcement, and if we are to distrust

Septimus' vision of the Unicorn as the supplanting beast, the whole play collapses. In some way, Septimus realizes that he and the players minister to the Unicorn; irrelevant though they will be in the reign of the Unicorn, they are still in his camp, against the townsmen and their "bad, popular poets." Septimus can be defiantly gay in welcoming his own destruction: "I will speak, no, I will sing, as if the mob did not exist. I will rail upon the Unicorn for his chastity. I will bid him trample mankind to death and beget a new race. I will even put my railing into rhyme, and all shall run sweetly, sweetly." And though Septimus realizes his own imminent superfluity he yet defends the Unicorn passionately, and even mixes his own identity with that of the glorious beast: "Because I am an unforsworn man I am strong: a violent virginal creature, that is how it is put in 'The Great Beastery of Paris.' " [25]

F. A. C. Wilson, in his discussion of *The Player Queen*, rightly says that the Unicorn "is perhaps the most celebrated of all emblems of alchemy as an image for the divinity"; and he mentions as well the esoteric significance of the unicorn in the Order of the Golden Dawn.[26] He points out too that Yeats may have identified Noah with poetry. Blake had spoken of "Poetry, Painting & Music, the three Powers in Man of conversing with Paradise, which the flood did not Sweep away," [27] and in Yeats's note on the passage, the three powers are identified as Noah, Shem, and Japhet.[28] What Mr. Wilson fails to do is to take the necessary next step and identify divinity's converse with man (the Unicorn's proximate mating with Decima) as a symbolic description of the poetic process: though all men to some degree unite with images, the poet is the master of that act. The hint in the play itself is a broad one: Septimus announces that "Man is nothing till he is united to an image. Now the Unicorn is both an image and beast; that is why he alone can be the new Adam." We have already seen that Decima is both woman and image, making her fit to be the new Eve. Septimus recognizes the affinity between his wife and the Unicorn: "She is terrible. The Unicorn will be terrible when it loves." [29]

The new images for poetry are incarnated in the Unicorn and Decima, and Septimus' grand gesture of saving the ancient images from destruction is futile. His images are irrelevant, though he speaks of them with pseudotragic bravado: "It is necessary that we who are the last artists — all the rest have gone over to the mob — shall save the images and implements of our art. We must carry into safety the cloak of Noah, the high-crowned hat of Noah, and the mask of the sister of Noah. She was drowned because she thought her brother was telling lies." [30] But because the mask of Noah's sister reminds him of Decima, Septimus leaves it behind, and ironically enough the drowned sister is resurrected at the end of the play when Decima dons the rejected mask. Lost images are restored in the revolution of the cycles, and the old images become out of date. The timid Queen is an old image, too; if the Unicorn has been coupling with her in the night, the union has been barren, and she, representing the negation of all experience, is only too glad to be obliterated from the scene. Decima, symbolically the daughter of a harlot and a drunken sailor,[31] assumes the gold brocade of the Queen, puts on a mask of burning gold, so to speak, and imposes her will on Septimus, the Players, the Prime Minister, and the people. She takes on her new role, foreseeing with liberty of impulse the destruction of her past, as she addresses the players: "You are banished and must not return upon pain of death . . . A woman player has left you. Do not mourn her. She was a bad, headstrong, cruel woman, and seeks destruction somewhere and with some man she knows nothing of; such a woman they tell me that this mask would well become, this foolish, smiling face! Come, dance." [32] There is an echo in this speech of the original tragic ending, in which Decima is forced to drink poison; Yeats's comedy is never total.

If we ask, finally, what emerges from *The Player Queen*

we can say dramatically, confusion; poetically, a few notable lines; symbolically, a vision of reality that is at best blurred. Yeats's late plays, when they are at all successful, are dramatized lyric pieces with the fewest possible characters. The crowded stage of *The Player Queen* obscures the one essential relation Yeats is interested in presenting: the Decima-Septimus-Unicorn triangle. Muse and Poet, Muse and unknown Divinity of inspiration; at moments the three are, logically enough, indistinguishable. When Decima sings she is the poet; when Septimus can scarcely distinguish himself from the Unicorn he is allying himself with the source of inspiration; when Decima casts off Septimus she becomes "fierce" and "terrible" like the Unicorn. We are, in fact, justified in saying that Decima, Septimus, and the Unicorn form a Yeatsian Trinity; three natures and one substance. They are artistic principles at war with each other, and we acknowledge in turn their conflicting claims. Septimus' human attachment to Decima is played off against a sense of the mind's primary duty to the image conveyed by Decima's unfaltering progress to her enthroned niche. The overruling sovereignty and despotism of the poetic image, Decima's banishing of Septimus, the forsaking of old loyalties for the sake of art — these are contrasted with the charm of the players and the romantic gallantry of Septimus' obsolete mode.

This is material intrinsically better suited to reflective poetry than to comedy, at least given the cast of Yeats's mind, and *The Player Queen* shows a certain uneasiness in its rather deliberate high spirits. (*The Herne's Egg* suffers from somewhat the same uncertainty of direction, except that being in verse, it is more tightly constructed.) When Yeats has stripped his theme, given up his attempts at heavy-handed folk humor, and abandoned prose for verse, the poetic value of the plays increases, as we shall see in *A Full Moon in March*, *The King of the Great Clock Tower*, and *The Herne's Egg*, all variants on the themes treated in *The Player Queen*.

Chapter VII

Desecration and
the Lover's Night

SINGING and dancing are consequent upon death, symbolic or real. This is what we are to conclude from the three plays to be discussed in this chapter. It has been pointed out often enough by Yeats himself [1] and by his commentators that his recurrent image of a severed head singing goes back to the 1897 edition of *The Secret Rose*, where, in the story "The Binding of the Hair," the minstrel Aodh, though beheaded in battle, continues his song in praise of the beauty of Queen Dectira, until "a troop of crows, heavy like fragments of that sleep older than the world, swept out of the darkness, and, as they passed, smote those ecstatic lips with the points of their wings; and the head fell from the bush and rolled over at the feet of the queen." [2] Thirty-seven years later, the image reappears in *The King of the Great Clock Tower*, and is used again in the reworking of the theme in *A Full Moon in March*. In the first version of *The King of the Great Clock Tower*, published by the Cuala Press in 1934, it is the severing of the head which causes poetry to appear; until that point, the play is in prose. The final version of the play which we find in the *Collected Plays* is in verse throughout, and is the better for it, but some of the impact of the singing of the head is lost in consequence. Even so, the verse of the singing head is in strong contrast to the rather slack blank verse of the body of the play, since blank verse is, after all, a dramatic convention for normal speech in prose.

Much has been made of the ritual origins of Yeats's last plays, and Yeats himself made quite certain that his anthropological interests were known to his commentators. But the invoking of Dionysus or Orpheus can be overdone. The Stroller in *The King of the Great Clock Tower* has affinities with Orpheus, but he has been metamorphosed into an Orphic figure of the twentieth century, and as usual, the differences are more interesting than the similarities. Yeats plucked images from all quarters, but their fruition, not their origin, is what appears in the play.

Just as the conceptual origins of the last plays have been sought in primitive ritual, so their formal origin has been sought in the Japanese drama, again on Yeats's authority. It seems to me more likely that the evidence of the Noh was for Yeats confirmatory rather than initiatory. In spite of his efforts to make himself into a dramatist, all he could ever do was to transfer a lyric situation onto the stage, and the essential stasis of the early plays (with *The Shadowy Waters* the best, or worst, example) betrays a meditative rather than a dramatic impulse. Yeats had no distinguished precedent for his plays in English literature, and certainly, judged by our normal canons for dramatic power, they are weak productions. When the Noh plays came to Yeats's attention, they encouraged him in his dislike for the realistic potpourri of the English stage, and enabled him with a clear conscience to dispense with all the minor characters who had only obscured his central themes. The formal roots of the plays, then, are not to be found in the formal principles determining the coherence of Japanese drama, but rather in the central lyric quality of their conception. Yeats said much the same thing — that the plays were conceived in order to make him write lyrics. "I made up the play," he wrote to Olivia Shakespear, referring to *The King of the Great Clock Tower*, "that I might write lyrics out of dramatic experience, all my personal experience having in some strange way come to an end." He repeated the same explanation to Dorothy Wellesley: "The prose version of *The King of the Great Clock Tower* was written to force myself to write lyrics." *The Herne's Egg* was projected in the same spirit: "I am trusting to this play to give me a new mass of thought and feeling, overflowing into lyrics (these are now in play)." [3] It is clear that the plays are dramatic neither in conception nor in end, but are rather devices within which to embody lyrics.

If this is true, and I believe it is, the lyrics in the later plays are the nuclei around which the plays grew, and they, far more than ritual or Japanese dramatic prescriptions, determine the structure of the plays. *The King of the Great Clock Tower* contains four of these lyrics, and all four are sung by the attendants, none by the dramatis personae in their own voices. That fact alone marks out the piece as one of basically lyric character. The intervening passages of blank verse, and even the brief stage appearances of the King, the Queen, and the Stroller, are purely incidental to the lyric meditation. The drama is perfunctory indeed: when it is time for the Captain of the Guard to enter and seize the Stroller one of the attendants simply speaks in the Captain's voice. Dramatic indifference cannot be carried any further, and in fact one feels that Yeats would have preferred a single voice to speak all the way through, with the simplest indication of his changing personae.

The first of the four lyrics, like the image of the severed head, harks back to earlier days. Forty-five years before, in "The Wanderings of Oisin" Yeats had written of Tir-nan-oge and of Oisin's vision there:

> We galloped; now a hornless deer
> Passed by us, chased by a phantom hound
> All pearly white, save one red ear;
> And now a lady rode like the wind

> With an apple of gold in her tossing hand;
> And a beautiful young man followed behind
> With quenchless gaze and fluttering hair.[4]

That dim and timeless flight with Niamh over the ocean in search of "vain gaiety, vain battle, vain repose" has been transmuted by its later incarnation in the play into a metaphysical state appropriate to the Stroller; the point being that time is both irrelevant and inimical to poetry. Yeats seems to have had some idea of creating a dramatic contrast between the King and the Stroller, but the plan never came to anything. Although the sinister king was dropped in the reworking of the play, his presence is the excuse for the first lyric, setting time against the otherworld:

> They dance all day that dance in Tir-nan-oge.
> There every lover is a happy rogue;
> And should he speak, it is the speech of birds.
> No thought has he, and therefore has no words,
> No thought because no clock, no clock because
> If I consider deeply, lad and lass,
> Nerve touching nerve upon that happy ground,
> Are bobbins where all time is bound and wound.
>
> O never may that dismal thread run loose;
> For there the hound that Oisin saw pursues
> The hornless deer that runs in such a fright;
> And there the woman clasps an apple tight
> For all the clamour of a famished man.
> They run in foam, and there in foam they ran,
> Nor can they stop to take a breath that still
> Hear in the foam the beating of a bell.[5]

It is almost unnerving to realize that "lad and lass" in the first stanza have certain unmistakable affiliations with "Hades' bobbin bound in mummy cloth"; that those "happy rogues" have something in common with the Shrouds in "Cuchulain Comforted" who "had changed their throats and had the throats of birds"; and that the scene from "The Wanderings of Oisin" has taken on a subtly different and somber cast. Originally, the scene was a Rossetti-like conception, located in a dream world lacking all human urgency: the hornless deer was not frightened, the beautiful young man was not famished. Most of all, the graceful pre-Raphaelite figures were, in the early poem, simply one of those inexplicable apparitions encountered in fairyland, coming from nowhere, going nowhere. In the play, on the contrary, they are threatened and fleeing, dreading some undefined species of capture by that beating of a bell (the Yeatsian equivalent of "time's winged chariot") which they hear in the sea.[6] The implication is that if ever "the dismal thread" were to run loose, and time to touch Tir-nan-oge, the figures in the scene would be engulfed by the waves and disappear. They are figures somewhat like Wordsworth's Bedouin bearing the stone and the shell, who

> Went hurrying o'er the illimitable waste,
> With the fleet waters of a drowning world
> In chase of him.[7]

Yeats had as much reason as Wordsworth to be apprehensive of "the waters of the deep/Gathering upon us" and his Country of the Young cannot be an unshadowed paradise. In fact, the first version of the opening lyric for *The King of the Great Clock Tower* (given in a letter to Olivia Shakespear) shows how much of the poetic strength of paradisal imagery comes from our perception of the impossibility of an unclouded Paradise:

> I call to mind the iron of the bell
> And get from that my harsher imagery,
> All love is shackled to mortality,
> Love's image is a man-at-arms in steel;
> Love's image is a woman made of stone;
> It dreams of the unborn; all else is nought;
> To-morrow and to-morrow fills its thought;
> All tenderness reserves for that alone.[8]

For Yeats, imperishable bliss is not a poetic subject by itself: it becomes one only when coupled with the haunting apprehension of death. "Death is the mother of beauty," says Stevens, and Yeats would have agreed. At some point, the Clock in the Great Clock Tower will toll midnight and, like Cinderella, the images will be divested of their glory. Septimus' banishment was comic, but the end of a cycle of imagery foreseen in *The King of the Great Clock Tower* is heroic, not tragic.

Before the next lyric is sung, the dramatic situation, such as it is, is roughed in. The King has married a remote, nameless, and beautiful Queen, whose mystery irritates him. It is quite clear that she is of a different sort from the King, and that she does not love him, nor he her; he insults her and she keeps a disdainful silence. F. A. C. Wilson alleges that the Stroller "succeeds in alienating her affections from her husband," but there never were any to be alienated. Wilson further identifies the King and Queen with Yeats's "golden King and silver lady" in "Under the Round Tower," [9] but a quotation will show the impossibility of the identification:

> That golden king and that wild lady
> Sang till stars began to fade,
> Hands gripped in hands, toes close together,
> Hair spread on the wind they made;
> That lady and that golden king
> Could like a brace of blackbirds sing.[10]

Solomon and Sheba are clearly intended, since other poems using them as symbols of married love were composed at the same time; and the King and Queen of the play are certainly inconceivable as symbols of perfect union. Nothing marks the King as a symbol of wisdom, as Wilson would have it,[11] and finally, only the King, not the Queen, is the governor of the Clock Tower. The Queen is not bound by time, since she can cross the barrier between death and life.

The Stroller has celebrated the Queen's beauty on hearsay, and now demands corroboration for the image he has created. Bringing his imagined image, he of course "finds a real image there," but shrugs off the discrepancy:

> Neither so red, nor white, nor full in the breast
> As I had thought. What matter for all that
> So long as I proclaim her everywhere
> Most beautiful! [12]

It is clear, from the description of Phase 14 given in *A Vision* (see Chapter I) that the Queen in *The King of the Great Clock Tower* and *A Full Moon in March* belongs to that phase of aloof beauty. As I have shown earlier, a beautiful and remote woman is Yeats's pre-eminent symbol of the poetic image — and consequently is also the symbol of the Muse. One distinction must be made here between Phase 14 and Phase 15. In Phase 14 the Image is considered as the thing-in-itself, unobserved, self-sufficient, like Helen in the poem, "Long-Legged Fly." [13] In Phase 15 the Image is considered as something absorbed into the poetic consciousness — the Image has struck the poet, impinged on him, and can therefore be called the Muse. In both *The King of the Great Clock Tower* and *A Full Moon in March* the Queen is first an aloof and solitary object of worship, the remote subject of the poet's song, the Image; but during the dance and the kiss, she unites with the poet, causes him to sing through her inspiration, and at this point may rightly be named the Muse.

The Stroller demands that the Queen dance for him; the enraged King orders his execution; the Stroller in return proclaims that he is under the protection of the god Aengus (the Irish Apollo), and retells Aengus's prophecy:

> O listen, for I speak his very words —
> 'On stroke of midnight when the old year dies,
> Upon that stroke, the tolling of that bell,
> The Queen shall kiss your mouth,' — his very words —
> Your Queen, my mouth, the Queen shall kiss my mouth. [14]

The second of the four lyrics follows upon the seizing of the
Stroller. In a tranced state, the Queen sings her strange song,
in which there is not only the equation of sexual climax with
death, but of gestation with destruction:

> O, what may come
> Into my womb?
>
> He longs to kill
> My body, until
> That sudden shudder
> And limbs lie still.
>
> O, what may come
> Into my womb,
> What caterpillar
> My beauty consume? [15]

The poet's domination of the Muse, his bending her to his
will, is the reciprocal image to the figure of Leda with the
Swan. In Yeats's imagery, the poet is alternately male and
female: ("You are doubly a woman, first because of yourself
and secondly because of the muses," wrote Yeats to Ethel
Mannin in 1935, "whereas I am but once a woman." [16]) Passive, the poet is visited by an infusion of poetic power, but
then he turns that power to his own use, and the hitherto feminine mind takes on an active role, correcting the disappointing
"real image" and creating a poetic one. Hopkins described
the process:

> Nine months she then, nay years, nine years she long
> Within her wears, bears, cares and combs the same:
> The widow of an insight lost she lives, with aim
> Now known and hand at work now never wrong. [17]

Each poem is, in its own way, the corrosion of that particular
experience which engendered it: there is a dissolution involved
in mastering the experience.

The Queen is right in seeing the Stroller's domination as a
destruction of her aloof beauty, since up to the present her

"inscape" has been her remoteness. "Why sit you there,"
asked the King as the play began,

> Dumb as an image made of wood or metal,
> A screen between the living and the dead?
> All persons here assembled, and because
> They think that silence unendurable,
> Fix eyes upon you.[18]

That hieratic seated posture of the Queen is disturbed by the
coming of the Stroller. Descending from her throne, she begins to dance, controlled by the power of the severed head,
which sings the third of the lyrics. The head has now become
one of the resurrected dead, and its lyric is about the union
of the dead with the living, or, as we are accustomed to find
it in Yeats's symbolism, of the image with the real. The incident behind the song is Aeneas' meeting with his father in
Hades, the most memorable example in literature of the attempt of the dead and the living to kiss. Three times Aeneas
tries to embrace Anchises, but fails:

> Ter conatus ibi collo dare bracchia circum
> ter frustra comprensa manus effugit imago,
> par levibus ventis volucrique simillima somno.[19]

In the climactic moment when the Queen kisses the Stroller,
the normal prohibitions on such embraces are relaxed. All the
desperate attempts of the living to make sexual intercourse
a final good are frustrate, sings the head, but in the brief meeting of the two worlds, image and real, the ultimate union is
consummated. The union is brief because the tolling of midnight will bring it to an end — time will intervene and break
the trance — but for the moment during which it lasts the
absorption is complete.

> Clip and lip and long for more,
> Mortal men our abstracts are;
> *What of the hands on the Great Clock face?*

> All those living wretches crave
> Prerogatives of the dead that have
> Sprung heroic from the grave.
> *A moment more and it tolls midnight.*[20]

It is worth noting that the Island of Heroes of the opening lyric, populated by Oisin, Niamh, and other mythical figures, has lost its fairy-tale quality, and in this song has been transmuted into human terms entirely. This is perhaps why Yeats rejected the alternative song for the severed head, in which the heroic figures of Irish legend are summoned up by the singing Stroller. The alternative song makes perfect sense in the play, since the resurrecting of heroic images is just what Yeats thought one function of the poet to be: but the more metaphysical quality of the song finally inserted fits better with the previous discussion of time and death, and can establish the richer quality of the imaginative world, of which the real world is only an "abstract."

The Head asks a question in its final stanza:

> What's prophesied? What marvel is
> Where the dead and living kiss?
> *What of the hands on the Great Clock face?*
> Sacred Virgil never sang
> All the marvel there begun,
> But there's a stone upon my tongue.
> *A moment more and it tolls midnight.*[21]

That question must somehow be answered in terms of the play. What *is* the marvel that results from the interaction of Muse and Poet? And what power over that marvel has the Great Clock face? No explicit answer is given in so many words: we have only the last of the four lyrics as a resolution to the play. At first, there seems no connection between the play as we have known it and the final lyric (and indeed, strictly speaking, there is no connection with the play's *action* — this is one more indication of how little the action of the play has to do with its meaning). The end of the play shows the re-

fusal of the "wicked, crooked hawthorn tree" to believe in
resurrected and transfigured images.[22] But when the "rambling,
shambling, travelling-man" describes his vision, we realize that
death is a necessity for that "solemn sight": in life, the dancers
of Castle Dargan did not shine with that supernatural radiance;
it is conferred only by their ghostly state. The hawthorn tree,
like the King, is blind to that truth, and wants only a Struld-
brugg immortality:

> O, but I saw a solemn sight;
> *Said the rambling, shambling travelling-man;*
> Castle Dargan's ruin all lit,
> Lovely ladies dancing in it.
>
> What though they danced! Those days are gone,
> *Said the wicked, crooked, hawthorn tree;*
> Lovely lady or gallant man
> Are blown cold dust or a bit of bone.
>
> O what is life but a mouthful of air?
> *Said the rambling, shambling travelling-man;*
> Yet all the lovely things that were
> Live, for I saw them dancing there.
>
> Nobody knows what may befall
> *Said the wicked, crooked, hawthorn tree.*
> I have stood so long by a gap in the wall
> Maybe I shall not die at all.[23]

The answer, finally, to the hawthorn's position is the intensity of the vision of Castle Dargan — a ruin with lovely
ladies dancing in it, destruction and joy interacting as they do
only in art. "All the lovely things that were, live": the gram-
matical paradox of the final spondee makes its own assertion.
   The defects of *The King of the Great Clock Tower* are
not difficult to find, and Ezra Pound was right in condemning
it as drama. Yeats took offense at this, and called the play
"theatrically coherent, spiritually incoherent," [24] but he was
wrong: interchanged, the terms would be more accurate.
Spiritually, the play is forceful enough, but it is complicated
by the presence of the King of the Great Clock Tower. Im-

potent, uncomprehending, and bound by time, he has no real relation to the Queen. In fact, he, not the Stroller, is the actual antagonist in the play, and the protagonist is the Queen-Stroller, a fusion of divine and human. However, in this version of the relation between Poet and Muse, the Muse is too passive. It is the King, not the Queen, who becomes insulted at the Stroller's comments, and the King, not the Queen, who orders the beheading of the Stroller. (In *A Full Moon in March*, which is the reworking of *The King of the Great Clock Tower*, Yeats eliminates the King entirely and gives the Queen-Muse an active role.)

By definition, in Yeats's system, the union of thought and image takes place outside of time and is not influenced by it: in Phase 15, time is irrelevant. Both Head and Queen transcend time, and although the Queen sings of her apparent degradation in entering the world of time, generation, and death, in letting the poet's blood enter her womb, and in suffering the symbolic death of "that sudden shudder," she is yet rapt into the dance by the experience, as death becomes a special form of the still trance of Phase 15. The Head, too, is caught up into the same trance, singing of the ecstasy of that Kiss experienced in death, exceeding all sexual or prophetical joy. In the 1925 *Vision*, Yeats explained in detail what he meant by the Kiss of Death: it is given, he says, by the Spirits at Phase 15 because they need help to be "set free." Yeats specifically calls such a spirit a Muse in this passage, and attributes to her the production of a work of art. The passage is muddled, but I reproduce it in full since it relates to all these plays where "the dead and living kiss":

It is said of the Spirits at Phases 15 and 1 that the first need help and the second give it . . . The first give what is called the "Kiss of Death." The Spirits at 15 need help that, before entering upon their embodied state, they may rid themselves of all traces of the *primary Tincture*, and this they gain by imposing upon a man or woman's mind an *antithetical* image which requires *primary* expression. It is this expression, which may be an action or a work of art, which sets them free, and the image imposed is an ideal form, an image of themselves, a type of emotion which expresses them, and this they can do but upon one man or woman's mind; their coming life depending upon their choice of that mind. They suffer from the terror of solitude, and can only free themselves from terror by becoming entirely *antithetical* and so self-sufficing, and till that moment comes each must, if a woman, give some one man her love, and though he cannot, unless out of phase and obsessed to the creation of a succuba know that his muse exists, he returns this love through the intermediary of an idol. This idol he creates out of an image imposed upon his imagination by the Spirit. This Spirit is said to give the "Kiss of Death" because though she that gives it may persecute other idols, being jealous, the idol has not come out of the man's desire. Its expression is a harmonisation which frees the Spirit from terror and the man from desire, and that which is born from the man, and from an all but completed solitude, is called an *antithetical Arcon*. Such *Arcons* deal with form not wisdom.[25]

In the kiss of the dead and the living, both Muse and Poet represent, like the image in "Byzantium," "death-in-life and life-in-death." The Muse is "dead" because she carries the tradition of the past (what Yeats calls, in *A Full Moon in March*, "all time's completed treasure") which must constantly be revivified by contact with the present; she is "alive" because she is the inspiring principle. (Wallace Stevens conveys somewhat the same idea when he addresses the Muse as one of "the sisterhood of the living dead."[26]) The poet is "dead" because he is passive under her inspiration; he is "alive" because he shapes that inspiration into poetry. Both of them participate momentarily in the same condition, that "Condition of Fire" which is the state of the Daimons. The Muse may temporarily escape from that state of isolation by contact with the impermanent, bringing Phase 15 into a fleeting relation with humanity, while the human partner in the meeting of Muse and poet experiences in an agonizing instant that "disengaging of a soul from place and history, its suspension in a beautiful or terrible light," which was Yeats's definition of art.[27]

The artistic imagination, if it could be in a permanent state of inspiration by the Muse, would inhabit Phase 15 uninterruptedly, but such is not the case. Consequently, the human mind can only account for moments of beatitude or harmony in human life by assuming intervention by a being from Phase 15, Muse or Daimon. Yeats describes the process in *Per Amica Silentia Lunae*:

> Daemon and man are opposites; man passes from heterogeneous objects to the simplicity of fire, and the Daemon is drawn to objects because through them he obtains power, the extremity of choice. For only in men's minds can he meet even those in the Condition of Fire who are not of his own kin . . . His descending power is neither the winding nor the straight line but zigzag . . . it is the sudden lightning, for all his acts of power are instantaneous. We perceive in a pulsation of the artery, and after slowly decline . . . Always it is an impulse from some Daemon that gives to our vague, unsatisfied desire, beauty, a meaning and a form all can accept.[28]

If we are in any doubt that Yeats is talking about poetry, a glance at his source reassures us: in the passage from *Per Amica Silentia Lunae* just quoted, he is remembering Blake's "Milton":

> For in this Period the Poet's Work is Done, and all the Great
> Events of Time start forth & are conceiv'd in such a Period,
> Within a Moment, a Pulsation of the Artery.[29]

The true result of the visitation of the Daemon is a work of art. In the sonnet on Leda, I am half in doubt whether the lines

> The broken wall, the burning roof and tower
> And Agamemnon dead

refer to the actual events of the Trojan War or to the events as retold in Homer and the Greek tragedies, but I incline to think the latter; Yeats's supreme instance of the contact between divine and human produced not only a supernatural progeny and a tragic war but also an immortal poem. Remem-

bering that all such unions, for Yeats, have to do with crea-
tion, we can go on from his initial sketch in *The King of the
Great Clock Tower* to the revision of his theme in *A Full
Moon in March*.

2

Simplification of *The King of the Great Clock Tower* produced *A Full Moon in March*, where the meeting of Muse and
poet takes place in a vacuum, uninfluenced by time and the
rational world, since this is a Queen without a King. Time is
no longer clock time, but astrological and mythical time. The
beginning of the mystical year comes at the vernal equinox,
the time of the full moon in March. Winter is about to turn
to spring, Genesis is about to take place, and all things are
about to be renewed. The Queen is still in the state of winter,
ice-bound, when the play begins; she is a symbol for the
Daimon, isolated in the Condition of Fire until he (or she)
exercises power through a human being. But the Queen,
stretching and yawning, is awakening from her hibernation,
and prepares for the kiss of union. The Stroller of the earlier
play has become a Swineherd, the ultimate symbol of the
"mire and blood" of human veins, and of all that "desecrates"
the Muse. The necessity of that desecration in the lover's
night, of the coupling of Queen and Swineherd, is the theme
of the play, just as it is the theme of so many of the later
poems:

> 'Fair and foul are near of kin
> And fair needs foul,' I cried . . .

> 'A woman can be proud and stiff
> When on love intent;
> But Love has pitched his mansion in
> The place of excrement;
> For nothing can be sole or whole
> That has not not been rent.' [30]

The "proud and stiff" Queen must be humbled in union, and
her humiliation will be signified by the dropping of her veil.

Until the actual moment of union, the Swineherd has not seen the face of the Queen, nor does he care, since he believes in her beauty and trusts to luck that he will see it eventually. He knows that the divine principle in itself is incomplete (just as the Queen's beauty, when seen, was disappointing), and that only by a seeming desecration can the Muse gain power and wholeness. It is the Muse who is doubtful, who is affronted by the idea: "O foul, foul, foul!" says the Queen, as she hears the Swineherd prophesy her destiny — a descent from her high station, a flight to an ignorant forest and the dung of swine, impregnation by blood, the final trance of conception.

Five lyrics form the core of the play, three of them sung by the attendants, and the others by the Queen and the Head. The first and last establish the common denominator of love. Possessing country boy or Pythagoras, scholastic or fool, love is no respecter of persons; it makes the foolish wise and the wise foolish, and is itself both gold and dung. The Queen, who will not admit that all ladders start in the earth, is not prepared to accept such a doctrine. Her idealizing of love causes her to react in horror, and when the Swineherd asserts that she will "bring forth her farrow in the dung" she orders him killed. The Attendant then sings a song deriving in a rather nebulous way from the story in *The Secret Rose* mentioned at the beginning of this chapter. For his own purposes, Yeats transforms the story into a parallel with his play. Though the Queen who speaks the verse denies that she has caused the death of her lover, we suspect that she protests too much. She ordered him beheaded, we imagine, to test the truth of his boast that death itself could not prevent him from singing her beauty:

> He had famished in a wilderness,
> Braved lions for my sake,
> And all men lie that say that I
> Bade that swordsman take
> His head from off his body
> And set it on a stake.

> He swore to sing my beauty
> Though death itself forbade.
> They lie that say, in mockery
> Of all that lovers said,
> Or in mere woman's cruelty
> I bade them fetch his head.[31]

The "ancient Irish Queen" is equivocating: perhaps she did not order the execution for those reasons adduced by "all men," but she did order it for the uniqueness of the experience with which it provided her, to see her lover become only a singing throat. Other women have "had their fling," but they lacked her triumph: they "never stood before a stake/And heard the dead lips sing." [32]

If we are to find this anything more than a rather gruesome fairy tale, we must look further for the symbolic meaning. Cruelty and ignorance, says Yeats in *A Vision*, "constitute evil . . . and are that which makes possible the conscious union of . . . the *Daimon* of the Living and a *Spirit of the Thirteenth Cone*, which is the deliverance from birth and death." [33] Cruelty on the one side, in the Queen's reduction of the poet to a singing throat; ignorance on the other side, on the part of the victim who is finally enlightened by the symbolic "death." It is again the situation of Leda and the Swan, ignorance violated by cruelty. This is why, after the brittle defiance of the Attendant's song, just quoted, we are immediately confronted with the explanatory love song of the Queen:

> Child and darling, hear my song
> Never cry I did you wrong;
> Cry that wrong came not from me
> But my virgin cruelty.
>
> Great my love before you came,
> Greater when I love in shame,
> Greatest when there broke from me
> Storm of virgin cruelty.[34]

The havoc wreaked by the Muse on her devotees is a proof of

her love: whom she loves she chastens, since all knowledge
and power arise, as Yeats says in *The Hour Glass*, from destruction and terror.

> Only when all our hold on life is troubled,
> Only in spiritual terror can the Truth
> Come through the broken mind.[35]

   The relation between Poet and Muse, reduced to its most
schematic form, appears in the song of the severed Head, as
Head and Queen, at this moment, laugh with the gaiety that
"transfigures all that dread."

> I sing a song of Jack and Jill.
> Jill had murdered Jack.
> *The moon shone brightly*;
> Ran up the hill, and round the hill,
> Round the hill and back.
> *A full moon in March.*
>
> Jack had a hollow heart, for Jill
> Had hung his heart on high;
> *The moon shone brightly*;
> Had hung his heart beyond the hill,
> A-twinkle in the sky.
> *A full moon in March.*[36]

The song of the Head continues, in fairy-tale form, the song
of the Queen, but the lesser ecstasy of love is sacrificed for
the greater ecstasy of art. Jack the Poet no longer has a complete heart (symbolizing the experience of love) because Jill
the Muse has hollowed out the substance of it and transformed
it into art — the light of Phase 15, the full moon in March.
To achieve song, Yeats would say, experience must be im-
molated. In being made into a poem, life is detached, made into
something external and public, and sacrificed on the altar of
form. The events of life are forsaken in favor of their metaphors:

> It was the dream itself enchanted me: . . .
> Players and painted stage took all my love,
> And not those things that they were emblems of.[37]

Experience is private, hidden in the heart, but poetry is public, on display, like Yeats's circus animals or the full moon.

I do not think much is gained by reading into the song of the severed Head, as F. A. C. Wilson does, references to Minerva and Dionysus, Calvary and Mount Abiegnos; nor do I agree with his characterization of the Queen as the "eternal feminine" and the Swineherd as "the masculine principle in nature, brutal, violent and disruptive." Mr. Wilson would have it that "one function of *A Full Moon in March* is to strip bare the relations between the sexes"; but that sociological interpretation makes the play even more peculiar than it is. Mr. Wilson's other view of the play is that it is a work "centring upon the Platonic theology" in which the Queen is "the type of pure spirituality" and the Swineherd is "spirit on the lowest, material plane." [38] I am uncomfortable with any view imputing mystical references to Yeats's plays, and consequently prefer to think that the theological symbols, when he uses them, have primarily aesthetic and human reference. This is so, I think, in all his talk of "divine" and "human"; and though we are at times constrained to talk in his own terms, we should be wary of forgetting that they are symbolic ones.

The final lyric in *A Full Moon in March* recapitulates the argument of the play. As in *The King of the Great Clock Tower*, the Second Attendant is the questioner, uncomprehending, about to be enlightened, while the First Attendant has the accents of conviction in affirming the necessity of "desecration and the lover's night." The Second Attendant is a visitor from another sphere, with "a savage, sunlit heart" and an incomplete understanding of the Queen's action, as, rapt in adoration of the Head she had earlier scorned, she sinks "in bridal sleep." The Muse might seem self-sufficient — she is of Phase 15, she has unity of being, she carries a pitcher with "all time's completed treasure tight therein." But pitchers are only useful for pouring; time's completed treasure is only good when spent in the lover's night; artifice is only art when it arises in the place "where all the ladders start." Grief and fright — the emotions of the Second Attendant — are the natural feelings on seeing the "holy, haughty feet descend/ From emblematic niches," because there is a temptation always to think of the sages standing in God's holy fire as emblems of a state of final independence from complexity. It is impossible to overestimate the strength of the pull in Yeats to just that point of view; his pre-Raphaelite roots were strong in him till the end of his life. *A Full Moon in March* springs from a decadent root — Wilde's *Salome* — and betrays affinities with its source, naturally, but the transformations outweigh the resemblances. The pre-Raphaelite remoteness, the flight to delicate and perverse ivory towers, withdrawal to the sphere of attenuated art — these refuges became impossible for Yeats. The final lyric sums up Yeats's demands on the imagination, and though the language is ceremonious, the conclusion is a harsh one:

> What can she lack whose emblem is the moon?
> But desecration and the lover's night.³⁹

3

The King of the Great Clock Tower and *A Full Moon in March* are, like "Leda and the Swan," serious and prophetic in attitude and tone, so much so that the levity of *The Herne's Egg* comes as a shock to anyone who expects the same reverential treatment to be accorded the Daimon always. Yeats called the play "the strangest wildest thing I have ever written" and wrote to Ethel Mannin, "I am sending you a copy of my very Rabelasian [*sic*] play *The Herne's Egg*, but do not ask me what it means." ⁴⁰ What it means is something more complicated, at any rate, than the meaning of the two earlier plays. No longer is Yeats proposing a simple Muse-artist relation. The Muse is there, in the person of the Great Herne, and the artist is there, in the person of Attracta, and the climax is there, when Attracta sings her Ledean song, but there is more to the play than its core.

Like the Unicorn in *The Player Queen*, the Great Herne, or heron, is another figure for the Daimon, and we may link it to the other "daimonic" bird, the Phoenix. For Yeats, the Phoenix is a favorite symbol for the Muse,[41] and poets exist to care for this Phoenix:

> We should ascend out of common interests, the thoughts of the newspapers, of the marketplace, of men of science, but only so far as we can carry the normal, passionate, reasoning self, the personality as a whole. We must find some place upon the Tree of Life for the Phoenix nest, for the passion that is exaltation and the negation of the will, for the wings that are always on fire, set high that the forked branches may keep it safe, yet low enough to be out of the little wind-tossed boughs, the quivering of the twigs.[42]

The quotation could easily serve as an epigraph to *The Herne's Egg*, and the central problem of the play, it seems to me, is the correct placing of the Phoenix nest. Attracta and Congal are both concerned with the problem, Attracta wishing to deny the connection of the Phoenix with the Tree of Life, Congal wishing to place the nest on the lowest branches. It is true that Attracta sings (and is therefore symbolic of the poet) but it is also true that she can sing of the power of the Great Herne only while she is being raped by Congal and his soldiers.[43] Attracta is in danger of thinking that the presence of the Great Herne is the only condition necessary for poetry; Congal is in danger of thinking that the Great Herne is a figment of Attracta's imagination, and that to beget, nothing is needed but a common man. The Herne's egg (like Leda's egg, a symbol of the product of union of Muse and poet — the completed poem) is consequently claimed by both sides, by Congal who thinks it is simply something utilitarian and therefore to be eaten, and by Attracta, who thinks it is something sacred and not to be violated. Actually, of course, it is something in between, and *The Herne's Egg* is a play of compromise.

In his long essay on *The Herne's Egg*,[44] F. A. C. Wilson makes the first really thorough attempt to explain the play, and he has done all critics that follow him a good service in establishing the Indian influences upon Yeats. As we might have expected, the Indian ideas strike us with an oddly familiar ring. Like the other source images which Yeats appropriated from time to time, they are, as I have said above about the Noh drama, confirmatory rather than initiatory. Yeats realized this, and wrote to Dorothy Wellesley about *The Herne's Egg*: "Shri Purohit Swami is with me, and the play is his philosophy in a fable, or mine confirmed by him."[45] Mr. Wilson, on this hint, finds the play an exposition of Indian theological doctrines; while he is discussing the specific incidents in the play, he is often interesting, but his allegorical exegesis is strained.[46] I prefer to see the play as Yeats's "philosophy" confirmed by Indian symbols rather than the other way round.

There is also a question of tone to be settled before anything can be said about the play. Mr. Wilson speaks of the various scenes and speeches as "moving," "exciting," "magnificent," "splendid," "beautifully modulated," "vivid," "beautiful and pregnant," and so on. But *The Herne's Egg* is none of these things. The adjectives might fit a Shakespearean tragedy, but certainly they do not apply to what is essentially a rather arid and contrived piece of theatrical writing. Yeats being Yeats, there are some good passages, though fewer than in *The King of the Great Clock Tower* and *A Full Moon in March*. The interesting thing about *The Herne's Egg* is *not* its humanity (it has very little) nor its stagecraft (bad, as usual) nor its language (apart from scattered speeches); it is interesting as a criticism on *The King of the Great Clock Tower* and *A Full Moon in March*. I find its "tragicomic levity," as Mr. Wilson chooses to call it, a tiresome and unsuccessful tone, uncongenial to Yeats's temperament. I suspect that *The Herne's Egg* was perhaps an attempt to exorcise the Leda theme by the method used in *The Player Queen* — to turn the tragedy into a farce, to mix the emotions, to take oneself somewhat less than seriously. Yeats was not entirely incapable of a detached attitude toward himself and his images, but his best works are the poems of "high seriousness," and *The Herne's Egg*, sporadically attractive as it is, loses out by its grotesquerie.

The Herne's Egg is the least lyric of the three plays considered in this chapter; that, too, it has in common with *The Player Queen*. We have only one genuine lyric, Attracta's marriage song, and though there are a few moments of poetic power scattered through the play as well, for the most part the lines, though in verse, lack force. Attracta's song, since it is the lyric core of the play, deserves the first comment:

> When I take a beast to my joyful breast,
> Though beak and claw I must endure,
> *Sang the bride of the Herne, and the Great Herne's bride*,
> No lesser life, man, bird or beast,
> Can make unblessed what a beast made blessed,
> Can make impure what a beast made pure.[47]

So she begins, and the old antithesis is set up — cruelty descending upon ignorance, purity and blessedness arising out of the impure and unblessed substratum of existence.

Attracta's second stanza is more puzzling:

> Where is he gone, where is that other,
> He that shall take my maidenhead?
> *Sang the bride of the Herne, and the Great Herne's bride*,
> Out of the moon came my pale brother,
> The blue-black midnight is my mother.
> Who will turn down the sheets of the bed? [48]

The song harks back to a scene involving the three girls, Agnes, Mary, and Kate (intended, one feels, to be attractive, but who come out finally as no more than silly). The three have been discussing Attracta's trysts with the Great Herne:

> *Agnes.* The last time she went away
> The moon was full — she returned
> Before its side had flattened . . .
>
> *Kate.* Those leaps may carry her where
> No woman has gone, and he
> Extinguish sun, moon, star.
> No bridal torch can burn
> When his black midnight is there.
>
> *Agnes.* I have heard her claim that they couple
> In the blazing heat of the sun.
>
> *Kate.* But you have heard it wrong!
> In blue-black midnight they couple.
>
> *Agnes.* No, in the sun.
>
> *Kate.*   Blue-black!
>
> *Agnes.* In the sun!
>
> *Kate.*   Blue black, blue-black! [49]

The completeness of experience claimed by Attracta cannot be restricted to any one state of light or darkness. It is clear that Yeats wants us to think of her as a creature from Phase 15, since all the symbolism of the moon points that way, but the enlightenment allied to the coupling demands the sun for a symbol, while the annihilation involved suggests midnight. Attracta claims all three states: moon and midnight in second stanza, and, as we shall see, dawn (or the sun) in the third. The reference to mother and brother (Attracta being a peculiarly nonhuman creature) is more odd. I can only suggest that the Great Herne is not only lover, but also brother and mother, and cite a good parallel in Wallace Stevens, when he addresses the Muse (the "One of Fictive Music") as "Sister and mother and diviner love." [50]

Attracta ends her song, as we might expect, by characterizing her union with the Great Herne in Yeats's favorite words — horror and terror.

When beak and claw their work begin
Shall horror stir in the roots of my hair?
Sang the bride of the Herne, and the Great Herne's bride,
And who lie there in the cold dawn
When all that terror has come and gone?
Shall I be the woman lying there? [51]

The Ledean question has been put even more acutely in this poem: Yeats raises the whole problem of the retention of identity after the new experience. In the sonnet on Leda, the question was phrased in relation to knowledge, and that is a painful enough spot. Here, the enlightenment is taken for granted (in "the cold dawn") and the difficulty is one of self-recognition. The play is in part, I think, an answer to Attracta's question; and the answer is No. She *is* changed by her experience, and the most appealing thing about the play is that Yeats leaves us suspecting that perhaps it was the sevenfold rape, and not the Great Herne, that changed Attracta.

So much for the center of the play; with that established, we can return to the beginning. The kings of Connacht and Tara are engaged in a symbolic "perfect battle" in which actions are mirror images, skills are perfectly matched, and losses are equal on both sides. Mr. Wilson would have it that the battle indicates Eden,[52] but it is made quite clear in the play that the stylized gestures are what we would call "going through the motions," the characteristic activity of one of the "final phases" in Yeats's system. To be bluntly allegorical, it is equivalent to repeating the gestures of a tradition when that tradition no longer has any vivid meaning, but only stands for a certain well-bred attitude. As Congal, King of Connacht, says,

Congal.   They had, we had
          Forgotten what we fought about,
          So fought like gentlemen, but now

> Knowing the truth must fight like the beasts.
> Maybe the Great Herne's curse has done it.
> Why not? Answer me that; why not?
>
> *Mike.*   Horror henceforth.
> *Congal.*   This wise man means
> We fought so long like gentlemen
> That we grew blind.[53]

The great shaking-up which Yeats so delighted in imagining in all possible manifestations is coming on Congal and
his men. As much as *The Player Queen*, as much as "The
Second Coming," *The Herne's Egg* is a work centered on
revolution. Just as in *The Player Queen*, the era which is
ending has its sympathetic side; Congal, like Septimus, is an
attractive figure. And just as Decima's coldness and oppor-
tunism are humanly chilling (even if allegorically necessary)
so Attracta's rather repulsive purity has its drawbacks.

Congal is not to be underestimated. He, like Septimus, is
unluckily the sacrifice to the new order, but it is with regret
that Attracta watches him be reincarnated into a donkey.
For his offense against the Great Herne, he is cursed:

> 'He that a herne's egg dare steal
> Shall be changed into a fool . . .
> And to end his fool breath
> At a fool's hand meet his death.' [54]

There is a double edge to the denouement: Congal escapes
the Fool, but we suspect that by his stubborn doubt of the
existence of the Great Herne he *has* deserved the name of
fool, and in dying by his own hand, yet fulfills the curse.
Yeats has a good deal of sympathy for Congal, shown in
one indubitable way — he gives him good verse. In fact,
Congal speaks the single most interesting passage in the play,
an argument for the fact that imagination creates experience,
and not the reverse:

> Women thrown into despair
> By the winter of their virginity
> Take its abominable snow,

As boys take common snow, and make
An image of god or bird or beast
To feed their sensuality:
Ovid had a literal mind,
And though he sang it neither knew
What lonely lust dragged down the gold
That crept on Danae's lap, nor knew
What rose against the moony feathers
When Leda lay upon the grass.[55]

There is truth in Congal's assertions; the "better world" of the imagination does arise out of disappointment with the images presented by the "real" world (based though it is upon these as a groundwork). As I have said earlier, the passage describing the Simplon Pass in Wordsworth's *Prelude* is the classic instance of the compensatory power of the imagination, but even Wordsworth shrank from saying so in plain words. Attracta recoils from the idea that she may be a participant in the reality of the Great Herne, that without her, he would not exist. "Was wirst du tun, Gott, wenn ich sterbe?" asks Rilke's monk [56] and Congal has proposed just the same reciprocal identity.

Congal is not, then, a stupid opponent of imagination; he simply stands firm on its root in sense, and cannot get past that point. Attracta is just as obtuse, in her own way, and as she repeats her doctrinal statements one has the feeling she is not listening to Congal at all:

There is no reality but the Great Herne . . .
There is no happiness but the Great Herne.

Congal is tart with her, and rightly:

It may be that life is suffering,
But youth that has not yet known pleasure
Has not the right to say so.[57]

Congal is voicing Yeats's own impatience with the cloistered view of life as a vale of tears, and there are moments when we sense that Attracta and the Saint Octema–ridden Queen in *The Player Queen* are related figures. Congal would have it that all art is sublimation, and Attracta would hold just the converse, denying all reality but art. Both are wrong, for, as Yeats said in *A Vision*, "the *Spirit* cannot know the *Daimons* in their unity until it has first perceived them as the objects of sense, the *Passionate Body* exists that it may 'save the *Celestial Body* from solitude.' " [58]

Yeats continues his exploration into the nature of art in the scene between Attracta and the three girls. Here, he seems to be considering an idea hinted at in "Long-Legged Fly," the idea that art creates the archetype of what is desirable, that Michelangelo's perfect Adam or Attracta's perfect marriage is a necessary antecedent to the Adams or marriages of the common people. The populace need to have images created for them, and put in their mind; only Attracta dares to accept any image, saying

> Whatever shape he choose,
> Though that be terrible,
> Will best express his love.[59]

After the "real" battle between Connacht and Tara (symbolic of the new brutality ushered in by Attracta's sovereignty) and after the rape of Attracta by Congal and his men, the play becomes largely a contest between Congal and Attracta concerning just what did happen. *Was* Attracta violated by contact with earthly men, or is she indeed the bride only of the Great Herne? Though the Great Herne causes thunder (with an evident Jovian parallel), Congal remains adamant, even till his death, affirming to the Herne that "Six men and I possessed his wife." [60] The six men, all cowards, deny the fact, and will be reincarnated in bestial forms. Congal, being truthful and brave, deserves something better, and Attracta, who has come to an admiration for Congal, hopes he will be reincarnated in human form — so much so that she is willing to participate in carnal intercourse (she who had been so appalled at the thought earlier) in order that he may be reborn a human being. Congal, on the other hand, who had defiantly disbelieved in the Great Herne, has come to a belief in his existence. Both Attracta and Congal, then, have modified their early positions, but Yeats is not ready to call it a draw. The old reverence for the super- natural concept of poetry elaborated in the earlier plays still operates, and Congal's sacrilege must be punished. Like the King of the Great Clock Tower, Congal has come round, but not sufficiently so, and therefore he is reincarnated as a donkey; there is a suggestion,[61] however, that Congal is to be the next servant-donkey for the Great Herne, which is a fitting end.

In the last analysis, both Attracta and Conga have been bettered by their enlightenment. Congal appears at the end "moon-crazed, moon-blind,/Fighting and wounded, wounded and fighting"; [62] and we realize he has somehow entered Attracta's sphere. Attracta, on the other hand, has realized that the Great Herne's potency is not alone sufficient for conception:

> I lay with the Great Herne, and he,
> Being all a spirit, but begot
> His image in the mirror of my spirit,
> Being all sufficient to himself
> Begot himself; but there's a work
> That should be done, and that work needs
> No bird's beak nor claw, but a man,
> The imperfection of a man.[63]

Once more we have returned to the rag-and-bone shop, Yeats's predictable goal, always, even when he is writing in the comic mode.

Although *The Herne's Egg* (like *The Player Queen*) takes a partially ironic and critical view of the relationship of the Daimon-Muse and man, it still presents the same view of poetic creation and of the Daimon which Yeats proposed in *A Vision* and which we have seen corroborated in *The King of the Great Clock Tower* and *A Full Moon in March*.

Chapter VIII

Plays of Death, Purgation, and Resurrection

WHEN we ask what the recurrent themes of death, purgatory, and resurrection meant to Yeats, we involve ourselves in a thicket of possible interpretations. F. A. C. Wilson thinks that Yeats found those themes in esoterica, and treats them as having their source in the documents of mystical revelation and cult rituals. Once again, I prefer to put things the other way round, and say that Yeats sought out esoteric doctrines about the afterlife because his imagination was already obsessed with the afterlife as symbol. The germ for "The Dreaming of the Bones," for instance, appeared as early as 1897, in *The Secret Rose*.[1] In many of the headnotes to *Irish Fairy and Folk Tales*, Yeats finds, with evident satisfaction, confirmatory beliefs in popular superstition. Clearly, death and purgation, like the idea of cataclysm, attracted him from the beginning of his poetic career, and are not genetically related to his interest in theosophy, séances, and Buddhism.

It is surprising, as I have said earlier, how literally critics have tended to take Yeats in his writings on death and the afterlife. Perhaps such critical solemnity of tone is a transference from Christian sentiments: "There is an afterlife: therefore Yeats's views on it are important and religious." Leaving aside the dogmatic question of the existence of an afterlife, I can only insist on the many hints Yeats throws out to clarify his symbolic position.

Of these hints, the strongest and most explicit comes in the introduction to *The Words upon the Window-Pane*, when Yeats makes it clear that a relation exists in his mind between "poets and artists" and "the dead." "We poets and artists may be called, so small our share in life, 'separated spirits,' words applied by the old philosophers to the dead." The myth of death and purgation which occupies such a large part of *A Vision* (together with the myth of resurrection which is only hinted at in places) is clearly allied in Yeats's mind with the creative function. The relation is not a one-to-one allegorical scheme, and some of its overtones must remain personal to Yeats himself, but as we have already seen in "Byzantium," Yeats's eccentric symbolism of death and the purgative state can yield a recognizably human and nonesoteric meaning. "A writer must die every day he lives," Yeats wrote in the *Autobiographies*, and "be reborn, as it is said in the Burial Service, an incorruptible self, that self opposite of all that he has named 'himself.' " [2] It is this alternation of states, which Yeats found in himself, that forms the substratum of the plays we are to consider in this chapter.

Before discussing the plays of purgation proper (*The Dreaming of the Bones*, *Words upon the Window-pane*, and *Purgatory* — to which might be added *The Only Jealousy of Emer*), we must look briefly at Yeats's very unsatisfactory "theological" plays, *Calvary* and *The Resurrection*. One is about death, one about rebirth, and both illustrate how uncomfortable Yeats was with Christian symbolism. (They provide incidentally a comment on his good sense in forsaking it for his invented system.) The plays illustrate too Yeats's mixed feelings in using Christ as a symbol, inherited, I think, from Blake's equally uncertain view. In the introductory memoir to the Yeats-Ellis edition of Blake's works, the editors quote from the 1869 *Reminiscences* of Crabb Robinson: Blake, when asked what he thought of Jesus, said "He is the only God. But then and so am I, and so are you." Robinson continues: "He [Blake] had just before . . . been speaking of the errors of Jesus Christ. Jesus Christ should not have allowed himself to be crucified and should not have attacked the Government." Later, Ellis and Yeats quote another saying of Blake's: "Christ took much after his mother, the Law,"[3] adding that Blake's view is puzzling only when his pairs of "mystic contraries" are not kept in mind. This is also true of Yeats, and explains why he can comment on Christ from two different points of view, sympathetic and hostile.

We have said above that Christ is a figure from Phase 15, and in this aspect, he symbolizes for Yeats the creative imagination. Yeats's easy passage from history to symbol, so basic to *A Vision*, is nowhere better illustrated than in his remarks on "the historical Christ": "The historical Christ was indeed no more than the supreme symbol of the artistic imagination, in which, with every passion wrought to perfect beauty by art and poetry, we shall live, when the body has passed away for the last time." "The historical Christ," the artistic imagination, and the resurrected body become in this passage another Yeatsian trinity-in-unity, and the same constellation of symbols (derived of course from Blake) appears in Yeats's account of Blake's life: "The creative imagination of William Blake — the Christ in him — had arisen from the tomb in the thirty-third year of his age."[4]

It is hardly to be denied, with these passages as evidence, that *Calvary* and *The Resurrection* must be in some sense plays about the creative imagination. But before looking at them we must insert a necessary qualification. Christ is a figure from Phase 15, true, but it is Phase 15 of the primary cycle, not the cycle of Yeats's sympathies. If Christ were to appear today, Yeats says, he would be out of place; his perfect beauty is not akin to our present temper, and might even appear repellent to our eyes. This is not only a comment on historical Christianity as Yeats chose to consider it, it is also, and more interestingly, a comment on the historical fluctuations of the imagination. By founding a church and instituting a common ritual, Christ (in Yeats's version of his character) became the symbol of corporate activity, abhorrent to a poet who would write:

> Some moralist or mythological poet
> Compares the solitary soul to a swan;
> I am satisfied with that . . .
> The wings half spread for flight,
> The breast thrust out in pride
> Whether to play, or to ride
> Those winds that clamour of approaching night . . .
> The swan has leaped into the desolate heaven.[5]

Christ's heaven is not desolate and has nothing in common with the solitude of the swan; rather, the perfection of the primary cycle comes in shared experience and in social unity.

2

Yeats's own note on *Calvary* is unusually full, and while it stays within the terms of the play itself, it is still useful in seeing the outline of action as Yeats viewed it. "I use birds as symbols of subjective life . . . Certain birds, especially as I see things, such lonely birds as the heron, hawk, eagle, and swan, are the natural symbols of subjectivity, especially when floating upon the wind alone or alighting upon some pool or river." So much is already clear from the poems and plays, if we recall the birds in "The Wild Swans at Coole," "Coole Park and Ballylee, 1931," "Meditations in Time of Civil War," *The Herne's Egg*, and so on. Yeats goes on to explain the heron in *Calvary*:

I have used my bird-symbolism in these songs to increase the objective loneliness of Christ by contrasting it with a loneliness, opposite in kind, that unlike His can be, whether joyous or sorrowful, sufficient to itself. I have surrounded Him with the images of those

He cannot save, not only with the birds, who have served neither God nor Caesar, and await for none or for a different saviour, but with Lazarus and Judas and the Roman soldiers for whom He has died in vain. "Christ," writes Robartes, "only pitied those whose suffering is rooted in death, in poverty, or in sickness, or in sin, in some shape of the common lot, and he came especially to the poor who are most subject to exterior vicissitude." I have therefore represented in Lazarus and Judas types of that intellectual despair that lay beyond His sympathy, while in the Roman soldiers I suggest a form of objectivity that lay beyond His help.[6]

This note explains why John Rees Moore decides to call the play "a study of types of human loneliness."[7] It may be that, and it may be a comment on historical Christianity as well, but it is something else besides. We come to that further meaning, I think, in considering Yeats's source, a story of Oscar Wilde's, told to Yeats by an actor. Yeats recalls the incident in the *Autobiographies*:

"Christ came from a white plain to a purple city, and as He passed through the first street, He heard voices overhead, and saw a young man lying drunk upon a window-sill. 'Why do you waste your soul in drunkenness?' He said. 'Lord, I was a leper and You healed me, what else can I do?' A little further through the town He saw a young man following a harlot, and said, 'Why do you dissolve your soul in debauchery?' and the young man answered, 'Lord, I was blind, and You healed me, what else can I do?' At last in the middle of the city He saw an old man crouching, weeping upon the ground, and when He asked why he wept, the old man answered, 'Lord, I was dead, and You raised me into life, what else can I do but weep?'"[8]

Yeats thought the story an allegory of Wilde's own sudden change from dandy to criminal: "A comedian, he was in the hands of those dramatists who understand nothing but tragedy." And though Yeats was dissatisfied with the story as Wilde published it ("spoiled . . . with the verbal decoration of his epoch") he thought that in its scenario form, as the actor had quoted it to him, it had a "terrible beauty."[9]

The types of "intellectual despair" and of "objectivity"

which the play sets in opposition to Christ are not, then, simply contrasts to Him: they have been made what they are by Christ. The play is concerned with the interaction of objective and subjective life, the double interlocking gyres. Yeats, an "antithetical" artist born out of phase into "this filthy modern tide," decided that the dead end of art had come about because his contemporaries had attempted to create from an exhausted symbolism.[10] The paralysis in which poetry found itself; the wasted lives of Wilde, Johnson, Dowson; Yeats's abortive early attempts to find a different technique — all these are reflected in the stasis of the white heron in *Calvary*.[11] He stands, famished and paralyzed, gazing upon his own reflection, unable to do anything but wait for a more propitious time. When Christ dies (or, symbolically speaking, when the primary cycle ends) the heron's cycle will come round in the new crescent moon. The opening lyric of the play implies that the heron's strength is just barely adequate to carry him on to the new crescent and save him from being "fishes' diet."

> Motionless under the moon-beam,
> Up to his feathers in the stream;
> Although fish leap, the white heron
> Shivers in a dumbfounded dream.
> God has not died for the white heron.
>
> Although half famished he'll not dare
> Dip or do anything but stare
> Upon the glittering image of a heron,
> That now is lost and now is there.
> God has not died for the white heron.
>
> But that the full is shortly gone
> And after that is crescent moon,
> It's certain that the moon-crazed heron
> Would be but fishes' diet soon.
> God has not died for the white heron.[12]

The fish of the primary cycle cannot nourish the heron any

more than the primary Redeemer can redeem him. To the heron, all primary things are destructive, and his only salvation is in fixed self-absorption, a narcissistic stare.

This is why, once again, the sympathies of the play are mixed. Yeats is on the side of the heron, we feel, but he will not accept the heron's stare as a final solution. At the same time, he experiences the usual human fear before change, and is afraid of the time when the heron will come into power with the "crucifixion" of Christ. Like *The Player Queen* and "The Second Coming," *Calvary* takes place at the moment of revolution. The First Musician voices the Yeatsian fear, as the crowd mocks Christ:

> O, but the mocker's cry
> Makes my heart afraid,
> As though a flute of bone
> Taken from a heron's thigh,
> A heron crazed by the moon,
> Were cleverly, softly played.[13]

The flute music, like the same music in *The Herne's Egg* played to summon Attracta, is the heralding of the new dispensation.

Meanwhile, Christ meets the first of those he has ruined — the resurrected Lazarus, who says to Christ, "You took my death, give me your death instead." He continues,

> Alive I never could escape your love,
> And when I sickened towards my death I thought,
> 'I'll to the desert, or chuckle in a corner,
> Mere ghost, a solitary thing.'[14]

Horrified by Christ's declaration that there shall be no more death, that all shall be raised up again, Lazarus, who prizes solitude above all things, goes off in a vain search to recover it. Doomed to the ceaselessly communal life of the Christian community symbolized by the three Marys, Lazarus disappears. The three Marys are incapable of independent existence:

> Take but His love away,
> Their love becomes a feather
> Of eagle, swan or gull,
> Or a drowned heron's feather
> Tossed hither and thither
> Upon the bitter spray
> And the moon at the full.[15]

Once Christ has disappeared, men and women of the primary dispensation become only bits of flotsam on the antithetical tide, under the new subjective moon, replacing the primary cycle with its opposite.

The second encounter of Christ is with Judas, whose effort to perform an *acte gratuit* by betraying Christ is indeed a protest against the primary system, but the act destroys Judas himself as well. We recall that in *A Vision*, Judas is the example given of the Hunchback: he is the man of Phase 26 (Christ dies at Phase 28) whose "greatest temptation may be to defy God, to become a Judas, who betrays, not for thirty pieces of silver, but that he may call himself creator." [16] It is clear that deformity, in this play, is associated *not* with Christianity, as Wilson would have us believe,[17] but with the opponents of Christianity. This is perfectly understandable, since the action of the play occurs during an objective cycle, where objective beauty is supreme, and subjective elements appear deformed. The victory goes to Christ, for the moment, and Judas finally hangs himself (we are meant, I think, to bring his death to mind although it is not explicitly present in the play) because he realizes that his gesture of defiance is in itself an acknowledgment of the power of the system over him. He has not freed himself from the influence of the primary at all. Though he denies God's power of predestination, asserting that he planned his betrayal all alone, with only a heron beside him, that heron ironically represents the imminent and predestined next cycle which he has unknowingly served.

Finally, at the Crucifixion, Christ encounters the Roman soldiers. Against them, he is powerless, and in the face of their dance he cries, "My father, why hast Thou forsaken Me?" In view of their limited part in the play, we are at first taken aback by their effect, but Yeats's notes on the play explain the intention. Robartes, in these notes, tells of a Job-like Arab who worships God's Chance: "Some worship His Choice; that is easy; to know that He has willed for some unknown purpose all that happens is pleasant; but I have spent my life in worshipping His Chance, and that moment when I understand the immensity of His Chance is the moment when I am nearest Him." [18] Those who worship God's chance, like the soldiers, stand outside the cycles of objectivity and subjectivity, and can regard them with indifferent eyes, needing neither support nor consolation. It is irrelevant to them which cycle is in the ascendant, and therefore they lie totally outside the scope of Christ's powers. It is they who will enlighten him, and not vice versa: they propose to do the dance of the dice-throwers because Christ has not yet seen it. It is when Christ sees the dance and perceives the parity of his "system" with all others that he feels abandoned by God, not when he sees the resistance and bitterness of Judas and Lazarus. The dance of the dicers reminds us of the Great Wheel, as Wilson has noted,[19] but it is not a noble reminder. The dicers have the last word in the play proper, making both Christ and Judas seem irrelevant: the play ends with a shrug of dismissal.

It is clear that the four encounters represent allegorically four types of response to life in the objective cycle. The Marys are those who lose their own individuality under the system and are therefore ephemeral; Lazarus is typical of those who choose the heron's self-absorbed solitude and brood in desert places, wishing for death and oblivion; Judas represents the futile inimical gesture ending in self-destruction; and the soldiers represent a studied indifference to the revolving cycles. Lazarus and Judas are men born out of phase, and neither the wish for death of the one nor the abortive thrashing in protest of the other can be a creative act. Nor is the aloof and uncommitted attitude of the soldiers: we are not meant to see their dance as anything but an image of the Great Wheel, so far as I can see, since it has none of the visionary exaltation of the dances which symbolize creation. The man born out of phase ("We Irish") must neither flee, nor attempt futile protest, nor withdraw from the struggle — but what other remedy is there? The play looks for a solution for the man out of harmony with his time, and finds none. In the final lyric Yeats asks why "the solitary soul" cannot find sufficient satisfaction in its own selfhood, hinting briefly that perhaps it can be content in an exaltation like the eagle's, but concluding on a note of restless unhappiness:

> Lonely the sea-bird lies at her rest,
> Blown like a dawn-blenched parcel of spray
> Upon the wind, or follows her prey
> Under a great wave's hollowing crest.
> God has not appeared to the birds.
>
> The ger-eagle has chosen his part
> In blue deep of the upper air
> Where one-eyed day can meet his stare;
> He is content with his savage heart.
> God has not appeared to the birds.
>
> But where have last year's cygnets gone?
> The lake is empty; why do they fling
> White wing out beside white wing?
> What can a swan need but a swan?
> God has not appeared to the birds.[20]

In a manuscript version of *Calvary* there is an oddly moving touch which Yeats later changed, rightly enough, aiming at a certain impersonality in the play. Still, the early draft gives us a hint of what the final poem sprang from, because we read in it:

Where have last year's cygnets gone?
Coole lake's empty . . .[21]

This is the fulfillment of the apprehension at the end of "The Wild Swans at Coole":

But now they drift on the still water,
Mysterious, beautiful;
Among what rushes will they build,
By what lake's edge or pool
Delight men's eyes when I awake some day
To find they have flown away? [22]

The society of the "cold companionable streams" is not enough for the swans: inevitably the migration takes place, and the swan leaps into the desolate heaven. The question "What can a swan need but a swan?" is a rhetorical parallel to the symbol of the heron staring at his own image. The self — or its mirror image, or its double — is not enough, Yeats suggests; only migration into a different sphere, a flinging of the self beyond its own absorption, can cure imaginative sterility.

Yeats's affirmation of the necessity of a new symbolism, of the adoption of the Mask, is usually phrased in resolute terms; *Calvary* is unusual in its frustration and uneasiness. As a piece of literary work, it is negligible, but it is interesting as a revelation of Yeats's decisive discarding of the Christian symbolism, his resentment of it, and his feeling of estrangement as he wanders between two worlds, one dead, the other powerless to be born.

3

The Resurrection shows us another side of the image of Christ. Unsympathetic to the reader in *Calvary*, here he becomes the vehicle of revelation, truly a figure from Phase 15. In this play Yeats is imagining what it would have been like to live in phase with Christianity, when it was a stimulus and not a shroud for the imagination. The body of the play is a somewhat sterile bit of conversation, with the Hebrew, the Greek, and the Syrian conveniently representing three dialectical positions: the Hebrew is *l'homme moyen sensuel*, rather glad that Christ has turned out to be human after all, because it would have been so troublesome to have to take a real Messiah into account; the Greek is the dispassionate intellectual, observing with analytical interest the Dionysian ceremonies in the streets; the Syrian is the believer in mystery, in the "something that lies outside knowledge, outside order." [23]

At the unfolding and folding of the curtain, the three musicians sing one of Yeats's most impressive songs, "I saw a staring virgin stand." Ellmann has cleared up most of the difficulties of interpretation in the appendix to *The Identity of Yeats*, but he does not mention the way the poem achieves its effect, which is, as he rightly says, "extraordinary even when imperfectly understood." [24] The poem in fact parallels the play in usuing shock tactics to bring about a new awareness of reality. Just as the skeptical Greek recoils in terror when he feels the beating of the resurrected Christ's heart, and is forced to look on history with different eyes, so we are disconcerted by Yeats's style and language. We are not accustomed to think of Dionysus as holy, nor of Minerva as a staring virgin, and certainly not to consider God's death as "but a play." The combination of savagery with harmony, of death with heartbeats, unnerves the reader, and prepares him to share the reversal of attitude embodied in the play.

> I saw a staring virgin stand
> Where holy Dionysus died,
> And tear the heart out of his side,
> And lay the heart upon her hand
> And bear that beating heart away;
> And then did all the Muses sing
> Of Magnus Annus at the spring,
> As though God's death were but a play.[25]

Yeats is forcing us to share his conviction that resurrection and genesis, as I have said above in Chapter IV, are the same: the Great Year is the celebration of the equal value of all revelations, primary or antithetical.

It cannot be pointed out too often that although Yeats's personal sympathies were with the antithetical cycle, in principle he held out for the absolute parity of antithetical and primary.[26] Each is a means of revelation appropriate to its time, and his aim in the first song is to make us grant to the antithetical forces the respect we automatically devote to the Christian revelation. Let us also call Dionysus holy; let us call the Virgin Mary fierce. Yeats makes his point to us, his contemporaries, in the opening song: *we* should reverence the antithetical. In the play, he makes his point in reverse to the contemporaries of Christ: *they* should reverence the primary. No one system is sacred.

The irreverence with which Yeats treats Troy and the Argonauts in the second stanza of the first song makes his point once more. As Jeffares reminds us,[27] the source for the second stanza is not only the Fourth Eclogue of Virgil, but also Shelley's *Hellas*.

Another Troy must rise and set,   A loftier Argo cleaves the main,
Another lineage feed the crow,   Fraught with a later prize;
Another Argo's painted prow   Another Orpheus sings again,
Drive to a flashier bauble yet.[28]   And loves, and weeps, and dies;
    A new Ulysses leaves once more
    Calypso for his native shore.[29]

Jeffares, in a note, quotes E. M. Tillyard's remark that "It is only when Yeats's fierce irony is set against the background of Shelley's most serene and passionate idealism that it gets its full force." [30] There is irony, true, but it is not only directed against the romanticizing of past history, as one might think seeing it in juxtaposition with Shelley. It is shock for the sake of shock; lest we agree too quickly with the earlier affirmation that indeed Dionysus is holy, we are immediately given, in the lines reminiscent of *Hellas*, a deliberately diminished view of Greece. The "fierce virgin and her Star" of the last stanza are, as Ellmann demonstrates,[31] complex figures, merging Minerva and Dionysus, Virgo and Spica, and Mary and Christ. Since he is working here with a triple meaning, Yeats can afford to do without the irony of the preceding lines, and can present to us the immemorial terror of one cycle confronting its successor:

> The Roman Empire stood appalled:
> It dropped the reins of peace and war
> When that fierce virgin and her Star
> Out of the fabulous darkness called.[32]

"It has seemed to me of late," Yeats wrote in the introduction to *The Resurrection*, "that the sense of spiritual reality comes whether to the individual or to crowds from some violent shock."[33] For the individual, read the Greek; for crowds, read the Roman Empire. Once again, Yeats is saying that we must be forcibly driven to any new apprehension; that of itself, human nature is conservative and resists its rebirth into a new state of knowledge. All the forcible verbs in the song bear out its message, and enact symbolically both the shock of revelation and the violence of the reaction to it.

I cannot agree with Ellmann that in *The Resurrection* "the pattern of the death and resurrection of Christ is treated as if it were a *re-enactment* under a new guise of the death and resurrection of Dionysus":[34] the two deaths and resurrections are parallel, but not similar. Ellmann's metaphor suggests the same god wearing different garments ("a new guise"), but Dionysus and Christ represent to Yeats two totally different forces: no cycle ever repeats another, as we saw in Chapter IV, and that is why it is so difficult for the inhabitants of one cycle to apprehend the reality of the succeeding revelation. Each revelation is unique.

Both the aloof, agnostic Greek and the comfortably mediocre Hebrew, as I have said, turn out to be mistaken —

Christ *has* risen. F. A. C. Wilson would have it that the Greek represents "the subjective point of view" [35] and the Hebrew the objective, and in one sense he is right; but what he does not mention is that both are being manifested in a debased form. To make this clear, we may think for a moment in present-day terms. We are now expecting, Yeats would say, an antithetical revelation, to which we can react in three ways. Those of us who are primary personalities, to whom the Christian revelation is congenial, can continue to cling defiantly to that gospel, refusing to recognize its exhaustion; those of us who are antithetical in personality but Christian in upbringing can refuse to change because of the psychological upheaval it would cause in us; and those of us who are wise, according to Yeats, will accept the new revelation. The first two choices are sterile ones, because those who adopt them are setting themselves against the stream of fate, and their efforts (like Judas' in *Calvary*) will come to nothing.

When we reverse the present-day terms and think of *The Resurrection*, it becomes clear that the Greek is indeed embodying a subjective point of view; but that view (like the Christian view in our own time, as Yeats would say) is no longer imaginative, ardent, and creative as it was in its perfection. The Hebrew, although he had been a believer in Christ (and consequently may be said to have an objective or primary personality) is glad that it all turned out to be untrue; he wants to marry and have children, not be possessed by the divine. Both Hebrew and Greek disapprove of the Dionysian rage in the streets, but for different reasons: the Hebrew simply finds the worshipers a mob of madmen and dismisses them impatiently, but the Greek, analyzing the performance, finds it an appalling instance of loss of control. The gods of whom the Greek approves are different: "What seems their indifference is but their eternal possession of themselves. Man, too, remains separate. He does not surrender his soul. He keeps his privacy." [36]

To equate the Greek with Yeats, as Mr. Wilson does,[37] is surely to forget Yeats's constant celebration of the visitations of the Daimon as the ultimate invasion of privacy. No one who agreed with the Greek's statement quoted above could have written "Leda and the Swan." When subjectivity is out of place it becomes deformed, and it is in that aspect that it manifests itself in the Greek, who disowns the ancient religious rites of his own civilization, having forgotten their meaning. At the end of the play, however, the Greek is convinced, and sees his world collapse: "O Athens, Alexandria, Rome, something has come to destroy you. The heart of a phantom is beating. Man has begun to die. Your words are clear at last, O Heraclitus. God and man die each other's life, live each other's death." [38] The Heraclitean phrase was a maxim Yeats had made his own; only in the moment of conversion does the Greek speak for the playwright.

The Resurrection went through several changes in composition, beginning as a "chaotic dialogue," progressing to "a play about Christ meeting the worshipers of Dionysus on the mountain side," and ending in its present form. As it now stands, it embodies Yeats's statement that "at moments . . . one could with a touch convey a vision — that the mystic way and sexual love use the same means — opposed yet parallel existences." [39] As usual, Yeats was seeing things "doubled" — if not tripled or quadrupled — and I do not wish to restrict illegitimately the meaning of *The Resurrection*. I can only say that I think it has suffered from being treated in theological terms, and that we might keep in mind, while reading it, the multiple meanings which the word "resurrection" had for Yeats, of which the most important may be Blake's. In *Vala*, or *The Four Zoas*, Blake invokes his Muse, the Daughter of Beulah, and exhorts her to sing of the "fall into Division" and the "Resurrection to Unity." [40] Resurrection and rebirth always imply for Yeats the restoration of a Unity of Being which has been damaged through

an inevitable attrition, and they imply as well a corresponding courage in acceptance of the revelation. Whether the
new being is religious, sexual, political, or artistic, the inner
core of the experience remains the same — the destruction
of the old, the appearance of the new. The Christian revelation, when it appeared, embodied "the difference that
heavenly pity brings":

> In pity for man's darkening thought
> He walked that room and issued thence
> In Galilean turbulence;
> The Babylonian starlight brought
> A fabulous, formless darkness in;
> Odour of blood when Christ was slain
> Made all Platonic tolerance vain
> And vain all Doric discipline.[41]

Originally the poem ended here,[42] but we can understand,
in retrospect, why Yeats added the final stanza. Without the
last stanza, we cannot understand what Resurrection really
is: it is a blaze of revelation, true, but it has been led up to
by a long process of preparation, and it will spend itself
slowly in an equally long process of attrition. Man creates
his moments of glory out of his own carefully built substance,
and suffers in their waning. The great necessity is to prepare
for the moment of revelation and rebirth, to welcome it as
it comes, and to be willing to exhaust oneself in sustaining it.

> Everything that man esteems
> Endures a moment or a day:
> Love's pleasure drives his love away,
> The painter's brush consumes his dreams;
> The herald's cry, the soldier's tread
> Exhaust his glory and his might:
> Whatever flames upon the night
> Man's own resinous heart has fed.[43]

As a conclusion to a theological piece about historical
Christianity, this stanza makes little sense. As a conclusion

to a play about the waning of one source of imaginative strength and the revivifying appearance of a new creative force, it becomes more satisfying. The stanza is affirming the transiency of any imaginative form: love dies, the Image is consumed in its imperfect artistic incarnation, glory and power are lost in the sordid aftermath of war. The only final statement is that the form remains; and to continue in Wordsworthian terms, the function never dies — that function of the "resinous" heart to serve as a torch constantly renewing its light as the imagination is resurrected.

4

Nothing so obsessed Yeats as the idea of purgation leading to a state purified of complexity. By a process of massive accretion, all sorts of subsidiary images encrusted the original idea, until finally, we meet it everywhere. It becomes involved with ghosts, spiritualism, poetic images, historical occurrences, personal experiences, theosophy, Irish myth, literary figures, and almost anything else we can name. Yeats devoted an entire book of *A Vision* to spinning out doctrines about a Swedenborgian Purgatory; the *Collected Poems* are full of references to purgation; and in at least three plays the idea is central, while it figures incidentally in others.

The earliest of the three purgatorial plays, *The Dreaming of the Bones*, is accompanied by a long explanatory note which will serve as well as any other to introduce this group. Yeats writes: "The conception of the play is derived from the world-wide belief that the dead dream back, for a certain time, through the more personal thoughts and deeds of life . . . The lovers in my play have lost themselves in a . . . self-created winding of the labyrinth of conscience." He continues with a description of the Dreaming Back and the Return, and adds: "In the spiritual world subjectivity is innocence, and innocence, in life an accident of nature, is now the highest achievement of the intellect." [44] To illustrate, he refers to the song of the goatherd from "Shepherd and Goatherd," his pastoral elegy for Robert Gregory:

> He unpacks the loaded pern
> Of all 'twas pain or joy to learn,
> Of all that he had made.
> The outrageous war shall fade . . .
> Knowledge he shall unwind
> Through victories of the mind,
> Till, clambering at the cradle-side,
> He dreams himself his mother's pride,
> All knowledge lost in trance
> Of sweeter ignorance.[45]

Yeats then quotes "a curious letter" from Michael Robartes to John Aherne (some of the former information about Purgatory had been attributed to that elusive tribe, the Judwalis) and so we learn deviously of the connection Yeats establishes between purgation and "our ordinary dreams": "There is an analogy between the dreaming back of the Body of Passion . . . and our ordinary dreams." Finally, Yeats says untruthfully, "I wrote my play before the Robartes papers came into my hands," [46] and neatly disavows his own creation.

Yeats did not need the Judwalis or Michael Robartes: thirty years before he wrote *The Dreaming of the Bones* he had professed a belief in the purgative activities of the dead. In *Irish Fairy and Folk Tales* we find his early declaration that "Ghosts . . . live in a state intermediary between this life and the next. They are held there by some earthly longing or affection, or some duty unfulfilled, or anger against the living . . . They are compelled to obey some one they have wronged." [47] In the final sentence quoted we can see the germ of the idea, expanded in Book III of *A Vision*, of Victimage for the Dead, as the Spirit pays for its earthly "sins." And in *The Secret Rose*, in the story called "The Vision of Hanrahan the Red," Yeats treated for the first time the story of

Diarmuid and Dervorgilla, which 20 years later would form the basis for *The Dreaming of the Bones*. There is as well a revised version of the story done in 1925 after the writing of the play; Yeats, when he found a congenial theme, could never let it alone.

This is not the place for a detailed comparison of the three versions of the story, but it should be said at least that the political overtones found in the play are incidental, and have only a very small part in the original story and in the revised prose version. Dermond and Dervadilla (as they are called in the early story) are not being punished principally for their treason in bringing about the Norman invasion of Ireland. They are condemned to their restless wandering because they had not loved each other properly:

> We loved only the blossom of manhood and of womanhood in one another, the deciduous blossom of the dust and not the eternal beauty. When we died there was no inviolate world about us, the demons of the battles and bitterness we wrought pronounced our doom. We wander inseparable, but he who was my lover beholds me always as a dead body dropping in decay, and I know that I am so beheld.[48]

Hanrahan's vision is one of different types of lovers. First he sees those who, unlike Dermond and Dervadilla, "sought in one another no blossom of mere youth, but a beauty coeval with the night and with the stars"; second, Hanrahan sees those who "sought only to triumph one over the other"; third, those who "desired neither to triumph nor to love, but only to be loved."[49] It is clear that the genetic nucleus of *The Dreaming of the Bones* is nonpolitical, and that the later topical analogies with Irish affairs which suggested themselves naturally to Yeats in 1917 are, if not irrelevant to the unraveling of the meaning of the play, at least not its central concern.

Hanrahan the Red is, of course, one of the many names (like Michael Robartes, Aedh, O'Sullivan Rua, and so on) which Yeats used to identify himself — or if not himself, to identify, as he said, "principles of the mind." [50] The identification of Yeats with Hanrahan we can take for granted; what is equally interesting in "The Vision of Hanrahan the Red" is the identification of Hanrahan and his beloved with the wandering and condemned couples of the story. In his lyric, Hanrahan imagines himself and Maive "amid the hovering, piteous, penitential throng," and later wonders "if he and his Maive would so wander and what their punishment might be." [51] Yeats, then, sees himself as a possible spirit in Purgatory.

On first sight, *The Dreaming of the Bones* might seem to be a political allegory or a spiritualist document. Though it has elements of both, I think enough has been said above to establish it primarily as another of Yeats's expeditions in mental travel. The plot is simple enough: a young man meets at night Diarmuid and Dervorgilla, not knowing that they are shades; they beg him to forgive them so that they can kiss; he refuses, the memory of their betrayal of Ireland swaying his decision; and the lovers vanish in a cloud, as day breaks. We realize that Yeats is working on a variant of the Dreaming Back, and we must stop a moment to consider the transformation the idea receives in this play.

In the usual description of the purgatorial state, one spirit works out its own salvation by reliving again and again the events of its life until it can accept them with equanimity, cast out remorse, and recover radical innocence:

> . . . all hatred driven hence,
> The soul recovers radical innocence
> And learns at last that it is self-delighting,
> Self-appeasing, self-affrighting,
> And that its own sweet will is Heaven's will.[52]

In other words, the spirit finally forgives itself. This is hardly an action given to dramatic exposition, and Yeats must, in his purgatorial plays, get around the difficulty somehow. In *The*

Dreaming of the Bones, he does it by inventing the young man, on whom the forgiveness depends. Since the young man refuses to forgive, we may say that the play is about an occasion on which the mind cannot cast out remorse for some reason or other, cannot come to terms with the events in its own memory.

Fear of the dreamlike images that haunt the night is the theme of the Musician's opening song:

> Why does my heart beat so?
> Did not a shadow pass?
> It passed but a moment ago.
> Who can have trod in the grass?
> What rogue is night-wandering?
> Have not old writers said
> That dizzy dreams can spring
> From the dry bones of the dead? [53]

It should be noticed that the First Musician speaks in two voices: his blank verse narration is that of a neutral observer, but his lyrics reflect the view of the young man even to the point of verbal echoes. Like the young man, the Musician is torn between the daylight and the world of dreams, oscillating between sympathy and resentment. The first song echoes the young man's fear; he had fought in the Easter Rising, and is in hiding from the British, waiting for a boat to take him to the Aran Islands. The young man disclaims all fear of ghosts, saying that they would not betray him, even if they could, being Irish; and he sees their "tumult of the fantastic conscience" as irrelevant to himself.

> Well, let them dream into what shape they please
> And fill waste mountains with the invisible tumult
> Of the fantastic conscience. I have no dread;
> They cannot put me into gaol or shoot me;
> And seeing that their blood has returned to fields
> That have grown red from drinking blood like mine,
> They would not if they could betray. [54]

Guided by the stranger and the young girl (Diarmuid and Dervorgilla) the young man climbs toward the top of the mountain, and as he climbs the Musician sings three stanzas of an enigmatic song. Each stanza has the same refrain:

> Red bird of March, begin to crow!
> Up with the neck and clap the wing,
> Red cock, and crow!

The refrain is an impatient protest against the night and the powers that inhabit it, those powers that make us remember, relive, and consider the past in all its mixed emotions. The Musician cries out for a discarding of the past (as March always symbolizes a new phase) and urges the morning to break and dispel the ghosts. The first four lines of each stanza are in oblique opposition to the refrain, and testify to the power of the windy, cloudy, image-haunted night:

> Why should the heart take fright?
> What sets it beating so?
> The bitter sweetness of the night
> Has made it but a lonely thing.

Here the Musician approximates the young man's feelings; engaged in corporate activity until now, he experiences in his flight a loneliness akin to the solitude of the shades.

Cloud is the element in which the shades wander, for obvious reasons: the period "between lives" is not phasal, so the moon must be hidden. We recall that at the end of the play Diarmuid and Dervorgilla are enveloped in cloud as they vanish:

> A cloud floats up
> And covers all the mountain-head in a moment;
> And now it lifts and they are swept away.[55]

So when, in the second stanza, the Musician sings:

> My head is in a cloud;
> I'd let the whole world go;
> My rascal heart is proud
> Remembering and remembering.

we are to understand that the young man, like the shades, is "dreaming back." Whatever the memory, he now shares the attitude of the ghosts — "the world well lost"; not even to undo their sin would Diarmuid and Dervorgilla renounce their love. By attributing to himself a "rascal heart" he has joined the ranks of the "rogues" who wander the hills. Finally, in the last stanza, he realizes that what daylight and clarity suppress, the clouds and the dark liberate:

> The dreaming bones cry out
> Because the night winds blow
> And heaven's a cloudy blot.
> Calamity can have its fling.[56]

"Can" in this stanza must be interpreted to mean "is permitted to" and "calamity" must be given its Yeatsian meaning of "ghostly suffering":

> No shade however harried and consumed
> Would change his own calamity for theirs,[57]

we are told of the ghostly lovers. If I insist on these points it is because Mr. Wilson's reading (where "calamity" is the "unsuccessful Easter rebellion" and "can" means "let," implying that "final victory is certain")[58] seems to me wholly mistaken, but likely to gain currency.

The young man, speaking through the Musician, pulls himself back, after each moment of sympathy for the lovers, by invoking the cock of daylight, which will crow out calamity and cloud (but will destroy as well the "bitter sweetness" of that proud remembering).

Meanwhile, the young girl tells the young man the plight of Diarmuid and Dervorgilla:

> Their manner of life were blessed could their lips
> A moment meet; but when he has bent his head
> Close to her head, or hand would slip in hand,
> The memory of their crime flows up between
> And drives them apart.[59]

Unable to forgive them for the destruction they have brought on Ireland, the young man looks on as the lovers dance, attempt to join, and vanish heartbroken. His only comment is,

> I had almost yielded and forgiven it all —
> Terrible the temptation and the place! [60]

The young man, still cherishing hatred for the betrayer, is incapable of "the spiritual intellect's great work," which is to acquire a breadth of judgment beyond the personal:

> Nor can there be work so great
> As that which cleans man's dirty slate.[61]

The young man is still a partisan, with all a partisan's bitterness. John O'Leary once said to Yeats that there was no cause that had not had good men on its side, and Yeats came to the same point of view about individual action:

> I am content to follow to its source
> Every event in action or in thought;
> Measure the lot; forgive myself the lot!
> When such as I cast out remorse
> So great a sweetness flows into the breast
> We must laugh and we must sing,
> We are blest by everything,
> Everything we look upon is blest.[62]

The young man's refusal to forgive the lovers is an image of the mind's refusal to accept as its own some past action; until such an action is admitted, measured, and forgiven it is a destructive force in the mind and unavailable for creative use, in Yeatsian terms. The young man is unwilling to make himself part of the history of all Ireland by a yielding to human sympathy — he turns irritably from the elusive demands of night to the grosser realities of day, and the Musician's final song embodies his refusal of experience:

> At the grey round of the hill
> Music of a lost kingdom
> Runs, runs and is suddenly still.
> The winds out of Clare-Galway
> Carry it: suddenly it is still.

> I have heard in the night air
> A wandering airy music;
> And moidered in that snare
> A man is lost of a sudden,
> In that sweet wandering snare.

The cadences of the verse here leave us no doubt of the beauty embodied in that "wandering airy music," played by "crazy fingers." We may recall Yeats's exhortation "To a Friend Whose Work Has Come to Nothing":

> And like a laughing string
> Whereon mad fingers play
> Amid a place of stone
> Be secret and exult.[63]

This is precisely what the young man is unable to do, and he sees defeat as motive for resentment.

> What finger first began
> Music of a lost kingdom?
> They dream that laughed in the sun.
> Dry bones that dream are bitter,
> They dream and darken our sun.
>
> Those crazy fingers play
> A wandering airy music;
> Our luck is withered away,
> And wheat in the wheat-ear withered,
> And the wind blows it away.

The final comment of the Musicians sums up the action of the play: the young man has been granted a vision, his heart has been stirred, he has seen the owl of night and heard the curlew cry, but he prefers to dismiss his chance to weigh the claims of night, and would rather welcome again the strident cock of day.

> My heart ran wild when it heard
> The curlew cry before dawn
> And the eddying cat-headed bird;
> But now the night is gone.

I have heard from far below
The strong March birds a-crow.
Stretch neck and clap the wing,
Red cocks, and crow! [64]

The main difficulty with *The Dreaming of the Bones* is
that there is no necessary connection between the lovers and
the young man. Hanrahan, in the early story, is simply a
spectator and the question of forgiveness never comes up.
When "principles of the mind" are projected into dramatic
personages, conflicts that are understandable as interior struggles run the risk of seeming artificial dramatic situations. The
vacillation of the young man between the "sweet wandering
snare" of sympathy and his political hatred is insufficiently
connected with the transgression of Diarmuid and Dervorgilla. This criticism can in fact be made general, and applies
to all the dramatic projections of the purgative process, as we
shall see in examining *Purgatory*.

5

I do not intend to write about *The Words upon the Window-Pane* for several reasons. It does not present the same
difficulties as the other late plays, and it is more a case study
for Yeats's convictions about the power of memory and imagination than a symbolic recasting of his own experience. Second, it was not written to form a matrix into which Yeats
could fit poetry, and this study concerns principally those
plays which embody lyrics. Third, the play is primarily a
theatrical tour-de-force; in fact, from a dramatic point of
view, it is probably the best thing Yeats did, with its steady
suspense, somewhat ironic view of the séance, and its moments
of passion. My concern, however, is not with Yeats as a playwright — I think his gifts in the purely theatrical direction
were limited, to say the least. The play is intelligible to anyone
acquainted with the speculations, if not the facts, about Swift,
Vanessa, and Stella, and I think any commentary on it here is
unnecessary.

Purgatory is another matter. Yeats's penultimate play is another effort in the same genre as *The Dreaming of the Bones*, by which I mean that the skeletal structure is the same. Again we have a troubled spirit compulsively repeating events out of the past, and again we have the spectator who is somehow involved in the spirit's action. But in the twenty-two years which intervened between the composition of the two plays, Yeats's mood changed decisively, and I would say for the worse.

Any critic who writes of *Purgatory* has to take into account, uncomfortable though it may make him, what Yeats himself said about it. The first unpalatable statement comes in a letter to Dorothy Wellesley: "I have put nothing into the play because it seemed picturesque; I have put there my own conviction about this world and the next." [65] F. A. C. Wilson, using this sentence as his justification, says of his own theological orientation: "In approaching [*Purgatory*] from the point of view of its theology, I imagine I am documenting it as he [Yeats] would have wished." [66] What Yeats wrote to Dorothy Wellesley is certainly true, in one sense, and is corroborated in her recollection of a conversation with Yeats on the same subject:

He had been talking rather wildly about the after life. Finally I asked him: 'What do you believe happens to us immediately after death?' He replied: 'After a person dies he does not realize that he is dead.' I: 'In what state is he?' W.B.Y.: 'In some half-conscious state.' I said: 'Like the period between waking and sleeping?' W.B.Y.: 'Yes.' I: 'How long does this state last?' W.B.Y.: 'Perhaps some twenty years.' 'And after that' I asked, 'what happens next?' He replied: 'Again a period which is Purgatory. The length of that phase depends upon the sins of the man when upon this earth.' And then again I asked: 'And after that?' I do not remember his actual words, but he spoke of the return of the soul to God. I said: 'Well, it seems to me that you are hurrying us back to the great arms of the Roman Catholic Church.' He was of course an Irish Protestant. I was bold to ask him, but his only retort was his splendid laugh.[67]

The comic element in all this is not to be missed — not only the "splendid laugh" with which Yeats could dismiss the whole subject, but also Dorothy Wellesley's naïve characterization of Yeats as an "Irish Protestant." The conversation sounds like a game, and probably was: Yeats's making up the length of purgation on the spot, and Dorothy Wellesley's teasing questions are not the hallmarks of a serious theological conversation.

But the theological view of *Purgatory* nevertheless dies hard, and T. S. Eliot has twice (at least) made disparaging remarks on *Purgatory*, criticizing it theologically. In his essay on the poetry of Yeats, he says, "The play *Purgatory* is not very pleasant, either . . . I wish he had not given it this title, because I cannot accept a purgatory in which there is no hint, or at least no emphasis upon Purgation." And in the general fault-finding in *After Strange Gods*, Yeats comes under particular censure: "Mr. Yeats's 'supernatural world' was the wrong supernatural world. It was not a world of spiritual significance, not a world of real Good and Evil, of holiness or sin, but a highly sophisticated lower mythology." [68] In both quotations, Eliot is taking an orthodox theological stand, and criticizing Yeats for not conforming to those canons of dogma which he chooses to invoke. There is no denying that Yeats left himself easy prey to such criticism by the tenor of his own statements, but this sort of comment never gets to the heart of the play at all.

There is another possible approach (*Purgatory* seems to have attracted more commentators than Yeats's other plays) and that is to see the play as historical allegory. John Heath-Stubbs has taken this view, as Wilson points out, and the play for him "symbolises the corruption of the old Anglo-Irish aristocracy, which allowed itself to become contaminated by contact with the rising bourgeoisie. The old man . . . represents the revolutionary generation of Yeats himself . . . His own son . . . typifies the younger generation of the new Ireland." [69] The play is undoubtedly in part a com-

ment on Yeats's Ireland, but Mr. Heath-Stubbs leaves out
the entire question of purgation and what it corresponds to
in historical terms.

Two things about purgation must, it seems to me, be kept
in mind. The first is that ideally it leads to rebirth; the
second is that the world where purgation takes place may be
called — we have it on Yeats's authority — the world of
imagination. Earlier in this chapter I quoted Yeats's remark
in the *Autobiographies* that a writer must die every day he
lives and be reborn an incorruptible self, that self opposite
to all that he has named "himself." We should recall in this
connection that one of the purgative states in *A Vision* is
called *The Shiftings*, and in it the soul experiences all that is
missed in life — all that is not "itself." Purgation, then, points
ideally toward creation via the mask, and in that sense is an
activity of the imagination, whose vehicle the mask becomes.
In "Swedenborg, Mediums, and the Desolate Places" Yeats
writes of the purgatorial state: "This earth-resembling life
is the creation of the image-making power of the mind,
plucked naked from the body, and mainly of the images in
the memory . . . Like the transgressions, all the pleasure
and pain of sensible life awaken again and again, all our
passionate events rush up about us and not as seeming imagination, for imagination is now the world." [70]

"Imagination is now the world." There are only two moments of which this can be said — the moment of creation
and the moment of purgation. Our suspicion that the two
are allied, if not precisely identical, is strengthened when we
read Yeats's description of "the dead" in *Per Amica Silentia
Lunae*. Like many sentences in that book, it gives, in embryonic form, a conception which Yeats elaborated at greater
length in *A Vision;* sometimes the only way to come to the
core of a grandiose Yeatsian mystification is to hunt down its
origin in the little book that might well have kept its original
title of *An Alphabet*. The vocabulary in the description of

the dead gives away a good deal: The dead "perceive, although they are still but living in their memories, harmonies, symbols, and patterns, as though all were being refashioned by an artist, and they are moved by emotions, sweet for no imagined good but in themselves, like those of children dancing in a ring." [71] Harmonies, symbols, and patterns; refashioning by an artist; dancing in a ring; spontaneous and self-directed activity: these are all Yeats's usual words for artistic form.

It is easy to make the objection that occurs at once — that the emotions in *Purgatory* are anything but sweet. That is very true, but it is also true that Yeats's poetry grows more bitter and more violent toward the end of his life, and that *Per Amica Silentia Lunae* may reflect an earlier mood. What has not changed, however, is the kernel of the idea — that Purgatory is a symbol of the imagination at work.

With this much in mind, we can look at the rather simple plot of the play itself. Years ago, the daughter of a wealthy house had married her groom; their son, now an old man, comes with his coarse and ignorant son to contemplate the ruin of his ancestral house. The old man sees the ghost of his mother reliving the night he was conceived, and in the hope that he can end her purgatory, he kills his son (as he had killed his father) but the ghost of his mother returns nevertheless — her purgatory continues.

At the beginning of the play, the Old Man distinguishes between the proximate and remote consequences of transgressions:

> The souls in Purgatory . . . relive
> Their transgressions, and that not once
> But many times; they know at last
> The consequence of those transgressions
> Whether upon others or upon themselves;
> Upon others, others may bring help,
> For when the consequence is at an end
> The dream must end; if upon themselves
> There is no help but in themselves
> And in the mercy of God.[72]

This is a new aspect of the Yeatsian purgatory; in *A Vision*, Yeats does not write in terms of consequences, and he probably devised the idea here partly as a dramatic expedient. We have already seen that the young man in *The Dreaming of the Bones* had no real connection with the lovers, and that this weakened the play. In *Purgatory*, we are tempted by the passage quoted above to believe that the Old Man can indeed cut short his mother's suffering, and therefore dramatic suspense is maintained. If we are willing to admit that the young man and the ghosts in *The Dreaming of the Bones* symbolize two fragmented halves of the remorseful mind, then the point of the play appears to be the Yeatsian doctrine that only self-forgiveness can halt the obsessive rehearsing of guilt. The same belief accounts for the denouement of *Purgatory*: it is the sufferer who has to accept past events, and exterior help is useless.

Enough has been said in commentaries on the play about the sparse symbolism — the bare tree, once green; the ruined house, once great; the animal imagery as the Old Man talks about his mother's marriage; the coarseness of the son, "a bastard that a pedlar got/ Upon a tinker's daughter in a ditch." [73] And critics have been quick to point out the Oedipal situation causing the Old Man's hatred of his father, and the echoes of Lear at the end of the play.[74]

What is more interesting in the play is the actual vision of the mother:

> She has gone down to open the door.
> This night she is no better than her man
> And does not mind that he is half drunk,
> She is mad about him.[75]

The mother is caught up in one of the moments of "intense pleasure" which it is the function of Purgatory to revive. If we choose to consider the Old Man as a dramatic projection of the part of her which detests her drunken husband, we can understand the passage about consequences somewhat

better. The Old Man's proper function is to forgive his
mother and father, since the real consequence in him of
their action is his mad hatred of them both, not the coarse
son he has begotten. In killing his son, he is intensifying the
consequences of his mother's action, rather than abrogating
them. The Old Man, maddened by the vision, exacerbates his
anger by bitter speculation:

> But there's a problem: she must live
> Through everything in exact detail,
> Driven to it by remorse, and yet
> Can she renew the sexual act
> And find no pleasure in it, and if not,
> If pleasure and remorse must both be there,
> Which is the greater? [76]

The Old Man has brought to our attention one of the
difficulties of detachment, whether moral or artistic: how
does the artist purify of "complexities of mire and blood"
an emotion which is integrally complex, mixed, and ambigu-
ous? "All hatred driven hence,/ The soul recovers radical
innocence," Yeats had once written in good faith; but the
later poems are full of questions like "Why should not old
men be mad?" Reproved by Dorothy Wellesley for some of
the imagery and emotions of his last poems, he replied with
"The Spur":

> You think it horrible that lust and rage
> Should dance attention upon my old age;
> They were not such a plague when I was young;
> What else have I to spur me into song? [77]

To Yeats at this point, hatred and rage begin to seem indis-
pensable, and detachment — even the detachment necessary
for creation — begins to seem impossible. I am fairly certain
that this dilemma was the genesis of *Purgatory*; and Yeats's
own bewilderment is reflected in the ending of the play.

The Old Man is briefly tempted to forgive his mother, as

he reflects on his father's youthful handsomeness. But he turns savagely on her again — "She should have known he was not her kind," — and in his anger, kills his son. For a moment he thinks he has succeeded in stopping the purgation:

> Study that tree.
> It stands there like a purified soul,
> All cold, sweet, glistening light.
> Dear mother, the window is dark again,
> But you are in the light because
> I finished all that consequence.[78]

At the sound of hoof beats, he realizes in horror that nothing is finished, and all goes on as before:

> Twice a murderer and all for nothing,
> And she must animate that dead night
> Not once but many times!
>   O God,
> Release my mother's soul from its dream!
> Mankind can do no more. Appease
> The misery of the living and the remorse of the dead.[79]

The play ends on a tone of frustration and incomprehension, as the Old Man discovers that lashing out at the world cannot cure an inner evil.

As a parable about the imagination (or, for that matter, as anything else) I find *Purgatory* thin and unsatisfying. I do not doubt that it is an exact representation of Yeats's state of mind in 1939; one has only to glance at *On the Boiler* (in which *Purgatory* was first printed) to understand how greatly Yeats's imagination was imbued with rage and hatred, and how remote any process of detachment, seemingly necessary for creation, must have seemed to him at the time. But the parable is split too many ways for coherence, and a good deal of any interpretation must be a mixture of prejudice and guesswork.

There is no doubt that the play is intended not only as a personal statement but as a bitter comment on modern Ireland as well. Ireland's purgation, too, seems destined to go on forever, in a sterile repetition without any new rebirth. The prayer at the end of the play—Yeats's version of "Mine, O thou Lord of life, send my roots rain"—is the conventional recourse in the face of frustration. The laboring and refining of life seem to come to no point: the dream cannot be liberated from its matrix and fixed in the stasis of art, but must go on writhing in a chaotic incoherence of passion. The immolation of experience which the poet hopes will produce a work of art is, at this point, impossible—he is still too deeply enmeshed in the emotions he has suffered to recollect them in tranquillity.

> All that I have said and done,
> Now that I am old and ill,
> Turns into a question till
> I lie awake night after night
> And never get the answers right.
> Did that play of mine send out
> Certain men the English shot?
> Did words of mine put too great strain
> On that woman's reeling brain?
> Could my spoken words have checked
> That whereby a house lay wrecked?
> And all seems evil until I
> Sleepless would lie down and die.[80]

That is the mood of *Purgatory*—that restless reliving of actions undertaken with mixed feelings and obligations. The poem I have just quoted goes on to undertake resolutely "the spiritual intellect's great work," but the play ends on a note of exhaustion and impotence. It is not Yeats's last word, however. As we shall see in the next chapter, his final pronouncement, in the person of Cuchulain, is heroic.

Chapter IX

The Saga of Cuchulain

O F YEATS's five Cuchulain plays, two precede *A Vision*: *On Baile's Strand* was published in 1903 and 1906; *The Green Helmet* in 1908 [1] and 1910. I do not include these plays in this study, first, because they are early works and second, because they did not serve Yeats as settings for lyrics. There is one lyric in *On Baile's Strand*, but it is peripheral, not central, and the conception of the two pre-1917 plays is utterly unlike the shaping idea of the three later Cuchulain dramas — *At the Hawk's Well* (1917), *The Only Jealousy of Emer* (1919), and *The Death of Cuchulain* (1939). Both *The Green Helmet* and *On Baile's Strand* are relatively uncomplicated plays. The first is a fairly trivial comment on the literary and political contentiousness which prevents the Irish from attaining effective unity, and the second is a straightforward drama of the struggle between heroism and political mediocrity. In *On Baile's Strand*, Yeats tries for an effect of depth by establishing a parallel between the Fool and Cuchulain, the Blind Man and Conchubar, but to my way of thinking he succeeds only in a rather trying and artificial way.

The contrast between the two earlier plays and *At the Hawk's Well* can be explained in several ways. Roughly ten years had passed, *A Vision* was under way, the example of the Noh had relieved Yeats of the obligation to write conventional plays, and most important, imagination had free rein in shaping the plot. *At the Hawk's Well* is not based on any one of the Cuchulain legends; though Yeats always used a free hand with his sources, he apparently did not want to attempt an adaptation of traditional legend at this time, preoccupied as he was with the structure of his first dance play.

The plot of the play is quickly told. Cuchulain, young and not yet famous, comes to a magic well of immortality, guarded by a hawklike woman. The well is dry, but an old man sitting by the well tells Cuchulain that from time to time the water rises in it. Cuchulain sits down to wait, the Guardian of the Well begins to dance, and Cuchulain, determined to conquer her, follows her offstage. As he leaves, the miraculous water rises, and disappears; both Cuchulain and the old man, who was asleep, have missed their chance to drink of it. The Guardian of the Well meanwhile has roused to arms the warrior-woman Aoife and her troops, and Cuchulain goes off to face them. The play ends as it had begun, with a lyric.

The first question that arises concerns the well: where did Yeats find his symbol, and what does he mean by it? As far back as 1898 he mentions a vision of a magic well in a record of three visions seen by members of the Order of the Golden Dawn,[2] and repeats the account in a letter to Dorothea Hunter. Allan Wade quotes her note to the letter in his collection: "The magic well of Connla lies at the foot of a mountain ash. Those who gaze therein may, if they can find a guide, be led to the Fount of Perpetual Youth. The ash berries fall into the waters and turn them to fire. Connla, the Druid, is the Guardian of the Well." [3]

Standish O'Grady gives a slightly different account of the well, substituting hazels for the mountain ash, queens or goddesses for the druid, and prescience, wisdom, or eloquence for immortality. "The Castalian well of our mythology was on Slieve Gullian. Thither Finn approached once; but the goddesses who guarded it, arose, and in their helplessness and confusion, dashed from the palms of their hands the water of the well against him. From what fell upon his lips the hero acquired the gift of prescience." O'Grady's second description is somewhat fuller, telling of

the hazels, whose magic clusters might assuage that hunger of the spirit which knows no other assuagement . . . Here beneath those hazels, their immortal green and their scarlet clusters, sprang the well of the waters of all wisdom. Three dreadful queens guarded it. Sometimes they smile, seeing afar some youth wandering unconsoled, o'erladen with the burthen of his thoughts, rapt with visions, tormented by the gods, a stranger in his own household, scorned by those whom he cannot scorn, outcast from the wholesome cheerful life of men — they smile, and, smiling, dart from rosy immortal fingers one radiant drop upon his pallid lips, and, lo! the word out of his mouth becomes a sword wherewith he shears through mountains; with his right hand, he upholds the weak, and with the left prostrates powers, and tyrants tremble before the light of his mild eyes.[4]

It is easy to see how O'Grady's essay could lead to a dramatic scenario, and easy to see as well how his female guardians replaced in Yeats's imagination the "venerable figure, luminous but human, the figure of a man with a white beard," who had represented to Yeats Connla the Druid.[5] But it is crucial to the interpretation of the play to realize that Cuchulain thinks of the well as a source not of wisdom or power but of immortality.

> He who drinks, they say,
> Of that miraculous water lives forever.[6]

Yeats may have attached symbolic meaning to the well, as we shall see presently, but on the literal level, the well is one of immortality, nothing else.

Birgit Bjersby suggests that it was from William Morris that Yeats derived the conjunction of Well and Tree, and quotes his essay on Morris in support of her suggestion: "When the water that gives a long and a fortunate life and that can be found by none but such a one as all women love

is found at last, the Dry Tree, the image of the ruined land,
becomes green. To him indeed as to older writers Well and
Tree are all but images of the one thing, of an 'energy' that
is not the less 'eternal delight' because it is half of the body."
Mrs. Bjersby comments, "In his play Yeats does not sing of
the green tree but of the dry one, and his well of immortality
is a mocking well." [7] This is not strictly true, as we shall see.

At the Hawk's Well is the most generalized account of a
meeting with the otherworld in the plays. In *The Player
Queen* and *The Herne's Egg*, the Daimon-like Unicorn and
the "subjective" Heron were clearly aesthetic symbols; in
A Full Moon in March and *The King of the Great Clock
Tower* the Queen is evidently a Muse; in *The Dreaming of
the Bones* and *Purgatory* the shades are metaphors for "unpurged images"; in *The Resurrection* the "phantom," Christ,
represents the vitality of a new source of imaginative strength;
and in *Calvary* the solitary heron once again represents the
aloof and indifferent quality of subjective art. But the Guardian of the Well, though she is allied with the Sidhe and has some
of the qualities of the image, cannot be identified with any
certainty as a symbol having primarily an aesthetic reference.
A "straight" reading of the play sees it as an espousal of
heroism, and I agree with this reading entirely. I would only
add that Yeats identified the ecstasy of saint, sage, and hero
with the ecstasy of the poet, and that in speaking of heroism
in battle or in learning or in sanctity he is often invoking
these types of courage as symbols of perseverance in the poetic
vocation. I do not think *At the Hawk's Well* gains anything,
however, in being translated into aesthetic terms, and I propose to discuss it here in terms of moral heroism.

One of the immediate problems that confronts us in reading the play is the assigning of "voices" to the musicians. In
the plays we have been considering, the musicians either spoke
clearly for one character or another, or else they served as
an impersonal chorus. Here, the "voice" changes in the middle

of a lyric: sometimes the musicians, so far as I can see, are speaking for the Old Man, sometimes for Cuchulain, and sometimes as a detached third person. As I come to the musicians' songs, then, I will indicate my conjectures about the speaking voice.

One final word must be said about the autobiographical elements in the play. Mrs. Bjersby has remarked that when Yeats was writing *At the Hawk's Well* he was considering marriage, and Richard Ellmann has gone further in making connections between the play and Yeats's life: "An autobiographical element in the play is difficult to overlook: the old man who had been patiently waiting at the well for fifty years is Yeats's intellect (he was exactly fifty at the time of writing the play), as the young Cuchulain is his instinctive self." [8] Such identifications are risky (for one thing, Yeats's intellect was never such a whining thing as the old man is shown to be) but there is no doubt that the play encourages autobiographical inferences. So do all the other plays, and there is nothing to do but admit it freely, and pass on. Nobody transformed experience more than Yeats (not only in his art, but in his entire personal "mask") and to find the historical "real" beneath the fiction is a task almost hopeless, it seems to me, in the plays.

The play opens with a lyric in two eight-line stanzas, of which the first is impersonal and sets the scene: the Well, the withered tree, Cuchulain climbing the mountain, and a mysterious "ivory face" with a "lofty dissolute air." I would guess, from the descriptions of Aoife in *On Baile's Strand*, which emphasize her pallor, amorousness, and nobility, that this is her face, not the old Man's, as Ure suggests, and probably not Cuchulain's, as Wilson would have it.[9] Cuchulain, after all, goes off at the end of the play to encounter Aoife in battle (and, as we know from the legends, to master her and become her lover). The second stanza of the opening lyric represents the point of view of the hero: a short valiant life is better than a long uneventful one. The poem forecasts the later use of the same idea in "Among School Children," as the Musicians sing:

> What were his life soon done!
> Would he lose by that or win?
> A mother that saw her son
> Doubled over a speckled shin,
> Cross-grained with ninety years,
> Would cry, 'How little worth
> Were all my hopes and fears
> And the hard pain of his birth!' [10]

The lyric immediately following, though it is broken up by interpolated commentary, consists of 3 quatrains: I will reproduce it, putting its parts together and indicating the voices, as the simplest form of explaining it. Like the first lyric, it sets the apathy of age against the enterprise of youth:

Old Man: The boughs of the hazel shake,
           The sun goes down in the west.

Cuchulain: The heart would be always awake,

Old Man: The heart would turn to its rest.

Cuchulain: 'Why should I sleep?' the heart cries,
           'For the wind, the salt wind, the sea wind,
           Is beating a cloud through the skies;
           I would wander always like the wind.'

Old Man: 'O wind, O salt wind, O sea wind!'
           Cries the heart, 'it is time to sleep;
           Why wander and nothing to find?
           Better grow old and sleep.'

The lyric makes it clear that these are two moods of the heart, and in that sense it is true to say that the Old Man and Cuchulain are both "principles of the mind" in Yeats. However, for the purpose of the play, they are two separate dramatic figures, and it makes commentary simpler to treat them as separate rather than as identical.

Meanwhile, in between the stanzas of this lyric, the First
Musician has been describing (in the disillusioned tones of
the Old Man), the Guardian of the Well, who sits

> Upon the old grey stone at its side,
> Worn out from raking its dry bed,
> Worn out from gathering up the leaves.
> Her heavy eyes
> Know nothing, or but look upon stone.[11]

At present, in her apathy and tiredness, the Guardian mirrors
the condition of the Old Man, while later, in her possession
and dance, she will mirror the condition of the aroused
Cuchulain. The Old Man reviles her for her petrified state:

> To-day you are as stupid as a fish,
> No, worse, worse, being less lively and as dumb.
> Your eyes are dazed and heavy . . .
>   Why do you stare like that?
> You had that glassy look about the eyes
> Last time it happened.[12]

With this apprehension, the stage is set for the entrance of
Cuchulain, who comes to seek the well. It is essential to realize
that in Yeats's play, the water is not said to cause either
perpetual youth or immortality in the sense of divinity: it
only makes one, like Tithonus, live forever. Cuchulain has
come in search of adventure, but the old man has long ago
abandoned any quest and has resigned himself to a resentful
waiting:

> O folly of youth,
> Why should that hollow place fill up for you
> That will not fill for me? I have lain in wait
> For more than fifty years, to find it empty,
> Or but to find the stupid wind of the sea
> Drive round the perishable leaves.[13]

We must not forget that in the end, Cuchulain's experience
is the same as the Old Man's, for he misses the water too.
But his response to the experience is different, and it is in

the quality of the response that his heroism lies. The old man
has become bitter, and Cuchulain rightly asks him,

> And who are you who rail
> Upon those dancers that all other bless?

The Old Man answers that he is "One whom the dancers
cheat." [14] So he is — but so is Cuchulain. Those dancers —
the Sidhe, the people of the otherworld — cheat everyone,
finally: fairy gold disappears; the fairy mistress deserts her
lover; and the victim is left with nothing but memories. The
only question is whether the encounter was worth the desertion, and the heroic answer is yes.

The Old Man is no hero, but a coward: when Cuchulain
says he will pierce his own foot to keep himself from sleep,
the Old Man demurs, "No, do not pierce it, for the foot is
tender,/ It feels pain much." [15] And he repeatedly urges
Cuchulain to flee without encountering the Woman of the
Sidhe or Aoife, admitting that he himself has never dared to
gaze on the "unmoistened eyes" of the Guardian of the Well.
Anyone who meets her gaze, he warns Cuchulain, is cursed:

> That curse may be
> Never to win a woman's love and keep it;
> Or always to mix hatred in the love;
> Or it may be that she will kill your children,
> That you will find them, their throats torn and bloody,
> Or you will be so maddened that you kill them
> With your own hand.[16]

The first curse reflects, probably enough, Yeats's view of his
own relation to Maud Gonne; the second reflects Blake's
maxim that sexual love is always accompanied by spiritual
hate; and the final curse is the one encountered, of course,
by Cuchulain — to kill his only son. The passage is a typically
Yeatsian mixture of autobiography, literary influence, and
legendary material, and though we may separate the elements
artificially, the play combines them.

At this point in the action, the Guardian cries out with

the voice of a hawk, and we must pause for a moment over her place in the play. Mrs. Bjersby has collected examples of Yeats's use of the hawk in the poetry and the plays, concluding that "the hawk is a symbol of nobility, of loneliness . . . or divine power, dangerous to mortals." [17] In *On Baile's Strand*, Cuchulain refers to his sun-god father as "that clean hawk out of the air," [18] so by inference, Cuchulain himself is half-hawk. Oliver St. John Gogarty said Yeats called the well "The well of immortality or of wisdom," and referred to the Hawk-Woman as "intellect"; [19] if she is intellect, her sudden "possession" can be said to represent one of those visitations of the Daimon that illumine the mind. I do not think that the Hawk-Woman symbolizes "logic and abstract thought" as Richard Ellmann would have it,[20] since in Yeats's frame of reference abstract thought never is possessed, never cries out in a supernatural voice, never dances. The Hawk-Woman is evidently kin to Attracta and the other medium-like figures of the plays, while her aloofness, indifference, and luring power link her with the women of Phase 14 and consequently with the image in its despotic power over the mind. Once again, in this play, the question of "Leda and the Swan" is implicitly asked: what knowledge remains in the mind as the residue of possession by the Daimon? The Old Man answers that the Hawk-Woman wakes to her former ignorance:

> It was her mouth, and yet not she, that cried.
> It was that shadow cried behind her mouth;
> And now I know why she has been so stupid
> All the day through, and had such heavy eyes.
> Look at her shivering now, the terrible life
> Is slipping through her veins. She is possessed.
> Who knows whom she will murder or betray
> Before she awakes in ignorance of it all,
> And gathers up the leaves? [21]

The Old Man's opinion, however, is always the cynical one, and I do not think we are meant to take his answer as the final word. As usual, Yeats's estimate of the knowledge correlative to power is equivocal.

At the Guardian's cry, the Old Man covers his head, unable to bear her "unfaltering, unmoistened eyes," and he sleeps, while the First Musician sings in the Old Man's voice a few lines echoing his earlier speech describing the possession:

> O God, protect me
> From a horrible deathless body
> Sliding through the veins of a sudden.[22]

Cuchulain, on the other hand, resolves to become immortal like the Guardian, but "maddened" by her dance, and swearing to conquer her, he follows her away from the well. Apparently, we are to think that Cuchulain sees the water of immortality rise in the well but disregards it in his pursuit of the Hawk-Woman and goes offstage without drinking from the well. At least, this is what I make of the comment of the First Musician and the song of the Musicians which follows it:

> I have heard water plash; it comes, it comes;
> Look where it glitters. He has heard the plash;
> Look, he has turned his head.
>
> He has lost what may not be found
> Till men heap his burial-mound
> And all the history ends.
> He might have lived at his ease,
> An old dog's head on his knees,
> Among his children and friends.[23]

What Cuchulain has lost and will not find except in the grave is rest, as we learn from the later speech of the Old Man:

> And never till you are lying in the earth
> Can you know rest.[24]

This is at first confusing — we would have said that Cuchulain had lost immortality, but apparently all he has lost is a species of vegetable ease. In letting himself be possessed by the power of the Sidhe, Cuchulain is gaining a type of immortality worth much more than the temporal longevity conferred by the well water. Yeats may have been influenced in writing the play by the legend of Cuchulain's taking of arms; Lady Gregory tells, in *Cuchulain of Muirthemne*, how the young Cuchulain heard Cathbad the Druid predict one day that any young man taking arms on that day would have a name greater than any other in Ireland, but his span of life would be short. Cuchulain asked and got Conchubar's permission to take arms, and said in answer to the King's later reproaches, "It is little I would care if my life were to last one day and one night only, so long as my name and the story of what I had done would live after me." [25] It is this Cuchulain whom we see in *At the Hawk's Well* — the hero who can tell the true immortality of brief remembered glory from false longevity. Attracted by the clash of arms, he goes out to face Aoife and her women, calling, as an epic hero might, "He comes! Cuchulain, son of Sualtim, comes!" [26] It is the Hawk-Woman who has led him away from the well and toward the conflict, and in thus leading him to his truest immortality, she can be called in some sense his Daimon, a Muse of battle.

The final lyric is a confusing one, and my attempt to reconstruct it here leaves me somewhat unsatisfied, as Wilson's interpretation also does.[27] I can only say that writing *At the Hawk's Well* must have taught Yeats something about the apportioning of speeches to the Musicians, since rarely again in the dance plays is the reader left in doubt concerning voices. As I see the lyric, it is spoken for the most part from the point of view of the Old Man, but the second stanza introduces Cuchulain's voice. The first stanza is clearly spoken by the Old Man — the vocabulary is his, the attitude is his:

> Come to me, human faces,
> Familiar memories;
> I have found hateful eyes
> Among the desolate places,
> Unfaltering, unmoistened eyes.

But Cuchulain, seeing the water of immortality plash in the well, disdaining it, and following the Hawk-Woman to battle, sings in return:

> Folly alone I cherish,
> I choose it for my share;
> Being but a mouthful of air,
> I am content to perish;
> I am but a mouthful of sweet air.

Wilson attributes the second stanza too to the Old Man, but the language argues differently. "O what is life but a mouthful of air?" asked the rambling, shambling travelling-man in the closing lyric of *The King of the Great Clock Tower*, and this view of life as a brief opportunity for daring action is consonant with Yeats's admiration for *sprezzatura*, the reckless heroic gesture. Cuchulain does not need a dragging physical immortality; content to perish, he praises

> Whatever life could make the pulse run quickly,
> Even though it were brief.[28]

The Old Man had taxed Cuchulain with folly earlier:

> O, folly of youth,
> Why should that hollow place fill up for you
> That will not fill for me? [29]

The folly that Cuchulain cherishes may be madness in the eyes of the world, but in a larger sense it is wisdom. Although the Old Man, in a moment of enlightenment, realizes that truth, his own cowardice (which we have seen in the play) keeps him from embracing it:

> O lamentable shadows,
> Obscurity of strife!
> I choose a pleasant life
> Among indolent meadows;
> Wisdom must live a bitter life.

The two stanzas differentiate between the Old Man and

Cuchulain still further. We must remember that the Old Man has never seen the well fill and hazel nuts drop from the tree: he has always through his cowardice fallen asleep at the crucial moment. Cuchulain has seen both and has chosen to follow the Woman of the Sidhe instead (compelled by her magical power, true, but still he has dared, unlike the Old Man, to gaze into her eyes — the element of choice is present).

The last two stanzas are spoken from the point of view of one who has never seen the full well and the fruitful tree:

> 'The man that I praise'
> Cries out the empty well,
> 'Lives all his days
> Where a hand on the bell
> Can call the milch cows
> To the comfortable door of his house.
> Who but an idiot would praise
> Dry stones in a well?'

> 'The man that I praise',
> Cries out the leafless tree,
> 'Has married and stays
> By an old hearth, and he
> On naught has set store
> But children and dogs on the floor.
> Who but an idiot would praise
> A withered tree?' [30]

The empty well and the withered tree on Slieve Gullian represent the unpromising nature of any heroic undertaking. One always takes a chance: the Guardian may not awake, the spring may not flow, the dance may not take place, the hazels may not ripen. It is not the well and tree in themselves that are important in these stanzas — we have seen that Yeats is unconcerned with the species of immortality they represent. It is truer to say, perhaps, that one finds one's own species of immortality at the well and tree. For Cuchulain it is battle and not the water, but he had to come to the well to find this out. The world counts praise of well and tree idiocy, and in those terms the last lyric criticizes Cuchulain — but such a criticism is actually praise.

This is why I cannot agree with Mrs. Bjersby's statement that Yeats's well of immortality is "a mocking well." She continues:

> The dry well and the leafless tree are symbols of [Yeats's] love. It is like a well, long choked up and dry, or like a tree without its greenery. If the well water surges up, it is not for his benefit, and without the water the tree is dry and dead. In his love, he feels like the young Cuchulain who imagines himself to be within reach of the miraculous water, when, on the contrary, it proves to be the very moment of deception.[31]

This view seems to me entirely mistaken, taking no account of Cuchulain's courage, the symbolic import of the dance of the Hawk-Woman, and the primarily heroic reference of the play. This is not a play about love. There is no doubt that the Old Man represents Yeats's occasional moments of resentment and hopelessness in his poetic vocation; but there is also no doubt, Wilson notwithstanding,[32] that the sympathies of the play are in the last analysis with Cuchulain. The Old Man has the final word, but that word is so limited and cowardly in the life it envisions that the Old Man is condemned out of his own mouth, and Cuchulain is the more enhanced. Yeats never ceased to praise obedience to the Muse and the consequent arduousness of life: in spite of its articulation of discouragement, this play is no exception to the general rule.

2

The Only Jealousy of Emer, the most confusing of the dance plays, can only be called the Hydra of Yeats's dramas: for each problem solved, another appears. It is even difficult to know in what category to place this play; by its characters it belongs among the Cuchulain plays, but by its content it should be assigned to the plays of purgation. There are problems in the source (it is composed of two stories welded together, not too well at that),[33] problems in the sequence of action, problems in the symbolic meanings, and problems in the autobiographical roots. It is written in verse of very great beauty, and has a larger proportion of lyric to dramatic verse than most of the plays — only *A Full Moon in March* equals it in that respect. To my mind, it is poetically the best of the plays, but my admiration for it cannot disguise the dramatic intransigence of the action.

The story, as Yeats tells it, shows Cuchulain in a magical trance: while his body lies as if dead, he is a captive in the otherworld, where he takes as mistress the sea goddess Fand (identified in the play with the Hawk-Woman whom Cuchulain had met and followed in *At the Hawk's Well*). Both Cuchulain's wife Emer and his earthly mistress Eithne Inguba want to reclaim Cuchulain from Fand: Emer thinks Eithne Inguba can call him back through love, but it turns out that only Emer can recall him, by renouncing forever her own claim to his love. She does finally renounce it, and must endure watching Eithne Inguba take the credit and embrace Cuchulain.

The plot is, in fact, the least important part of the play. The central issue is Cuchulain's relationship with each of the three women: Fand, Emer, and Eithne Inguba — Muse, wife, and mistress. I do not think that much is gained by insisting, as Wilson does,[34] on a rigid adherence to *A Vision* in classifying the characters of the play, since only Fand is clearly a "pure" incarnation, the others far more mixed. The source story is a triangle: Emer is jealous of Fand and is ready to take up arms against her, when Fand of her own accord renounces Cuchulain. Eithne Inguba is simply the name given Cuchulain's wife in one of the two versions of the story — it was Yeats who made the story into a quadrangle, and invented a mistress for Cuchulain.[35] The autobiographical implications are obvious, but there were literary reasons for the changes as well. Eithne serves as a surrogate for Emer who, being middle-aged, can no longer symbolize human beauty.

The action of the play has three parts: in the first, Cuchulain's wife and mistress attempt to call him back to consciousness; in the second, Emer sees a vision of Cuchulain with Fand; in the third, Cuchulain awakes and the play ends. We might say, given the resolution of the action, that *Emer* is a play about the triumph of human obligations and human memories over aesthetic experience. The play is linked autobiographically with two poems from *Michael Robartes and the Dancer* (1921), "An Image from a Past Life" and "Under Saturn." Both poems are about the persistence of the image of Maud Gonne in Yeats's mind even after his marriage; and though he reassures his wife that that image is powerless over him now, the protestations do not ring true:

> Do not because this day I have grown saturnine
> Imagine that lost love, inseparable from my thought
> Because I have no other youth, can make me pine;
> For how should I forget the wisdom that you brought,
> The comfort that you made?

Far more convincing than the protestations is the image of the vanished love:

> A sweetheart from another life floats there
> As though she had been forced to linger
> From vague distress
> Or arrogant loveliness,
> Merely to loosen out a tress
> Among the starry eddies of her hair.[36]

Similarly in the play the image of Fand in the central scene overpowers both Emer and Eithne Inguba in poetic value. The reason I do not say that the play is primarily about love is that Fand is identified throughout with Phase 15, which as we have seen is the phase where "all thought becomes an image" and aesthetic activity occurs. There is not much doubt that the play sprang from a domestic situation, but it has been transfigured in the writing, and emerges as a play which best reveals itself, I think, if the aesthetic reference, so clearly indicated by the terminology of *A Vision*, is uppermost.

So far as I can judge, the average reader sees *Emer* as a play about a selfless wife, a weak and straying husband, and a wicked temptress. Moral norms coerce this reader into approval of Emer, condemnation of Cuchulain, and dislike of Fand, but it is important, I think, not to impose alien moral norms on these plays while interpreting them. Against the common view, I point out that the play is called *The Only Jealousy* (not the *Renunciation*, or the *Self-Sacrifice*) of *Emer*; second, that Cuchulain's choice is predetermined because he is bewitched; and third, that Cuchulain is throughout a passive character, manipulated by otherworld powers (Fand's beauty and Bricriu's spite). Literary tests, rather than moral norms, must decide where Yeats wanted our sympathies to lie. Whether he failed in leading our sympathies there is another question.

The lyric which opens the play sets up one of the central oppositions in the action — the conflict between the turbulent and bitter sea and fragile human beauty. Some primal energy in the sea is responsible for the origin of that beauty (which Yeats compares to a sea bird thrown by the storm onto the land, or to a shell tossed upon the sand by the waves) but the savage strength of the sea does not accord well with its delicate inhabitants, whether bird or shell. In terms foreshadowing "The Statues," Yeats asks,

> How many centuries spent
> The sedentary soul
> In toils of measurement
> Beyond eagle or mole,

> Beyond hearing or seeing,
> Or Archimedes' guess
> To raise into being
> That loveliness?

The evolution is slow, it is true, but it must not be forgotten that the origin of art is nevertheless, in Yeats's view, from the brutal and the primitive. We see in the second stanza that rhythm of violence followed by elegance which, as I have said in Chapter I, is characteristic of Yeats. The Muses may drink tea from porcelain cups, but they search out sailors on the wharves as well; and in the second stanza, with its echoes of Blake and Keats, we see the harsher side of creation:

> What death? What discipline?
> What bonds no man could unbind,
> Being imagined within
> The labyrinth of the mind,
> What pursuing or fleeing,
> What wounds, what bloody press,
> Dragged into being
> This loveliness? [37]

The two aspects of creation (measurement and violence) may seem incompatible with each other, and even with their joint achievement, so much so that the sea disowns its own frail, unserviceable shell, the matrix rejecting its product. In the same way, although Emer and Eithne Inguba are participants in the beauty of which Fand is the absolute, there is only enmity, no recognition, between them.

The play takes place during Fand's reign over Cuchulain's mind — during his visit to the otherworld — and therefore, since Yeats conceives of Fand as a sea goddess, the sea is represented as victorious over the "fragile" loveliness of Emer or Eithne Inguba. The original title of the play was *A Sword Blade Against the Foam*,[38] and the certain triumph of Fand is implied by the impotence of any earthly weapon against the sea. Yet Emer and Eithne are resolved to combat the forces of the sea without really understanding them, and therefore Eithne, approaching the sickbed of Cuchulain, hears the sea cry out in hostility to her beauty.

> White shell, white wing!
> I will not choose for my friend
> A frail, unserviceable thing
> That drifts and dreams, and but knows
> That waters are without end
> And that wind blows.[39]

It was in fighting the waves (after killing his son on Baile's Strand) that Cuchulain fell into his trance; consequently Emer guesses that a sea god has entered his body in revenge. The source which Yeats used does not connect Cuchulain's trance with the killing of his son; this is Yeats's invention to link his plays one with the other. Neither does the source have the sea god Bricriu speak through Cuchulain's body; to explain Yeats's invention of Bricriu requires a glance at an earlier version of the play.

The version of *Emer* printed in the *Collected Plays* assigns a reduced and diminished role to Bricriu: we know only that he is an enemy to Fand, and that he has a withered arm. We may say, then, that he represents a "deformed" image, like the Hunchback in *A Vision*, inimical to that aesthetic perfection incarnated by Fand. In the early version of the play printed in *Four Plays for Dancers* Bricriu has a larger role. After Cuchulain deserts Fand (as he does in this earlier version) Fand reproaches Bricriu for having taught Emer how to prevail against her, and we learn that our guess about Bricriu is right: he does inhabit the same crescent as the Hunchback. Fand addresses him as

> . . . you that have no living light, but dropped
> From a last leprous crescent of the moon.[40]

Fand threatens Bricriu with punishment for his actions, and we realize that Emer has been a tool in a battle she knew

nothing of. The forces hostile to the imagination enlist on
their side things good in themselves — human loveliness, human bonds, human obligations — and use such instruments as
cloaks for their destructive designs. Emer's love for Cuchulain
has been used as a pawn in a strategy of the immortals, and
our last glimpse of Fand and Bricriu shows them trying to out-
ride each other to the court of their common sovereign, the
sea god Manannan, to have their quarrel judged.

In the final version of the play, the emphasis has been
shifted. The interest is centered on Cuchulain, and the struggle for power between Fand and Bricriu is barely indicated.
There is no conversation between the immortals, and no
recourse to Manannan; Fand vanishes with Cuchulain in
pursuit of her just before he is recalled, and Bricriu disappears
as Cuchulain returns. The play is better, I think, as it now
stands, since it hardly needed additional confusion of theme.
But still, the variation in emphasis between the two versions
is one more indication of Yeats's extremely personal application of the Cuchulain legend. He could not follow the source
and have Fand renounce Cuchulain — that would be to have
the Muse abandon her follower, and such an action was unthinkable. Neither could he have Cuchulain renounce Fand
— that would be to implicate himself in treason against the
Muse, and that was unthinkable too.[41] Nor could he have a
purely human person like Emer defeat the Muse — that
would upset all his hierarchies. Bricriu was a dramatic necessity, though nobody corresponding to him existed in the
source, and so Yeats invented him.[42] Once invented, Bricriu
tended to outgrow his niche in the play; but realizing the
symbolic difficulties inherent in the idea of a "deformed"
image conquering an image of the Fifteenth Phase, Yeats
prudently cut him down to size, so that Bricriu exists in the
final version as a sketchy blocking force.[43]

As Cuchulain lies in his trance, his mistress Eithne attempts
to call him back by kissing him, and she thinks, when his

body moves, that she has succeeded. It is Bricriu, though, who speaks through the body, not Cuchulain. Eithne's peculiar powerlessness throughout the play (she tries twice to summon Cuchulain and fails both times) indicates, I think, that her sovereignty is only partial. Emer can call Cuchulain back, but only at the price of renouncing his love, signaling the definitive end of her reign. Essentially, the play belongs to Fand, in spite of the fact that she is in the end defeated, and it belongs to her by virtue of her poetic impact.

Emer resists the demand of the sinister Bricriu that she renounce her hope of Cuchulain's love, but Bricriu puts one telling question, quenching her expectation that Cuchulain will tire of Fand:

> You've watched his loves and you have not been jealous,
> Knowing that he would tire, but do those tire
> That love the Sidhe? [44]

The answer of course is no, and Emer's resolution is weakened. At this point, Bricriu allows her a vision of the otherworld, and she sees, to her dismay, the Ghost of Cuchulain with Fand. Once again, in the link he establishes between death and the otherworld and trance, Yeats forewarns us of the meaning of Emer's vision. That constellation of images represents the mind in aesthetic suspension; and all the purgatorial terms used in relation to the Ghost of Cuchulain (who, incidentally, is never explicitly said to be dead, although he is "among the dead") have no reference to real death at all. One cannot legitimately see the play, I think, in Peter Ure's terms, as a conflict "between love and the abstraction of death": [45] an interpretation of the play which sees Fand as symbolic of actual physical death can get nowhere.

The dialogue between Bricriu and Emer just before the vision has the advantage of defining Fand further for us: Bricriu tells Emer that Fand is a shape-changing Woman of the Sidhe who fishes for men "with dreams upon the hook." [46]

At this point we may question Fand's motives in seducing Cuchulain. Bricriu sees her as an acquisitive temptress, collecting men as she might catch fish, bewitching Cuchulain "that he/ May glitter in her basket." [47] But Bricriu hates Fand, and is an untrustworthy source of information. Fand herself says mysteriously:

> Because I long I am not complete . . .
> When your mouth and my mouth meet
> All my round shall be complete
> Imagining all its circles run.[48]

Wilson thinks that by this speech Fand "tells Cuchulain that his kiss will bring her freedom from all the cycles of rebirth; without it, she would have to progress through the objective incarnations." [49] But as we saw earlier in Chapter VII, the creatures of Phase 15 give the "Kiss of Death" to be freed, not from the cycles, but from "all traces of the *primary Tincture* . . . They suffer from the terror of solitude, and can only free themselves from terror by becoming entirely *antithetical*." [50] They impress by a kiss an image of themselves on a human who then expresses that image in some action or work of art. Yeats says:

It is of that kiss I thought when I made Emer say:

> "They find our men asleep, weary with war,
> Or weary with the chase, and kiss their lips
> And drop their hair upon them; from that hour
> Our men, who yet know nothing of it all,
> Are lonely, and when at fall of night we press
> Their hearts upon our hearts, their hearts are cold." [51]

We are certain that Fand needs Cuchulain, but she needs him to attain perfection of self, not to escape the cycles. And she offers not empty inducements but a true gift — the simplicity of fire: "Daemon and man are opposites; man passes from heterogeneous objects to the simplicity of fire, and the

Daemon is drawn to objects because through them he obtains power, the extremity of choice." [52]

Fand, then, is neither a benevolent angel nor a wicked vampire, but something in between. Emer, of course, sees her as exclusively evil, and calls Fand's disguise a "lie." Bricriu corrects her, saying that dreams are not lies, but are holy, and in fact constitute existence as we know it:

> A dream is body;
> The dead move ever towards a dreamless youth
> And when they dream no more return no more. [53]

Once finished dreaming, the dead become "bodiless." Yeats's assertion that the world of image is the nearest thing we know to "reality" has here reached its logical conclusion, where existence and identity are contingent upon the image-making faculty. *Emer*, in this passage, raises the same question as *At the Hawk's Well*, the question of "Leda and the Swan": what is the residue of possession? Emer says it is ignorance: "Our men awake in ignorance of it all." [54] But again, like the Old Man, she is a prejudiced witness, neither understanding the phenomenon nor sympathizing with it. Some influence in the subject remains, in spite of her denial, for she cannot pierce the contemplative aftermath of the experience.

Fand, resembling an idol in her golden robes, as Yeats tells us, dances for Cuchulain as the vision of Emer opens. It is hardly necessary to remind the reader of all the characters in the plays with whom she is linked by her dance — the Player Queen, Attracta, the Queen of the two dance plays, Diarmuid and Dervorgilla, the Hawk-Woman. We should recall, too, at this point, that Cuchulain's heroism and energy are dependent somehow on his alliance with the Sidhe. In *At the Hawk's Well* he finds his immortality in battle through the guiding of the Sidhe, and in *On Baile's Strand* his extorted oath of obedience is marked by an exorcism of the Sidhe, as the women of the court sing,

> May this fire have driven out
> The Shape-Changers that can put
> Ruin on a great king's house
> Until all be ruinous.
> Names whereby a man has known
> The threshold and the hearthstone,
> Gather on the wind and drive
> The women none can kiss and thrive,
> For they are but whirling wind,
> Out of memory and mind.[55]

Shape-Changers like Fand are Cuchulain's natural kin, but they are also the natural enemies of "threshold and hearthstone" — Emer's world. Cuchulain, agreeing to forsake the Sidhe and obey Conchubar, initiates his own ruin, and the shadow of that tragedy on Baile's Strand hovers over *Emer*. We are not meant to feel relieved that Cuchulain has been torn away from Fand, I think — we are meant to regret it. In the source, Fand renounces Cuchulain freely, and he returns to Emer with a divided mind, but a drink of forgetfulness erases the experience entirely in the end. In Yeats's play, Fand is not to be so easily obliterated.

The division of loyalties that unmanned Cuchulain in *On Baile's Strand* — loyalty to the Sidhe (or his own self) against loyalty to his men who wish the oath — unmans him again in his encounter with Fand. She is his Muse, and the terms in which he describes her make this more than clear:

> Who is it stands before me there
> Shedding such light from limb and hair
> As when the moon, complete at last
> With every labouring crescent past,
> And lonely with extreme delight,
> Flings out upon the fifteenth night? [56]

The central importance of the otherworld scene appears when we realize that in *Fighting the Waves*, the prose version of *Emer* (written *after* the poetic version), the entire dialogue in octosyllabic verse is omitted as unfit for the lay ear. Yeats expected the common audience to disregard even the other lyrics, and makes in his introduction to the cut version the astonishing statement: "I have left the words of the opening and closing lyrics unchanged, for sung to modern music in the modern way they suggest strange patterns to the ear without obtruding upon it their difficult, irrelevant words." [57] Irrelevant to what, we may ask, and we suppose that Yeats must mean irrelevant to the play as it now stands. They must be relevant, then, to the excised portion — the dialogue of Cuchulain with Fand. This scene is the "esoteric" core of the play, in its concern with beauty, solitude, remorse, and memory.

Fand incarnates the lineaments of gratified desire, but Emer is Cuchulain's wife, and the weight of his memories, his wrongs towards Emer, weigh him down. Though Fand reminds him that he was glad to follow her at the Hawk's Well, he answers,

> I am not
> The young and passionate man I was,
> And though that brilliant light surpass
> All crescent forms, my memories
> Weigh down my hands, abash my eyes.[58]

These memories are not those productive recollections in tranquillity which produce poetry, but are rather "the night's remorse," the haunting images from the past which must be exorcised before creation can take place. Cuchulain has not yet cast out remorse — he is in a purgatorial state, as I have said above. The Woman of the Sidhe offers her kiss (that "Kiss of Death" which symbolizes the union of thought and image at Phase 15), and Cuchulain asks incredulously,

> And shall I never know again
> Intricacies of blind remorse? [59]

Fand answers, and her succeeding dialogue with Cuchulain, the climax of the play, is one of the few times in which Yeats succeeds in dramatic pathos. The allurements of the Muse, coupled with her intolerance of human demands, stretch

Cuchulain upon the rack of choice. In reply to his question, Fand prophesies,

> Time shall seem to stay his course;
> When your mouth and my mouth meet
> All my round shall be complete
> Imagining all its circles run;
> And there shall be oblivion
> Even to quench Cuchulain's drouth,
> Even to still that heart.

Ghost of Cuchulain.
> Your mouth!
> [They are about to kiss, he turns away.
> O Emer, Emer!

That moment of remorse, of distraction from her beauty, angers Fand:

> So then it is she
> Made you impure with memory.

Yielding to his memories, Cuchulain, overcome by remorse, remembers his marriage day:

> O Emer, Emer, there we stand;
> Side by side and hand in hand
> Tread the threshold of the house
> As when our parents married us . . .
> O my lost Emer!

Fand cuttingly accuses him of sentimentality: he had no such devotion to Emer, she says, when he deserted her during life for common sluts. On the other hand, she adds, Emer should not have expected fidelity from Cuchulain because he was born to live in the otherworld,

> Where no one speaks of broken troth,
> For all have washed out of their eyes
> Wind-blown dirt of their memories
> To improve their sight.[60]

Human moral conditions are incompatible with the demands of the Muse, and Cuchulain must decide where he casts his lot — this is Fand's ultimatum.

Yeats cannot incriminate himself by deciding for either

alternative, so he puts the power of dramatic resolution in Emer's hands. She hesitates, but Bricriu cries out,

> Fool, fool!
> I am Fand's enemy come to thwart her will,
> And you stand gaping there. There is still time . . .
> Renounce him, and her power is at an end.[61]

Emer does renounce him, and Cuchulain awakes in Eithne Inguba's arms, saying

> O Eithne Inguba,
> I have been in some strange place and am afraid.[62]

At least, that is how the play reads in the definitive edition. In an early version, however, there is a long and interesting scene in which Cuchulain's future is not left up to Emer. He indeed does make the choice Fand calls upon him to make — and he decides against Fand. Resenting her demands, resenting her dismissal of human bonds, and scornful of her dread of human memories, he says to her:

> I know you now in all your ignorance
> Of all whereby a lover's quiet is rent.
> What dread so great as that he should forget
> The least chance sight or sound, or scratch or mark
> On an old door, or frail bird heard and seen
> In the incredible clear light love cast
> All round about her some forlorn lost day?

He tells Fand that

> . . . man is held to those whom he has loved
> By pain they gave, or pain that he has given,
> Intricacies of pain.

Finally, he decides against the otherworld, saying

> . . . there's a folly in the deathless Sidhe
> Beyond man's reach.[63]

That positive forsaking of the Muse must have displeased Yeats; it was too unequivocal an action, and unworthy of his Mask. Far better to let Emer pluck Cuchulain back. And so the change was made.

The final lyric shows Yeats at his most maddening, and here I must differ with Wilson, with whom I agree in general on *Emer*. The first two stanzas are common ground, but on the third, and on the refrain, we part company. Before I say more, I will print the lyric as I conceive it divided into voices:

Emer to Fand:	Why does your heart beat thus?
Emer to us:	Plain to be understood, I have met in a man's house A statue of solitude, Moving there and walking; Its strange heart beating fast For all our talking.
Emer to Fand:	O still that heart at last.
Emer to us:	O bitter reward Of many a tragic tomb! And we though astonished are dumb Or give but a sigh and a word, A passing word.
Emer to Fand:	Although the door be shut And all seem well enough, Although wide world hold not A man but will give you his love The moment he has looked at you, He that has loved the best May turn from a statue His too human breast.
Fand to us:	O bitter reward Of many a tragic tomb! And we though astonished are dumb Or give but a sigh and a word, A passing word.
Emer to Fand:	What makes your heart so beat? What man is at your side?
Fand to Emer:	When beauty is complete Your own thought will have died

> And danger not be diminished;
> Dimmed at three-quarter light,
> When moon's round is finished
> The stars are out of sight.

Emer to us: O bitter reward, etc.[64]

This arrangement of the poem is open to charges of over-ingenuity, but so is any other reading, given the inherent difficulty of the stanzas. It will be seen that in my reading Emer taunts Fand, then Fand taunts Emer, each claiming a victory of sorts. I am led to this reading partly by earlier versions of the closing lyric. In a manuscript draft at Harvard the play ends with a song bearing only a slight resemblance to the present lyric; in it, we can clearly see that Yeats's sympathies are equally divided between Fand and Emer:

> How may that woman find
> Being born to ill luck as it seems
> And groping her way half blind
> In labyrinths of his dreams
> A little friendship and love
> ⟨For all the delight of the chase⟩
> ⟨A passionate man [*unrecoverable word*] enough⟩
> ⟨When he finds her not of his race⟩
> ⟨A lover his courtship done⟩
> ⟨Will weary likely enough⟩
> ⟨Of the alien thing he has won⟩
> For all its chase and its jest
> Passion soon has enough
> Of an alien thing on its breast.
>
> O bitter reward
> Of many a tragic tomb!
> And we though astonished are dumb
> Or give but a look and a word
> A passing word.
>
> And how could I dream that this wife
> Busied at her hearthstone
> And a mere part of our life
> Could speak with a gentle tongue

> And give him the hand of a friend?
> Could she not see in ⟨his⟩ that eye
> That ⟨she⟩ it must endure to the end
> Reproach of jealousy?
>
> O bitter reward
> Of many a tragic tomb!
> And we though astonished are dumb
> Or give but a look or a word
> A passing word.[65]

The first stanza is one of commiseration for Fand for the faithlessness of earthly lovers, and in reading it we must recall that in the early version which ends with this lyric Cuchulain eventually turns on Fand with recriminations: "That face, though fine enough, is a fool's face." [66] He deserts Fand for Emer; not simply plucked back, he makes a deliberate choice against the alien, in favor of the familiar. And the refrain, too, seen in this light, is sympathetic to Fand: Cuchulain's tragic tomb has brought her only a bitter reward of momentary hope eventually frustrated. But the second stanza changes the perspective: Emer's unexpected nobility of behavior touches the narrator too. Far from being a mindless drudge, Emer has revealed depths of generosity and forgiveness: but she too has won bitter rewards from Cuchulain's sojourn among the dead — the loveless continuation of her marriage, reproaches for her jealousy. In short, the bewitchment has yielded only bitter fruit in all directions, and the play ends on a stalemate.

This is, I think, the mood in which the final version ends as well. We may glance for a moment at an intermediate draft. Dissatisfied with the version I have just quoted, Yeats wrote the lyric as we now have it, substantially the same except for the closing stanza:

> What makes ⟨her⟩ your heart so beat?
> Some one should stay at her side
> When beauty is complete
> Her own thoughts will have died

And danger not be diminished;
Dimmed at three-quarter light
When moon's round is finished
The stars are out of sight.[67]

It is clear that the first question is addressed to Fand, whose
beating heart is mentioned in the otherworld scene. We must
then account for the woman in the second line, and it seems
most probable that it is Emer, who will fade into insignifi-
cance beside the full moon. In her danger of extinction she
needs a protector, a companion, a husband; powerless to help
herself (because "her own thoughts will have died") she
should not be left alone. Fand, though to be pitied perhaps,
is an inhuman creature hardly in need of a guardian or com-
forter.

We may now return to the final version of the lyric. The
speaker of the first manuscript version is clearly a spectator
whom for convenience we may call Yeats. The second version is less clearly objective, lacking as it does the reflective
tone ("And how could I dream," etc.) of the first. By the
time we arrive at the final version, I am not sure whether any
objective speaker is intended. The last stanza seems to be so
clearly a dialogue of two warring positions that I am inclined
to see the entire lyric in that way, but I may be mistaken.

To recapitulate: a speaker, sharing Emer's view, asks of
Fand, "Why does your heart beat thus?" implying that Fand's
heartbeat is somehow strange or excited, being so close to the
otherworld of death. Then the speaker explains the question
by describing the unwonted appearance of "a statue of solitude," as Fand is described, in Cuchulain's house. Emer's
fear of the Sidhe is reflected in the speaker's language, and
since Cuchulain's time among the Sidhe is a tragic death in
Emer's eyes, the refrain embodies her reaction to the bitter
reward of her renunciation — a loveless life. The impotence
in the refrain echoes Emer's earlier speech of frustration, in
which she says that after men are bewitched by the Sidhe
their wives cannot penetrate their abstraction:

> Our men awake in ignorance of it all,
> But when we take them in our arms at night
> We cannot break their solitude.[68]

"And we though astonished are dumb" — the reaction is Emer's.

In the second stanza, Emer momentarily asserts her victory over the "statue of solitude": though Fand may have supreme beauty, and can lure whom she will, still men may find themselves too human to be permanently happy with a Woman of the Sidhe. This is not true, and Emer knows it: Cuchulain did not return of his own accord — he was plucked away. But it is the perennial human hope, and it is Emer's dramatic function to voice the claims of human attachment. Her refrain, however, once again repeated, immediately negates her vaunted power. Fand replies victoriously in the third stanza, comparing humanly beautiful women like Emer and Eithne to stars which vanish in the light of the full moon. Cuchulain has no choice, she says: all human attraction is eclipsed when the Muse displays her sovereignty. Though human beauty may have temporary victories, in reality these are ephemeral, and the danger of losing Cuchulain to the otherworld is not diminished by this temporary setback.[69] The hapless human residue doomed to extinction at Phase 15 ("your own thought will have died," says Fand) can only look on and sigh, murmuring perhaps a protest which is unheard and vanishes as soon as it is uttered. Officially, Emer has Cuchulain back; officially, Eithne has his love; but we notice that Yeats has not given Cuchulain the drink of forgetfulness mentioned in the source. His Cuchulain will not forget the Woman of the Sidhe.

We cannot overlook, on the other hand, the harshness of the Sidhe. Fand's language is scornful, intolerant, edged with sarcasm, and peremptory — when it is not seductive or unearthly or triumphant. She is a mixed creature, and inspires mixed feelings, representing as she does an absolute both inhuman and superhuman. The play, it is true, repudiates her on one level: she does not gain, in the *action*, that completion for which she needs Cuchulain's kiss. But in the final lyric she does: "When beauty is complete . . ./When moon's round is finished,/The stars are out of sight." There is a victory in those lines, and it is Fand's. The lyric ends with the splendor of the full moon, Fand's planet, eclipsing lesser lights.[70]

Emer, as she appears in this play, represents what Yeats called "daily circumstance" — the quiet, decent, everyday life of constancy and convention.[71] She is life, but Yeats thought the Irish writer needed something larger than life. "The Irish story teller," he says in his preface to Lady Gregory's *Cuchulain of Muirthemne*, "could not interest himself . . . in the way men like himself burned a house, or won wives no more wonderful than themselves. His mind constantly escaped out of daily circumstance . . . his imagination was always running off to Tir-nan-oge." That, in brief, is the plot of *Emer*: the Ghost of Cuchulain runs off to Fand in Tir-nan-oge. The passage in the preface to *Cuchulain*, one of Yeats's most eloquent statements on the poetic process, goes on to say of the storyteller: "He understands as well as Blake that the ruins of time build mansions in eternity, and he never allows anything, that we can see and handle, to remain long unchanged. . . . A wandering lyric moon must knead and kindle perpetually that moving world." The wandering lyric moon which transforms the world from drabness to beauty is Fand's planet, and the great emotions inhabit her world, according to Yeats: "The Irish stories make one understand why the Greeks call myths the activities of the daemons. The great virtues, the great joys, the great privations come in the myths, and, as it were, take mankind between their naked arms, and without putting off their divinity." The encounter between the daimon and mankind is the one encounter worth going out to meet, in Yeats's view, but it is not to be found without the journey to Tir-nan-oge: it is certainly not to be found by the hearthstone with Emer. The proportions of life are diminished ones beside the proportions of art: "The imagination which remembers the proportions of life is but a long wooing . . . it has to forget them before it becomes the torch and the marriage-bed." [72]

That, briefly put, is the abstraction which lies behind *Emer*. Yeats gives the proportions of life their due, in the pathos associated with Emer, in her self-abnegation, and in her subdued acquiescence at the end, but Fand has the poetry, and consequently the victory. In spite of vacillation and stalemate, both implicit in the play, the Muse receives the final allegiance, as we have come to expect; and Emer, like Septimus in *The Player Queen*, appears in the end touching but superfluous.

3

Three times in his life Yeats wrote about the death of Cuchulain: as early as 1892 his long narrative poem with that title appeared,[73] and almost fifty years later his last play was given the same name; the late poem "Cuchulain Comforted" in a coda to the play and must be considered with it. It is no accident that Cuchulain's death interested Yeats so early, since the death of the epic hero is always, from one point of view, the climax of the saga. George Moore says of Yeats in *Hail and Farewell* that "he had long been dreaming an epic poem to be called 'Cuchulain,' " [74] but Yeats had no epic gift. Climaxes, paradoxical moments, and tragic recognitions formed the substance of his poetry, and the steady flow required of the epic poet would have bored him. So we have the fragmentary Cuchulain plays instead, and of these the most disconnected and jerky is the last. It was still under revision when Yeats died, but the main outlines are clear enough.

The early narrative poem (endlessly worked over) deals with the events retold in *On Baile's Strand*, and so does not concern us here. The death of Cuchulain, as Yeats finally envisages it, brings together all the aspects of his life, symbolized by four women — Emer, Eithne Inguba, Aoife, and the Morrigu. Cuchulain must not die young, as he does in the sagas, but must be Yeats's age (we notice that Aoife has white hair) and the circumstances of his death must be freely invented and symbolic.[75]

That invention is, in fact, the substance of the introduction by the Old Man. Yeats had contemplated an introduction of this sort (to be spoken by Frank Fay's uncle) for *The King's Threshold*,[76] but later discarded it. That speech made the same effort for a commonplace offhand tone that we notice in the prologue to *The Death of Cuchulain*, but like most of Yeats's attempts at a popular touch, failed. We can hope that Yeats might have discarded the Old Man in his last play if he had lived to do more revising, but as it is, we can only say that most of his speech is simply rant, and that the few interesting sentences articulate a perilous dramatic theory — "Where there are no words there is less to spoil." [77] Though Yeats's wishful thinking made the Old Man "the son of Talma" (the celebrated French actor) the play is no more compelling, dramatically speaking, than the other late plays, which is to say almost not at all. I agree with T. R. Henn that the last plays must be read as dramatic poems,[78] as variations on a given mythological theme. The Old Man makes his contempt for "that old maid history" very clear, and I suspect that for Yeats "history" in that sense included mythology taken pedantically. There is absolutely no justification in legend for this parade of women through Cuchulain's death scene, but Yeats was never averse to making up his own legends.

In a way, *The Death of Cuchulain* is the logical outcome of Yeats's efforts toward a corpus of plays for a coterie theater. The Old Man's intemperate speech, with none of the bitter grandeur of Yeats's poetic invective, reaches a shrill

frenzy in its vision of society as "people who are educating
themselves out of the Book Societies and the like, sciolists
all, pickpockets and opinionated bitches." [79] This is giving
up on society altogether — a much more tenable position for
a lyric poet than for a dramatist. Once a dramatist reaches
the point where he thinks that "no wood-carving can look as
well as a parallelogram of painted wood," [80] that the more
abstraction the better, he is no longer talking to an audience:
he is talking to himself. I have no qualms about equating the
Old Man with Yeats, in regard to his theatrical theories at
least, and the hysteria of his speech is precisely the hysteria
of *On the Boiler*. The fact that Yeats recognizes it for what
it is ("If you were as old you would find it easy to get excited") [81] does not make it any less unpalatable on stage.

The contempt for the audience which disfigures the Old
Man's introduction shows up just as strongly in the construction of the play. There is almost no exposition; the Old
Man has already said that the audience is expected to know
"the old epics and Mr. Yeats' plays" [82] — an unfair demand
nowadays, when Yeats is famous, and twenty years ago a
preposterous one. Eithne Inguba comes in speaking of Emer,
Maeve, Emain Macha, and Muirthemne in her first six lines,
with no one to serve the purpose that the Fool and the Blind
Man served in *On Baile's Strand* — to fill in the background
of the story. The action of the first scene is as confused as the
references. We finally gather that Eithne Inguba has been
bewitched by Maeve, Cuchulain's enemy, and for that reason
sends Cuchulain to his death. She still carries in her hand the
letter from his wife, which bids him be safe by delaying to
set out. Cuchulain reads the letter, but disregards it, believing Eithne's summons to come from her desire for a younger
lover:

> All that is written, but I much prefer
> Your own unwritten words. I am for the fight,
> I and my handful are set upon the fight:
> We have faced great odds before.[83]

At this point, the Morrigu, the goddess of war, appears to Eithne. She is the presiding genius over this play, as the Hawk-Woman was over *At the Hawk's Well*; she appears twice, once silently to Eithne, and once later in the play. Although she does not, as we might expect, perform the dance at the end of the play, she sets it in motion, and Emer is in that sense her surrogate, as we shall see. Meanwhile, the quarrel between Cuchulain and Eithne continues, as Eithne says it was Maeve who put her in a trance and caused her to speak the words of treachery. She represents Maeve as a monster:

> Though when Cuchulain slept with her as a boy
> She seemed as pretty as a bird, she has changed,
> She has an eye in the middle of her forehead.[84]

Cuchulain was not Maeve's lover in the legends, but in the play Maeve and Aoife blend into one warrior-woman, once Cuchulain's mistress but now his ultimate destruction. Yeats could not bear that one woman should be Cuchulain's great love and another his destroyer: one must be both. Once again the sagas are tailored to suit Yeats's autobiography, as Maud Gonne, the "stone-pale" Aoife of *On Baile's Strand*, becomes the older Maeve. The quotation I have just cited cannot fail to remind us, I think, of "A Bronze Head":

> Here at right of the entrance this bronze head,
> Human, superhuman, a bird's round eye,
> Everything else withered and mummy-dead.[85]

The mood of "A Bronze Head" has something in common with the tone of the last play, but its bitterness is softened by backward glances toward earlier days. *The Death of Cuchulain* has no such moments of nostalgia. Cuchulain himself, for the first time, seems confused in his allegiances, so that when Eithne asserts her power over him, he retorts that it was Emer who saved him after his battle with the sea. Later, in his scene with Aoife, an earlier bond than his marriage to

Emer claims him, and he cannot be harsh with his former mistress. He cannot be harsh with anyone, it seems; forgiving Eithne's treachery, agreeing with Aoife that she has a right to kill him, and standing passive while the Blind Man beheads him, Cuchulain is unrecognizable as an epic hero. The total impression is not at all that given by the sagas, where Cuchulain's savage anger in battle is the prelude to his death. Here, Cuchulain's indifferent stoicism is the obverse of the Old Man's hysteria: both spring from a conviction of the futility of effort. An epoch is dissolving; the heroic age is coming to an end with the death of Cuchulain as the images of deformity conquer the images of strength and beauty. The Blind Man belongs with the Hunchback, at the end of the cycle, and at this point in the waning of the moon, Cuchulain is nothing more than an anachronism.

Theoretically, when "Hector is dead and there's a light in Troy," we that look on should "laugh in tragic joy." [86] I do not find tragic joy, or indeed joy of any description, permeating the play; weariness and indifference come nearer its note. The peculiar insistence on the change from beauty to monstrosity, from strength to weakness, from love to treachery, comes close to deforming the play. First we have Eithne's reflections on Maeve's aging, quoted earlier; next Eithne's accusation of Cuchulain:

> You're not the man I loved,
> That violent man forgave no treachery.
> If, thinking what you think, you can forgive,
> It is because you are about to die.

Cuchulain, unlike Eithne, believes in the necessity of change:

> . . . Everything sublunary must change,
> And if I have not changed that goes to prove
> That I am monstrous.[87]

But an epic hero does not change, does not weaken, does not grow forgiving. In making Cuchulain his spokesman for the decay of nature, Yeats decides for the inevitability of the

declension into "the base sort now growing up." If Cuchulain
had been a foil for the Old Man — if he had been unvan-
quished, even in death (as he is in the sagas) the closing lyric
of the play would have been given more dramatic value. As
it is, the lyric applies to the sagas, but not so well to the
death of Cuchulain as we see it in Yeats's play.

There are occasional flashes of the old Cuchulain: to a
servant who asks whether Eithne's confession of treachery is
true, Cuchulain answers in a gesture of command, "I make
the truth!" And so he does, in saving Eithne from the consequences of her betrayal: she, being of two minds about him,
both exults in his death and is apprehensive of it. Certain of
his own doom, Cuchulain goes out to battle, and when the
stage lights up again, we see him at the pillar stone, wounded
with "six mortal wounds." Aoife enters, and there is a brief
recapitulation of their meeting at the Hawk's Well and the
birth of their son. When Aoife declares that she has come
to kill Cuchulain in revenge for his having killed their son,
Cuchulain assents, and Aoife adds:

> But I am an old woman now, and that
> Your strength may not start up when the time comes
> I wind my veil about this ancient stone
> And fasten you to it.

Cuchulain, remembering her beauty, answers her:

> But do not spoil your veil.
> Your veils are beautiful, some with threads of gold.[88]

We realize now that Aoife cannot kill Cuchulain, not within
Yeats's terms. She, by Cuchulain's reminiscence, is associated
with all those that wear gold (the Player Queen, the Queen in
A Full Moon in March, Fand, in fact all queens) and as such
can no more harm Cuchulain than could Fand in *The Only
Jealousy of Emer*. Those magical women may have been the
agents of disaster, but they can never be the agents of destructive violence. That mission is reserved for the deformed
inhabitants of "the last leprous crescents of the moon."

At the close of his dialogue with Aoife, Cuchulain sums up the tragedy: "I cannot understand," he says, and I think we must take this to mean he cannot understand everything — his encounter with Aoife and his killing his son; his infidelity to Emer; the treachery of Eithne; the seductiveness of Fand; and finally his predestined death. It is at this point that the Blind Man enters, and reminds us that he was present at the fight with the sea, which was, by its cutting off of Cuchulain's issue, the beginning of the end. Maeve, who was at least partial cause of Eithne's treachery, has suborned the Blind Man to bring Cuchulain's head; she, now grown monstrous (as Cuchulain and Eithne have made clear), is in league with the other forces of deformity. "Twelve pennies!" says Cuchulain ironically, "What better reason for killing a man?" That irony, betraying no surprise, is consistent with Cuchulain's persistent view that the wicked have inherited the earth and are, in fact, the only ones in phase with civilization. "I think that you know everything, Blind Man," Cuchulain adds (and we recall that another of the inhabitants of the end of the cycle, the Fool, would know everything if he were capable of knowing anything; this simply means that his primitive rapport with the inarticulate and brutal system of which he is a part never reaches a conscious level, but is nevertheless real enough). The Blind Man continues his unconsciously malignant misrepresentations of value:

> How could I have got twelve pennies for your head
> If I had not good sense?

After this speech, Cuchulain ceases to talk to his betrayers — Eithne, Aoife, and the Blind Man — and muses to himself:

> There floats out there
> The shape that I shall take when I am dead,
> My soul's first shape, a soft feathery shape,
> And is not that a strange shape for the soul
> Of a great fighting-man? [89]

As the Blind Man kills him, Cuchulain speaks his last words: "I say it is about to sing."

In another play, we might have had a song for the severed head, of the sort we have encountered before, but here Cuchulain does not sing; the ageless Street-Singer sings for him. Before the closing ballad, however, there is a dance, arranged by the Morrigu, but executed, unfortunately enough, by Emer. It is easy to see why Yeats destined Emer for the dance — it is the only way she could be made physically present in the play — but dramatically it is an imposition on the audience, who, unless she is to wear a placard proclaiming her identity, have no means of knowing who the dancer is. It is typical of the play that Emer, who has no magic about her, should have the last word, metaphorically speaking. The time of the Fifteenth Phase has passed, and all the wildness, beauty, and glory symbolized by Aoife, Fand, and even Eithne Inguba, have ceased to have a place in the scene. Emer, the representative, as we have seen, of domesticity and resignation to the routine of life, is the victor here, as she was theoretically in *The Only Jealousy of Emer*. The difference is that in the earlier play the vigor of Fand's claim extinguished Emer's milder light, where in the final play a general pall settles over the stage. The Morrigu operates as an impartial destiny in "arranging" this dance; she has no relation of intimacy with Emer or the other characters.

There is a hint of immortality in the "few faint bird notes" which end the play, but Cuchulain's true immortality lies in the poetry of a later age. The song of the Street-Singer is peculiarly dissociated from the action of the play (unlike the songs of the earlier plays which are integral to the action). The burden of the song is that the decline and degradation of the heroic age are somehow avenged by the poetry that is made out of that defeat: that the Fifteenth Phase catches up and transforms the "blood-dimmed tide" of the final phases. There are syntactical difficulties in the song, and we are justified, I am sure, in assuming with Wilson [90] that Yeats would have corrected it in revision, but we must deal with it as it stands. The point of the song, as I see it, is a question: Of what use are the images of the imagination, of which Cuchulain is one? We have seen him die in indifferent and weary exhaustion; we have seen the Blind Man and his monstrous associates become the rulers, by force and cunning; only the memory of Cuchulain's heroic exploits is left. Against that exalted memory, preserved only in snatches of folk poetry, we set all the ordinary demands and attractions of daily life, the things we can encounter in the flesh, those realities which at times seem the only satisfactions, unsatisfactory though they are. The Harlot in the song compares spirit lovers to physical lovers, raising once again the question that tormented the Lady in "The Three Bushes." The Lady, as we recall, sang,

> I am in love
> And that is my shame.
> What hurts the soul
> My soul adores,
> No better than a beast
> Upon all fours.[91]

She both adores and loathes the fact of physical union, and this is the condition of earthly love, as Yeats so often insisted. The Harlot knows this:

> . . . The flesh my flesh has gripped
> I both adore and loathe.

On the other hand, physical love is not the only sort of love. There are the unattainable spirit lovers, the heroic images, of whom the Harlot says,

> I adore those clever eyes,
> Those muscular bodies, but can get
> No grip upon their thighs.[92]

So, to put things for a moment in a schematic form, we may

say that "love" is divisible into two sorts: the pure adoration directed toward the images who remain perpetually elusive, unable to be gripped in physical embrace; and the mixed adoration-and-loathing directed toward the physical lovers who can be immediately apprehended. We are tempted to dismiss the images as an illusion, and the Harlot poses the central question of the song in the two lines,

> Are those things that men adore and loathe
> Their sole reality?

If the answer were yes, then Cuchulain is superfluous; if we can find all reality in the graspable present, we have no need for tradition, for the past embodied in poetic and mythological images. But the Harlot answers her own question in the negative, not by a blank denial, but by another question:

> What stood in the Post Office
> With Pearse and Connolly? [93]

The answer is of course that the thought of Cuchulain, the heroic and imitable ideal, was what engendered the courage of the Easter Rebellion. Historically, this is debatable, but the core of Yeats's answer is a true one: that "resemblances and the repetitions of resemblances are a source of the ideal," as Wallace Stevens has put it. The two questions following demand similar answers. The thought of the hero can summon up an image which so informs the soul that "it seemed / He stood where they had stood." [94]

If the song ended there, I would be more willing to grant the presence of "tragic joy": but much as Yeats admired the heroes of 1916, his pessimistic view of his own time refused to let him call Pearse and Connolly the Cuchulains of his epoch.

> No body like his body
> Has modern woman borne,
> But an old man looking on life
> Imagines it in scorn. [95]

The Old Man of the Prologue makes a shadowy reappearance
here, and it is his mood of bitterness that closes the poem. In
spite of honor and exploits, courage and battles, the twentieth
century cannot equal the heroic period. Poetry and imagination in our age must take their inspiration from the ancient
images, from the statue of Cuchulain by Oliver Sheppard
in the Dublin Post Office and, we presume, from the resurrection of the ancient stories accomplished by Yeats's poetry
and plays.

The only detailed commentary on this play has been done
by Wilson, and although he is burdened by his usual apparatus
of neo-Platonic and theological interpretation, his pages on
the image of the harlot in Yeats's poetry and plays are among
the best in his book.[96] But when he comes to the final lyric,
he proposes that it is the images, and not human lovers, which
are both adored and loathed, a view which destroys the
contrast the lyric sets out to make, and which the play implicitly embodies.

This is probably the place to make clear the statement
about the imagination which I believe the play makes. It is
of course a play about human death (a subject necessarily in
Yeats's mind at the writing) but I think the Street-Singer's
song, with its concern for the interaction between mind and
image, justifies us in reading the same concern into the play.
Cuchulain, as usual, is a figure for Yeats, and the defections
of Eithne Inguba, Aoife, Maeve, and even the Morrigu represent, I think, another version of the circus animals' desertion.[97]

> And when the Fool and Blind Man stole the bread
> Cuchulain fought the ungovernable sea;
> Heart-mysteries there, and yet when all is said
> It was the dream itself enchanted me:
> Character isolated by a deed
> To engross the present and dominate memory.
> Players and painted stage took all my love,
> And not those things that they were emblems of.

> Those masterful images because complete
> Grew in pure mind, but out of what began?
> A mound of refuse or the sweepings of a street,
> Old kettles, old bottles, and a broken can,
> Old iron, old bones, old rags, that raving slut
> Who keeps the till. Now that my ladder's gone,
> I must lie down where all the ladders start,
> In the foul rag-and-bone shop of the heart.[98]

Those old images with their power to bind and enchant —
the goddess, the tyrannical woman, the mistress, the beloved
— one by one desert Cuchulain, leaving only Emer. Yeats,
like Cuchulain, is alone and "must be satisfied with [his]
heart," [99] symbolized here by his wife. The images have
ceased to be their own reward, and the only present consolation is in the thought of the perennial youth of imaginative
creation. Just as Cuchulain's only thought at the moment
of death is of the song that his soul will sing in the afterlife,
Yeats's only thought is of the survival of his images in the
poetry of the streets. If poetry, poets, and the poetic process
are indeed destroyed by the barbaric and deformed civilization of which Yeats felt himself to be a member, something
will survive underground, in the obscure memory of the
common people, to arise in a more receptive time. However
the world may deceive itself into self-sufficiency, at some
point it must realize, like the Harlot, that the Sidhe and all
they represent are necessary to existence.

I do not share Wilson's admiration for the play; for me its
obscurity and confusion heavily counterweigh its occasional
"authentic cadence." I prefer to consider the play a rough
draft, and to read it as a tentative final statement rather than
as a finished piece of work. The same cannot be said of the
poem that Yeats called a sequel to the play, "Cuchulain Comforted." A polished exercise in *terza rima*, it represents Cuchulain's arrival in the otherworld after his death. Though Wilson
would place Cuchulain among Dante's negligent rulers,[100]

I cannot see that any precise location in the Inferno is justified from the poem, in spite of its Dantean reminiscences.
Wilson regards Cuchulain as a spiritual failure, as I have mentioned before in regard to *At the Hawk's Well*, but that seems
to me inconsistent with Yeats's admiration for the heroic
mask. We are not to see Cuchulain's purgatory as a punishment for his wars and battles, but rather as a complement
to them.

To understand the poem we must see with what attitude
Yeats finally dismissed his hero, and the place to begin is at
the end. Wilson rightly says that the conclusion of the prose
draft of the poem has a Dantean inflection, and later mentions
the allusion to *Inferno XV* in the threading of needles,[101] but
he does not combine the two in order to determine the precise
passage in Dante to which the end of the draft bears a resemblance: "Then they [the Shrouds] began to sing, and they
did not sing like men and women, but like linnets that had been
stood on a perch and taught by a good singing master." [102]
The syntactic resemblance is to the close of *Inferno XV*,
when Dante must bid farewell to Brunetto Latini:

> Poi si rivolse, e parve di coloro
>   che corrono a Verona il drappo verde
>   per la campagna; e parve di costoro
> quegli che vince e non colui che perde.

There is the same finality of approval in both passages, I find,
expressed in the "not like . . . but like" turn of phrase. The
approval has been mitigated in the final version of the poem,
which reads, "They had changed their throats and had the
throats of birds." [103] But we should not forget the original
impulse in looking at the finished product, nor should we overlook the glance back to "Sailing to Byzantium," to the bird
that was

> Set upon a golden bough to sing
> To lords and ladies of Byzantium
> Of what is past, or passing, or to come.[104]

There is a kinship, at least, between the linnets and the
golden nightingale.

We may now return to the poem itself, which is an unset-
tling one in all respects. It is called "Cuchulain Comforted"
and we might think of things which had comforted Cuchulain in the past: the joy of battle, the love of women, pride
in his son, independence, and sovereignty. What comforts
him in the poem is none of these, but rather the communal
and timid sewing of a shroud. The antithesis is clear enough,
but by it we are made to realize that this purgatory is very
different from the otherworld in which Cuchulain moved
during his bewitchment by Fand. That bewitchment corre-
sponded to the *Meditation* (containing the Dreaming Back,
the Return, and the Phantasmagoria) described in *A Vision*;
this purgatory rather corresponds to the *Shiftings*. I give
again the passage I quoted in Chapter III:

> At the end of the *Return* . . . the *Spirit* is freed from pleasure
> and pain and is ready to enter the *Shiftings* where it is freed from
> Good and Evil, and in this state which is a state of intellect, it lives
> through a life which is said to be in all things opposite to that lived
> through in the world, and dreamed through in the *Return* . . . This
> is brought about by no external law but by a craving in the *Principles*
> to know what life has hidden, that the *Daimon* who knows intellect
> but not good and evil, may be satisfied . . . All now is intellect and
> he [the man] is all *Daimon*, and tragic and happy circumstance alike
> offer an intellectual ecstasy at the revelation of truth, and the most
> horrible tragedy in the end can but seem a figure in a dance.[105]

Yeats adds, we recall, that in the *Shiftings* the soul is brought
"to quiescence," and this is what comforts Cuchulain. I give
the poem before proceeding any further:

> A man that had six mortal wounds, a man
> Violent and famous, strode among the dead;
> Eyes stared out of the branches and were gone,
>
> Then certain Shrouds that muttered head to head
> Came and were gone. He leant upon a tree
> As though no meditate on wounds and blood.

A Shroud that seemed to have authority
Among those bird-like things came, and let fall
A bundle of linen. Shrouds by two and three

Came creeping up because the man was still.
And thereupon that linen-carrier said:
'Your life can grow much sweeter if you will

'Obey our ancient rule and make a shroud;
Mainly because of what we only know
The rattle of those arms makes us afraid.

'We thread the needles' eyes, and all we do
All must together do.' That done, the man
Took up the nearest and began to sew.

'Now must we sing and sing the best we can,
But first you must be told our character:
Convicted cowards all, by kindred slain

'Or driven from home and left to die in fear.'
They sang, but had nor human tunes nor words,
Though all was done in common as before;

They had changed their throats and had the throats of birds.[106]

It is necessary to realize that the Shrouds are not in the same purgatorial state as Cuchulain. He is learning what cowardice is like by being placed among cowards, and is therefore undergoing the *Shiftings*, while they are probably still in some stage of the *Meditation*, not yet having cast off entirely what they were in life. I do not think that they are "pure souls who have escaped from the round of birth and death," as Wilson would have it; [107] they are far too timid, mindful of their former life, and submerged in common activity to be freed spirits. Nor do they yet sing with the effortlessness of the golden nightingale, but must "sing the best [they] can." Yet they have a lesson to teach Cuchulain, paralleling the lesson that the dice-throwers teach in their dance at the end of *Calvary* — that one must watch one form of life succeed another with detachment, like the three old men in "Lapis Lazuli." That is the only comfort to be found for tragedy, and Yeats insists on it:

> All things fall and are built again,
> And those that build them again are gay.[108]

The thought was in Yeats's mind at the time he wrote "Cuchulain Comforted" and it completes his tragedy of Cuchulain if we are to believe his words in *On the Boiler*: "The arts are all the bridal chambers of joy. No tragedy is legitimate unless it leads some great character to his final joy." [109]

Cuchulain himself was hardly led to his final joy in *The Death of Cuchulain*, except in his momentary vision of his soul. The poem incarnates that vision, but in an odd way, and I think we are right to be discomfited by such an end for Cuchulain. It leaves him suspended in the otherworld among his opposites, participating in a life which reminds us uncomfortably of the Christian life in *Calvary*: timid, resigned, communal, obedient. There is no suggestion of the resurgence of the hero after such discipline; the poem is almost an abdication of the heroic life in favor of the mild and persuasive placidity of the Shrouds. I do not agree with Mrs. Bjersby that Yeats "is Cuchulain linen-shrouded, and his comfort is that in spite of all — even though he might be counted among the crowd of cowards — he may look upon himself as a hero of the spiritual intellect." [110] There is no hint of such heroism in the poem.

We must realize that the death of Cuchulain symbolized for Yeats roughly what the death of Christ symbolized for Christians. Cuchulain is the antithetical man, and his death is the end of an antithetical age. Another age, whose tutelary spirits will be not unlike the Shrouds, will follow, and with that primary age Yeats is profoundly out of sympathy, for all his attempts at detachment. "Cuchulain Comforted" is a poem of intellectual consolation at change, telling us that a dead end has been reached, and any further development of the image of Cuchulain along previous lines will be fruitless. He must be buried for the time being, change his shape, undergo a purgatorial transformation, and then be resurrected. We are meant to find it a good sign that when we last see Cuchulain he is in Purgatory, since it guarantees his rebirth. This may sound like whistling in the dark, and in part, judging from the apathy of the last play, I think it was. Yeats's real consolation comes, not in picturing the interim between heroic ages, but in imagining their resurrection:

> Conduct and work grow coarse, and coarse the soul,
> What matter? Those that Rocky Face holds dear,
> Lovers of horses and of women, shall,
> From marble of a broken sepulchre,
> Or dark betwixt the polecat and the owl,
> Or any rich, dark nothing disinter
> The workman, noble and saint, and all things run
> On that unfashionable gyre again.[111]

The mood is the same as that of the closing lyric in *The Death of Cuchulain*, and has a vigor we do not find in "Cuchulain Comforted." The perennial vitality of a heroic mythology when informed by a poetic mind was the basis of Yeats's hope, and reminding himself that a fallow period was a necessity did not calm his impatience. The final image of Cuchulain that we receive may not be the conclusion we could have wished for the saga, but as the affirmation of a literary creed it makes a satisfactory last testament.

Conclusion

"**P**ERSONALLY I think your philosophy smells of the fagot . . . All these gyres and cones and wheels are parts of a machine that was thrown on the scrap-heap when Ptolemy died. It won't go. There is no petrol for such." [1] So one friend told Yeats, and the critics have, more politely, agreed with him. Even A.E., sympathetic as he was to esoteric literature, had "a growl about the *Vision*," and confessed a desire to rewrite it, "leaving out almost all that overprecise movement of his cycles." [2] This condemnation of Yeats's system has generally been extended to the late plays as well.

But these works to which Yeats gave so many years are worth reading, it seems to me, on several grounds. The post-1917 poetry is made clearer, Yeats's characteristic thought processes emerge, his symbols are further defined. Both *A Vision* and the plays have intrinsic worth too. They contain splendid pages, and they incarnate Yeats's poetics. Yeats writes repeatedly of the growth of the poet's mind, and would even agree at times with Wallace Stevens that "Poetry is the subject of the poem"; but while Stevens is concerned with the constructive power of the imagination, Yeats is obsessed by the nature of poetic inspiration — not its definition, but rather its workings in the poetic mind. In *A Vision*, as we have seen, Yeats traces the waxing and waning of inspiration in the individual life and in the life of history, while describing the types of mind receptive to that inspiration. He continues by describing inspiration in its unconscious sources as well as in its conscious labors, gives an exposition of the state of the mind being purified in order to create, and finally invokes historical symbols to convey his sense of the power and order of the creative act.

The plays take up the primary questions posed by *A Vision*: how do we account for the perpetual vigor of the imagination, and how should we react in the presence of an obsolete poetic tradition? In *The Player Queen*, we are counseled to cast the old tradition aside, without regret, and accept whatever bizarre inspiration the new dispensation may provide. The Dance Plays insist on the mutual subjugation of poet and Muse, and the mixed nature of all art. The "religious plays," *Calvary* and *The Resurrection*, show that the symbols which are the vehicles of inspiration lose their validity with time, and must be discarded in favor of a new revelation, which is generally the direct opposite of the preceding gospel. In the purgatorial plays, Yeats is concerned with the process whereby experience is "abstracted" from its context in life and made suitable for art; and finally, in the Cuchulain plays, Yeats shows us the conflicting claims laid by life and Muse upon the artist.

Yeats has come a long way in these plays from George Moore's description of his theatre as "a little mist, some fairies, and a psaltery." [3] It is nevertheless true, as Donald Pearce has said, that "one may indeed see in the symbolic Rose of the Nineties the nucleus of *A Vision*": [4] there has been no fundamental change needed to produce the strange work of Yeats's last period. The most vivid criticism of *A Vision* and the late plays comes from I. A. Richards, and I quote it here because it sums up the commonly accepted view of these works:

After a drawn battle with the drama, Mr. Yeats made a violent repudiation, not merely of current civilisation but of life itself, in favour of a supernatural world. But the world of the 'eternal moods,' of supernal essences and immortal beings is not, like the Irish peasant stories and the Irish landscape, part of his natural and familiar experience. Now he turns to a world of symbolic phantasmagoria about which he is desperately uncertain. He is uncertain because he had adopted as a technique of inspiration the use of trance, of dissociated phases of consciousness, and the revelations given in these dissociated states are insufficiently connected with normal experience.[5]

This neat separation of Yeats's work into good and bad is not true to fact. The late poems certainly do not repudiate life itself, and the constant message of the plays is of the necessary connection between the "supernatural" and the gross raw material of life. It is a surprise to find so Platonic a critic as Mr. Richards saying that the world of the eternal moods was not part of Yeats's natural and familiar experience. The ideas in *A Vision* are jumbled, it is true, and hampered by Yeats's attempts at "scientific" exposition, but it is not so certain that they are "insufficiently connected with normal experience." It has been my aim to show that they *are* symbolic statements about normal experience (insofar as Yeats's experience, as a poet, can be called normal), and that in any case, they are intelligible statements about the poetic process, the poetic mind, and the poetic product. As such, they deserve sympathetic reading and consideration, not dismissal out of hand. Looked at in this light, *A Vision* and the late plays provide a poetics which is rarely available elsewhere in Yeats's work.

Works Cited

Adams, Hazard. *Blake and Yeats: The Contrary Vision*. Ithaca, New York, 1955.

Becker, William. "The Mask Mocked: Or, Farce and the Dialectic of Self (Notes on Yeats's *The Player Queen*)," *Sewanee Review*, 61:82–108 (Winter 1953).

Bjersby, Birgit. *The Interpretation of the Cuchulain Legend in the Works of W. B. Yeats*. Upsala, 1950.

Blackmur, R. P. *The Expense of Greatness*. New York, 1940.

Blake, William. *Complete Writings*, ed. Geoffrey Keynes. London, 1957.

Brooks, Cleanth. "Yeats: The Poet as Myth Maker," in *The Permanence of Yeats*, ed. James Hall and Martin Steinmann. New York, 1950, pp. 85–92.

Coleridge, Samuel Taylor. *Biographia Literaria*, ed. J. Shawcross. Oxford, 1907. vol. I.

Cross, Tom Peete, and Clark Harris Slover, eds. *Ancient Irish Tales*. New York, 1936.

de Man, Paul. Unpublished notes on early drafts of W. B. Yeats's *The Player Queen*.

Eliot, T. S. *After Strange Gods*. New York, 1934.

——— "The Poetry of W. B. Yeats," in *The Permanence of Yeats*, ed. James Hall and Martin Steinmann. New York, 1950.

Ellmann, Richard. *The Identity of Yeats*. New York, 1954.

——— *Yeats, the Man and the Masks*. London, 1949.

Frost, Robert. *Complete Poems*. New York, 1949.

Gogarty, Oliver St. John. *It Isn't This Time of Year at All!* New York, 1954.

Graves, Robert. *Collected Poems, 1959*. London, 1958.

Gregory, Lady. *Cuchulain of Muirthemne*. London, 1902.

Hall, James, and Martin Steinmann, eds. *The Permanence of Yeats*. New York, 1950.

Heath-Stubbs, John. *The Darkling Plain*. London, 1950.

Henn, T. R. *The Lonely Tower*. London, 1950.

Hone, Joseph. *W. B. Yeats, 1865–1939*. New York, 1943.

Hopkins, Gerard Manley. *Poems*. New York and London, 1948.

Jeffares, A. Norman. *W. B. Yeats, Man and Poet*. New Haven, Conn., 1949.

Keats, John. *Complete Poetical Works*, ed. H. Buxton Forman. Oxford Standard Edition, New York, undated.

Lowell, Robert. *Poems, 1938–1949*. London, 1950.

Moore, George. *Hail and Farewell*. New York, 1914. 3 vols.

Moore, John Rees. "Evolution of Myth in the Plays of W. B. Yeats." Unpublished dissertation, Columbia University, 1957.

Newman, John Henry. *Discussions and Arguments on Various Subjects*. London, 1888.

Newton, Norman. "Yeats as Dramatist: *The Player Queen*," *Essays in Criticism*, 8:269–284 (July 1958).

O'Grady, Standish. *Selected Essays and Passages*. Dublin, undated.

Pater, Walter H. *Studies in the History of the Renaissance*. London, 1873.

Pearce, Donald. "Philosophy and Phantasy: Notes on the Growth of Yeats's 'System,'" *University of Kansas City Review*, 18:169–180 (Spring 1952).

———— "Yeats's Last Plays: An Interpretation," *ELH*, 18:67–76 (March 1951).

Poe, Edgar Allan. *Complete Tales and Poems*. Modern Library Edition, New York, 1938.

Rilke, Rainer Maria. *Gedichte*. Leipzig, 1927. vol. II.

Robinson, Henry Crabb. *Diary, Reminiscences, and Correspondence*. Selected and edited by Thomas Sadler. 2 vols. Boston, 1869.

Russell, George (A.E.). *The Living Torch*, ed. Monk Gibbon. London, 1937.

Saul, George Brandon. *Prolegomena to the Study of Yeats's Plays*. Philadelphia, 1958.

Seiden, Morton Irving. "William Butler Yeats: His Poetry and His Vision, 1914–1939." Unpublished dissertation, Columbia University, 1952 (date of microfilming; dissertation undated).

Shelley, Percy Bysshe. *Complete Poetical Works*, ed. George Edward Woodberry. Cambridge Edition, Boston, 1901.

Spitzer, Leo. "On Yeats's Poem, Leda and the Swan," *Modern Philology*, 51:271–276 (May 1954).

Stevens, Wallace. *Collected Poems*. New York, 1955.

—— *The Necessary Angel*. New York, 1951.

—— *Opus Posthumous*. New York, 1957.

Tillyard, E. M. W. *Poetry, Direct and Oblique*. London, 1948.

Trowbridge, Hoyt. "Leda and the Swan: a Longinian Analysis," *Modern Philology*, 51:118–129 (November 1953).

Ure, Peter. *Towards a Mythology*. London, 1946.

—— "Yeats's Christian Mystery Plays," *Review of English Studies*, New Series, 11:171–182 (May 1960).

Valéry, Paul. *Selected Writings*. New York, 1950.

Virgil, *Eclogues, Georgics, Aeneid 1–6*. Loeb Classical Library, Cambridge, Mass., 1932.

Wilson, F. A. C. *W. B. Yeats and Tradition*. New York, 1958.

—— *Yeats's Iconography*. New York, 1960.

Wordsworth, William. *The Poetical Works*, ed. Thomas Hutchinson. Oxford Standard Edition, New York, 1933.

Yeats, J. B. *Letters to His Son W. B. Yeats and Others, 1869–1922*, ed. Joseph Hone. London, 1944.

—— *Passages from the Letters*, selected by Ezra Pound. Dundrum, Ireland, 1917.

Yeats, W. B. *Autobiographies*. New York, 1953.

—— *The Cat and the Moon and Certain Poems*. Dublin, 1924.

—— *Collected Plays*. New York, 1953.

—— *Collected Poems*. New York, 1956.

—— *Correspondence with T. Sturge Moore, 1901–1937*, ed. Ursula Bridge. New York, 1953.

—— *The Cutting of An Agate*. New York, 1912.

—— *Essays, 1931–1936*. Dublin, 1937.

—— *Four Plays for Dancers*. New York, 1921.

—— *A Full Moon in March*. London, 1935.

—— *Ideas of Good and Evil*. London, 1907.

—— *Irish Fairy and Folk Tales*. Modern Library Edition, New York, undated.

—— *The King's Threshold*. MS Collection, Houghton Library, Harvard University (MS Eng 338.3).

—— *Letters*, ed. Allan Wade. New York, 1955.

—— *Letters on Poetry to Dorothy Wellesley*, New York, 1940.

—— *Letters to the New Island*, ed. Horace Reynolds. Cambridge, Mass., 1934.

Yeats, W. B. *Mythologies*. London, 1959.

——— *On the Boiler*. Dublin, 1939.

——— *On the Road to Calvary*. MS Collection, Houghton Library, Harvard University (MS Eng 338.8).

——— *The Only Jealousy of Emer*. MS Collection, Houghton Library, Harvard University (MS Eng 338.7).

——— *Per Amica Silentia Lunae*. New York, 1918.

——— *The Player Queen* in *The Dial*, 73:486–506 (November 1922).

——— *Plays in Prose and Verse*. London, 1922.

——— "Preface" to Lady Gregory's *Cuchulain of Muirthemne*. London, 1902, pp. vii–xvii.

——— *The Secret Rose*. London, 1897.

——— "Swedenborg, Mediums, and the Desolate Places," in Lady Gregory's *Visions and Beliefs in the West of Ireland*. New York and London, 1920, vol. II, pp. 295–339.

——— *Two Plays for Dancers*. Dundrum, Ireland, 1919.

——— *The Variorum Edition of the Poems*, ed. Peter Allt and Russell K. Alspach. New York, 1957.

——— *A Vision: An Explanation of Life Founded upon the Writings of Giraldus and upon Certain Doctrines Attributed to Kusta Ben Luka*. London, 1925.

——— *A Vision*. New York, 1956.

——— *Wheels and Butterflies*. New York, 1935.

——— ed., *The Poems of William Blake*. Modern Library Edition, New York, undated.

——— ed., with Edwin John Ellis. *The Works of William Blake*. London, 1893. 3 vols.

Notes

Introduction

1. See "William Blake and His Illustrations to 'The Divine Comedy'" and "Symbolism in Painting" in *Ideas of Good and Evil* (London, 1907), pp. 176, 227.

2. William Blake, "A Vision of the Last Judgment" in *Complete Writings*, ed. Geoffrey Keynes (London, 1957), p. 604. Hereafter cited as *Writings*.

3. W. B. Yeats, *A Vision* (New York, 1956), p. 5. Hereafter cited as *Vision*, B.

4. Blake, "A Vision of the Last Judgment," *Writings*, p. 617.

5. *Vision*, B, pp. 24–25.

6. Blake, "A Vision of the Last Judgment," *Writings*, p. 611.

7. "Symbolism in Painting" in *Ideas of Good and Evil*, p. 234.

8. *Vision*, B, p. 8.

9. J. B. Yeats, *Passages from the Letters*, selected by Ezra Pound (Cuala Press, Dundrum, Ireland, 1917), pp. 19–20.

10. W. B. Yeats, *Letters*, ed. Allan Wade (New York, 1955), p. 606. Hereafter cited as *Letters*.

11. *Vision*, B, pp. 12, 20, 22.

12. *Ibid.*, pp. 23, 24.

13. *Ibid.*, p. 24.

14. Mr. R. P. Blackmur, in what is clearly the best brief comment on Yeats's system, has warned against this sort of translation; but his particular concern has been with reading Yeats's poetry and "keeping judgment in poetic terms." ("The Later Poetry of W. B. Yeats," in *The Expense of Greatness*, New York, 1940, p. 96.) *A Vision*, in its own terms, has been so consistently misread that a process of translation seems the only solution. The translation should not be allowed to oversimplify poems, of course.

Chapter I. The Great Wheel.

1. *Vision*, B, p. 73.

2. Although Yeats used italics to describe many aspects of his

system, I think there is nothing to be gained by keeping them, and so I drop them except when they become necessary for reasons of clarity, for example in dealing with Book III.

3. *Vision*, B, pp. 73–74.

4. *Ibid.*, p. 81.

5. *Ibid.*, p. 82.

6. William Butler Yeats, *A Vision: An Explanation of Life Founded upon the Writings of Giraldus and upon Certain Doctrines Attributed to Kusta Ben Luka* (London, 1925), p. xi. Hereafter cited as *Vision*, A.

7. *Vision*, B, p. 83.

8. My basic text in discussing *A Vision* has been the second, and commonly available, edition. However, from time to time I will quote the first edition when its formulation is clearer or when it helps to support the point at issue. Although there are differences between the two editions, they are clearly not so great as to forbid this sort of auxiliary function for the first edition. I see no startling "evolution" in Yeats's thought which would make free quotation across several years fundamentally inaccurate. His ideas changed, but not drastically. The second edition moves toward greater precision and, at the same time, greater sophistication. Sometimes, however, precision becomes verbiage and sophistication becomes mystification; at those times I resort to the more primitive version.

9. *Vision*, A, pp. 14–15.

10. *Vision*, B, p. 83.

11. W. B. Yeats, *Per Amica Silentia Lunae* (New York, 1918), pp. 84, 86. Hereafter cited as *Per Amica*.

12. *Ibid.*, pp. 29, 54.

13. *Ibid.*, p. 39.

14. *Vision*, A, pp. 27–28.

15. *Vision*, B, pp. 83–84.

16. Wallace Stevens, *Collected Poems* (New York, 1955), p. 497.

17. *Per Amica*, p. 47.

18. *Vision*, B, p. 85.

19. *Vision*, A, p. 14.

20. *Letters*, pp. 626–627.

21. Donald Pearce, "Philosophy and Phantasy: Notes on the Growth of Yeats's 'System,'" *University of Kansas City Review*, 18:177 (Spring 1952).

22. *Letters*, p. 625.

23. Edgar Allan Poe, "Sonnet — To Science." The poem is the classic statement of the romantic poet to science.

24. W. B. Yeats, *Autobiographies* (New York, 1953), pp. 70–71. Hereafter cited as *Autobiographies*.

25. *Letters*, p. 916. For an unpublished summation by Yeats of

his "private philosophy," see also Hazard Adams, *Blake and Yeats: The Contrary Vision* (Ithaca, New York, 1955), pp. 287–288.

26. *Letters*, p. 887.

27. *Autobiographies*, p. 93.

28. *Ibid.*, p. 116.

29. *Letters*, pp. 888–889.

30. *Ibid.*, pp. 210–211.

31. "The Philosophy of Shelley's Poetry" in *Ideas of Good and Evil*, p. 91. Yeats's father argued for a loose, rather than strict, linkage between poets and systems. See J. B. Yeats, *Letters to His Son W. B. Yeats and Others, 1869–1922*, ed. Joseph Hone (London, 1944), pp. 220–221.

32. It was probably similar to his father's. The more one reads J. B. Yeats, the more one realizes how totally his son assimilated his ideas.

33. "The Philosophy of Shelley's Poetry" in *Ideas of Good and Evil*, pp. 127–128.

34. *Ibid.*, p. 90. Cf. Wallace Stevens, "Two or Three Ideas," in *Opus Posthumous* (New York, 1957), p. 208: "The great and true priest of Apollo was he that composed the most moving of Apollo's hymns."

35. "Magic" in *Ideas of Good and Evil*, p. 64.

36. *Ibid.*, pp. 68–69.

37. *Letters*, p. 781.

38. John Henry Newman, "The Tamworth Reading Room," in *Discussions and Arguments on Various Subjects* (London, 1888), p. 293.

39. *Vision*, A, p. xii.

40. Paul Valéry, "On Poe's *Eureka*," in *Selected Writings* (New York, 1950), p. 123.

41. W. B. Yeats, *Collected Poems* (New York, 1956), p. 162. Hereafter cited as *Collected Poems*.

42. "Poetry and Tradition" in *The Cutting of an Agate* (New York, 1912), p. 130.

43. *Collected Poems*, p. 162.

44. *Vision*, B, p. 135.

45. *Ibid.*

46. *Ibid.*

47. *Collected Poems*, p. 175.

48. *Vision*, B, p. 136.

49. W. B. Yeats, *Letters on Poetry to Dorothy Wellesley* (New York, 1940), 192. Hereafter cited as *Letters to Dorothy Wellesley*. See also A. Norman Jeffares, *W. B. Yeats, Man and Poet* (New Haven, Conn., 1949), p. 267.

50. *Vision*, B, p. 136.

51. *Ibid.*, pp. 187, 189.
52. *Ibid.*, p. 125.
53. *Per Amica*, pp. 33–34, 46.
54. *Ibid.*, p. 91.
55. *Collected Poems*, p. 246.
56. *Vision*, B, pp. 106, 107.
57. *Ibid.*, pp. 108–109. Professor John V. Kelleher has pointed out to me the similarity of this scene to some of Calvert's paintings; Yeats said of Edward Calvert in "Under Ben Bulben" that he, like the other religious romantic painters, "prepared a rest for the people of God." (*Collected Poems*, p. 343.)
58. *Vision*, B, pp. 110, 113.
59. *Ibid.*, pp. 114, 116.
60. *Ibid.*, p. 125.
61. *Ibid.*, p. 134.
62. *Collected Poems*, p. 236.
63. *Vision*, B, pp. 129, 130.
64. *Ibid.*, pp. 132, 134.
65. *Ibid.*, p. 132.
66. *Ibid.*, pp. 132, 133, 182, 135. The phrase "expressionless, expresses God" is Robert Lowell's.
67. W. B. Yeats, *Irish Fairy and Folk Tales*, Modern Library Edition (New York, undated), p. 156; *Vision*, B, pp. 133, 137.
68. *Vision*, B, pp. 139–140.
69. *Ibid.*, pp. 138–139.
70. "Behold me well: indeed I am, I am Beatrice."
71. *Ibid.*, pp. 141, 142.
72. Cf. Valéry, "Literature" in *Selected Writings*, p. 147: "In the poet . . . it is the lack and the blank that create."
73. *Vision*, B, pp. 144–145.
74. *Ibid.*, p. 144. According to the first edition of *A Vision* (p. 29) those idealists who hope for a "final conquest" see only the Vision of Good; those who are content to struggle with no final conquest, who can love tragedy, have not only the Vision of Good but also that of Evil.
75. *Vision*, B, p. 147.
76. *Ibid.*, p. 151.
77. *Ibid.*, p. 154.
78. *Ibid.*, pp. 164, 165.
79. *Ibid.*, pp. 167, 168, 169, 167.
80. *Ibid.*, pp. 177, 180.
81. *Letters*, p. 825.
82. *Collected Poems*, p. 286.
83. *Letters*, p. 826. See also *Vision*, B, p. 100, "Four Contests."
84. *Vision*, A, p. 141.

85. *Collected Poems*, p. 164.
86. *Ibid.*, p. 165.
87. *Ibid.*, p. 163.
88. *Vision*, B, p. 182.
89. *Ibid.*, pp. 178, 179, 181.

Chapter II. The Completed Symbol.

1. *Vision*, B, p. 207.
2. *Ibid.*, pp. 189n, 212, 213, 262.
3. *Ibid.*, p. 189n.
4. Blake, *Writings*, p. 426.
5. *Vision*, A, pp. 134, 139.
6. Blake, *Writings*, p. 426.
7. *Ibid.*, pp. 426–427.
8. W. B. Yeats, ed., *Irish Fairy and Folk Tales*, pp. 86, 156.
9. *Vision*, B, p. 262.
10. *Ibid.*, p. 187.
11. *Ibid.*, p. 188.
12. *Ibid.*, p. 187n.
13. *Ibid.*, pp. 191–192.
14. *Ibid.*, p. 189.
15. *Ibid.*; *Collected Poems*, p. 242.
16. *Collected Poems*, p. 192.
17. W. B. Yeats, *Letters to the New Island*, ed. Horace Reynolds (Cambridge, Mass., 1934), p. 94.
18. Blake, Letter to George Cumberland, 12 April 1827, in *Writings*, p. 878.
19. *Autobiographies*, p. 329.
20. Stevens, *Poems*, p. 15.
21. *Vision*, B, p. 189.
22. Blake, *Writings*, pp. 425, 427.
23. *Vision*, B, p. 189.
24. John Keats, "Lamia," Part II, ll. 234–237.
25. *Vision*, B, pp. 209, 189.
26. Gerard Manley Hopkins, "As kingfishers catch fire," ll. 1–8.
27. Stevens, *Poems*, p. 441.
28. *Vision*, B, pp. 192–194.
29. *Ibid.*, p. 195.
30. *Collected Poems*, p. 210.
31. *Vision*, B, p. 202.
32. *Ibid.*, pp. 196, 203–204.
33. I draw here on Book V, *passim*.
34. See *Vision*, B, p. 204, for Yeats's view that the classical era lasted from 1000 B.C. to A.D. 1000.
35. *Ibid.*, p. 268. This makes for a total of three thousand years

between the divine impregnation (2000 B.C.) and the end of the
era which that event occasions, in this case, the classical era ending in
A.D. 1000. So thirty centuries elapse between the birth and the
collapse, although only twenty centuries elapse between "divine"
incarnations (as Christ appears in A.D. 1, and the Rough Beast in A.D.
2000). Perhaps this confusion explains Yeats's hesitation over the
time span in "The Second Coming": the first printed version in
The Dial (November 1920) reads "thirty centuries of stony sleep,"
but Yeats later changed it to "twenty centuries."

36. *Ibid.*, p. 249.
37. *Letters*, p. 887.
38. *Collected Poems*, p. 286.
39. *Vision*, B, p. 206. Yeats compares Christ to Achilles in this
passage. For the other comparisons cited see "Leda and the Swan,"
"*Whence had they Come?*" and "The Second Coming."
40. *Collected Poems*, p. 287. Cf. *Letters*, pp. 827–828, where Yeats
writes of the horoscopes of his children which prompted this poem.
41. *Vision*, B, p. 207.
42. *Ibid.*, p. 211.
43. *Collected Poems*, p. 444.
44. *Vision*, B, pp. 210–211.
45. *Ibid.*, p. 240.
46. Richard Ellmann, *The Identity of Yeats* (New York, 1954),
pp. 221, 166. The bracketed words have been supplied by Mr.
Ellmann.
47. *Collected Poems*, p. 268.
48. *Vision*, B, p. 213.
49. Robert Graves, "To Juan at the Winter Solstice."
50. *Vision*, B, pp. 213–214.

Chapter III. The Soul in Judgment.

1. *Vision*, B, pp. 219–220. Cf. Crazy Jane's lines (*Collected Poems*,
p. 254): "Men come, men go, *All things remain in God.*"
2. She is derived, of course, from Orpheus, whose book this is:
his saying "The Gates of Pluto cannot be unlocked, within is a people
of dreams," gave the book its original name. See *Vision*, A, p. 220.
3. *Vision*, B, pp. 220, 222, 221.
4. Recall Valéry cited in Chapter I: "In the poet it is the lack
and the blank which create."
5. Stevens, *Poems*, p. 534.
6. William Wordsworth, *The Prelude*, Book VI, ll. 603–608,
635–640.
7. The relation of these six states to Swedenborgian doctrines is
discussed, not very helpfully, by Morton Seiden in his unpublished
dissertation (Columbia University, 1952), "William Butler Yeats:

His Poetry and His Vision, 1914–1939." I think it is generally true that
Yeats took only hints from Swedenborg, and shaped his six states
to reflect his own aesthetic experiences.

8. I defer to a later chapter discussion of "Purgatory" as it appears
in the plays; there is a brief account of the purgatorial state in W. B.
Yeats, *Four Plays for Dancers* (New York, 1921), pp. 129–131; cf.
also *Letters to Dorothy Wellesley*, p. 195. In the first edition of *A
Vision* there are eight stages, by my count. The reworking into six
is concerned, predictably enough, with creating the tripartite *Meditation*, the state which Yeats used most often in literary works — cf.
all the purgatorial poems and plays. In the first edition five of the
eight states are analogous to five of the present six:

1) *Vision of the Blood Kindred*	1) *Vision of the Blood Kindred*
2) *Separation of the Four Principles*	
3) *Awakening of the Spirits*	2) *Meditation*
	a. Dreaming Back
4) *Return*	b. Return
	c. Phantasmagoria
5) *Shiftings*	3) *Shiftings*
6) *Beatitude*	4) *Beatitude*
7) *Going Forth*	5) *Purification*
8) *Foreknowledge*	6) *Foreknowledge*

9. *Vision*, B, p. 223.
10. *Ibid.*, pp. 225, 230.
11. *Ibid.*, p. 225
12. *Collected Poems*, pp. 337–338.
13. *Vision*, B, p. 226.
14. *Collected Poems*, p. 338.
15. *Vision*, B, p. 226.
16. *Ibid.*, p. 227.
17. *Collected Poems*, p. 338.
18. *Vision*, B, p. 230.
19. *Ibid.*, p. 231.
20. See my introduction to Chapter VIII, especially the quotation
from Yeats's introduction to *The Words upon the Window-Pane*:
"We poets and artists may be called . . . the dead." See also *Per
Amica*, pp. 74–75.
21. *Vision*, B, pp. 230, 229, 230.
22. *Ibid.*, p. 231.
23. *Vision*, A, pp. 229–231.
24. *Ibid.*, p. 231.
25. *Ibid.*, p. 235; *Vision*, B, p. 232.
26. The first edition, from which I have been taking the descrip-

tion of the *Beatitude*, is here much freer, less inclined to vatic statement, than the second edition. Besides the marriage of idea and image,
a Vision occurs in this state: the soul sees the images which express
its capacities for wisdom, beauty, or power. Quality and image must
merge just as idea and image do. One may describe not only events
and ideas, but also oneself.

27. *Autobiographies*, p. 226; *Collected Poems*, p. 187.
28. W. B. Yeats, *Essays, 1931–1936* (Dublin, 1937), pp. 55–56.
29. J. B. Yeats, *Letters to His Son W. B. Yeats and Others*, p. 179.
30. *Vision*, B, p. 236.
31. *Vision*, A, pp. 237, 220.
32. *Vision*, B, p. 233.
33. *Ibid*. The affinity with the lines from "A Prayer for My
Daughter" is unmistakable.
34. *Ibid.*, p. 234.
35. *Ibid*. Cf. *Autobiographies*, p. 53.
36. There is an interesting parallel in an early poem by Robert
Frost, "The Trial by Existence."
37. *Vision*, B, pp. 234, 235.
38. *Ibid.*, pp. 235–236.
39. *Ibid.*, p. 214.
40. Wallace Stevens, *The Necessary Angel* (New York, 1951),
p. 81.
41. *Vision*, B, pp. 235, 236.
42. *Collected Poems*, p. 243.
43. *Vision*, B, p. 237.
44. The idea of expiation is insisted upon far more in the 1925
Vision, where it exhibits a striking similarity to the creation of a
work of art. Why the two appeared analogous to Yeats is not entirely
clear, but the fact is certain. In a typical text (p. 249) we read:
"There is, however, communication of waking man and *Sleeping*
Spirit, the communication during expiation and during the creation
of a work of art, let us say." The curious relation of art and death
in Yeats's mind, so evident in "Byzantium," is also more freely explained in the earlier "system." Yeats is at pains to argue that the
origins of art lie in funeral images (p. 240), and the Spirits of Phase
15 are said to give the "Kiss of Death," imprinting on the mind of
the receiver an image which may be expressed as a work of art.
Yeats explicitly calls the Spirit of Phase 15 the Muse in this unusually
open passage (pp. 241–242) which I quote at length in Chapter VII,
in connection with *The King of the Great Clock Tower*.

45. *Vision*, B, p. 236.
46. Stevens, *Poems*, p. 91.
47. *Vision*, B, p. 240.
48. *Ibid*.

49. Walter Pater, Conclusion to *Studies in the History of the Renaissance* (London, 1873).

50. Yeats said of the aesthetic movement in the *Autobiographies*, "Surely the ideal of culture expressed by Pater can only create feminine souls" (p. 289), and we recall his own predilection for the antithetical and masculine.

51. *Vision*, B, p. 239.

52. The refusal of experience in one direction may, however, cause a compensatory flowering in another "life": "Did Dante acquire in the Thebaid the frenzy that he offered to Beatrice?" *Vision*, A, p. 243.

53. Pater, Conclusion to *The Renaissance*.

54. *Vision*, B, pp. 239–240.

55. *Ibid.*, p. 240.

56. Joseph Hone, *W. B. Yeats, 1865–1939* (New York, 1943), p. 401.

57. *Vision*, B, p. 240; *Collected Poems*, p. 323.

Chapter IV. The Great Year of the Ancients.

1. *Vision*, B, p. 248.
2. *Ibid.*
3. *Vision*, A, p. 155.
4. *Vision*, B, p. 246.
5. Stevens, *Poems*, pp. 403–404.
6. *Vision*, B, p. 249.
7. *Collected Poems*, pp. 253–254.
8. *Vision*, B, p. 249. Professor John V. Kelleher reminds me that March in Ireland, unlike March in New England, is truly a spring month.
9. *Per Amica*, p. 58.
10. *Vision*, B, p. 255.
11. *Ibid.*, p. 257.
12. *Ibid.*, p. 263.
13. *Letters*, p. 892.
14. *Vision*, B, p. 263.
15. W. B. Yeats, *Wheels and Butterflies* (New York, 1935), pp. 101, 103.
16. *Collected Poems*, pp. 184–185.
17. For Yeats's probable source in Hermes Trismegistus for "The Second Coming," see F. A. C. Wilson, *W. B. Yeats and Tradition* (New York, 1958), pp. 149–150, hereafter cited as *Yeats and Tradition*. But the passage assumes the malignity of the world, whereas Yeats does not.
18. *Collected Poems*, pp. 185, 187.
19. *Ibid.*, p. 185.

20. *Autobiographies*, p. 189.

21. Richard Ellmann, in his commentary on the poem (*The Identity of Yeats*, pp. 257–260) writes only in terms of historical antitheses: "While Yeats is not fond of Christianity, and regards its suppression of individual personality as having led to the present anarchy, yet at the end of the poem he envisages something far worse." Jeffares, in his identification of the falconer with Christ (*Yeats, Man and Poet*, p. 203) falls into the same error. If the poem embodied only Yeats's view of Christianity and its probable historical replacement, it would be of no more than transient interest. It is unfair to the poem to reduce it to historical observation, but the only way to escape such a blind alley is to see the statements about Christianity as symbolic, not dogmatic. As symbols, they have a plurality of meaning, granted; my concern here is to establish a neglected meaning — the relevance of the poem to Yeats's theory of poetic inspiration.

22. Wilson, *Yeats and Tradition*, pp. 66–67. Professor Reuben Brower suggests that Yeats may have been thinking of the fifth Eclogue of Virgil, in which the apotheosis of Daphnis refers allegorically to Julius Caesar.

23. *Vision*, B, p. 245.

24. Stevens, *Poems*, p. 67.

25. *Vision*, B, p. 262.

Chapter V. Dove or Swan.

1. There have been many points of view on the meaning of this poem; of them all, Adams' (in *Blake and Yeats*, pp. 203–205) is closest to mine. Leo Spitzer's subtle article — "On Yeats's poem, Leda and the Swan," *Modern Philology*, 51:271–276 (May 1954) — is vitiated in part by his belief that the poem is about "the tragedy of procreation by rape" (276). Hoyt Trowbridge would have it that the poem treats of "sexuality as a manifestation of the divine," — "Leda and the Swan: a Longinian Analysis," *Modern Philology*, 51:118–129 (November 1953) — which seems an unduly sectarian interpretation. Leda's "knowledge" has also been variously guessed at.

2. See also Yeats's proposal (in *The Herne's Egg, Plays*, p. 409) that it was Leda's "lonely lust" which invited and indeed created the Swan. The theory is proposed by Congal, but he, like Attracta, is a "principle" of Yeats's mind, rather than an autonomous dramatic character.

3. *Collected Poems*, p. 212.

4. Ellmann, *The Identity of Yeats*, pp. 176–179.

5. *Ibid.*, p. 176.

6. *Ibid.*, p. 177.

7. W. B. Yeats, *The Cat and the Moon and Certain Poems* (Dublin, 1924), p. 37.

8. Yeats, in his historical speculations, belongs to a large company of writers-with-a-thesis: his is not the only Procrustean bed, if we think of Spengler and Toynbee, T. S. Eliot and Ezra Pound.

9. *Vision*, B, pp. 267–268, 273.

10. *Ibid.*, pp. 270–271. See also the closing speech in *The Resurrection*.

11. *Collected Poems*, p. 322.

12. See F. A. C. Wilson, *Yeats's Iconography* (New York, 1960), pp. 290–303, for the most complete unraveling of these difficult stanzas. I cannot agree that the poem is one of "inner reconciliation" since the objective dark is never a congenial location for Yeats. The poem ends on wish, not accomplishment.

13. *Collected Poems*, p. 323.

14. *Vision*, B, pp. 279–281.

15. *Ibid.*, p. 281.

16. *Ibid.*, p. 277.

17. *Collected Poems*, p. 243.

18. See *Inferno*, I. The resemblance is noted by Wilson, *Yeats's Iconography*, p. 305.

19. See, for example, Cleanth Brooks, "Yeats: The Poet as Myth Maker," in *The Permanence of Yeats*, ed. James Hall and Martin Steinmann (New York, 1950), pp. 85–92.

20. See Wilson, *Yeats and Tradition*, pp. 231–243.

21. Ellmann, *The Identity of Yeats*, pp. 219–222.

22. *Vision*, B, p. 291.

23. *Ibid.*, p. 293.

24. *Ibid.*, pp. 295, 298.

25. *Ibid.*, pp. 299, 300.

26. Stevens, *Poems*, p. 250.

27. *Ibid.*, p. 251.

28. Wallace Stevens, *Opus Posthumous* (New York, 1957), p. 206.

29. *Collected Poems*, p. 292.

30. Stevens, *Opus Posthumous*, pp. 207, 209.

31. *Ibid.*, p. 213.

32. *Collected Poems*, p. 338.

33. Stevens, *Poems*, pp. 496–497.

Chapter VI. The Player Queen.

1. W. B. Yeats, *Plays in Prose and Verse* (London, 1922), pp. 428–429.

2. See the early manuscript draft of *The King's Threshold* (MS Eng 338.3) in Houghton Library, Harvard University.

3. I am indebted for this information to Professor Paul de Man of Cornell University, who kindly let me read his notes on the manuscript versions of *The Player Queen*.

4. The case for the theatrical possibilities of *The Player Queen* has been most persuasively argued by William Becker, in his very intelligent article "The Mask Mocked: Or, Farce and the Dialectic of Self (Notes on Yeats's *The Player Queen*)," *Sewanee Review*, 61:82–108 (Winter 1953). Mr. Becker understands the play better than any other critic, but it seems from his description of its failure in the theater that audiences, like critics, do not share his insight. Even with Mr. Becker's responsible and informed directing, the play mystified the playgoers.

5. W. B. Yeats, *Collected Plays* (New York, 1953), p. 273. Hereafter cited as *Plays*.

6. The claims of *The Player Queen* to political significance have been put forth by Norman Newton in his article "Yeats as Dramatist: *The Player Queen*," *Essays in Criticism*, 8:269–284 (July 1958). Mr. Newton says, in fact, that *The Player Queen* "is still one of the best plays about politics of the past hundred years" (276). It may be Mr. Newton's political preconceptions which make him misread the play so badly as to say of Decima, "It must not be thought that Yeats presents her with paradoxical approval. She is the bad ruler of a bad people; *The Player Queen* was contemporaneous with the 'Paudeen' poems" (275).

7. *Plays*, pp. 270, 256.

8. *Ibid.*, p. 249.

9. *Ibid.*, p. 250.

10. *Ibid.*

11. *Ibid.*, pp. 250, 252.

12. *Ibid.*, pp. 253–254.

13. *Ibid.*, p. 254.

14. *W. B. Yeats and T. Sturge Moore: Their Correspondence, 1901–1937*, ed. Ursula Bridge (New York, 1953), p. 91. The letter is dated May 27, 1926.

15. *Plays*, p. 255.

16. *Collected Poems*, pp. 297–298.

17. *Ibid.*, p. 296.

18. This information comes from notes on the early drafts taken by Professor Paul de Man.

19. *Plays*, pp. 259–260.

20. *Collected Poems*, p. 93.

21. *Plays*, p. 260.

22. *Collected Poems*, p. 214.

23. *Plays*, p. 265.

24. *Ibid.*, p. 264.

25. *Ibid.*, pp. 265–266, 269.

26. Wilson, *Yeats and Tradition*, p. 182.

27. Blake, "A Vision of the Last Judgment," *Writings*, p. 609.

28. Wilson, *Yeats and Tradition*, p. 183.

29. *Plays*, pp. 267, 268.

30. *Ibid.*, p. 267.

31. In Septimus' poem, *ibid.*, p. 259.

32. *Ibid.*, p. 273. This ending has been changed from the first printed version of the play (*The Dial*, 73:506, November 1922). There, the Prime Minister banishes Septimus and the players, and there is no ironic hint that Decima herself will be superseded. In general, no important differences separate the early and later versions.

Chapter VII. Desecration and the Lover's Night.

1. It was pointed out first by Yeats himself in the preface to *A Full Moon in March* (London, 1935), and subsequently by various commentators. For the preface, see *The Variorum Edition of the Poems of W. B. Yeats*, ed. Peter Allt and Russell K. Alspach (New York, 1947), p. 857. Hereafter cited as *The Variorum Poems*.

2. W. B. Yeats, *The Secret Rose* (London, 1897), pp. 9–10.

3. *Letters*, pp. 819, 845, 846.

4. *Collected Poems*, p. 355.

5. *Plays*, p. 398.

6. Wilson (*Yeats and Tradition*, p. 84) wrongly says the bell "resuscitates" the lovers. The text presents the bell as a threat, not an aid, to love.

7. William Wordsworth, *The Prelude*, Book V, ll. 136–138.

8. *Letters*, p. 817.

9. Wilson, *Yeats and Tradition*, pp. 75, 76.

10. *Collected Poems*, p. 135.

11. *Yeats and Tradition*, p. 76.

12. *Plays*, p. 400. I differ from Wilson, who thinks the Stroller coarsely unappreciative (*Yeats and Tradition*, p. 77).

13. *Collected Poems*, p. 328.

14. *Plays*, pp. 400–401.

15. *Ibid.*, p. 401. Compare the songs in "The Three Bushes."

16. *Letters*, p. 831.

17. Gerard Manley Hopkins, "To R. B." And cf. Blake's "Mental Traveller," for the alternation from passive to active.

18. *Plays*, p. 399.

19. "Thrice there he strove to throw his arms around his neck, thrice the form, vainly clasped, fled from his hands, even as light winds, and most like a winged dream." Virgil, *The Aeneid*, VI, ll. 700–702. Wilson (*Yeats and Tradition*, p. 77) thinks the reference is to the Fourth Eclogue.

20. *Plays*, p. 402.

21. *Ibid.*

22. Wilson's reading of the final stanza (in *Yeats and Tradition*,

p. 81), "The tree then cynically voices the clinging belief of humanity in its own immunity to change," is a tenable one; I retain my own interpretation principally because it provides an antithesis to the type of immortality praised by the travelling-man.

23. *Plays*, p. 403.

24. *Letters*, pp. 827, 830.

25. *Vision*, A, pp. 241–242.

26. Stevens, *Poems*, p. 87.

27. W. B. Yeats, *The Cutting of an Agate*, p. 191.

28. *Per Amica*, pp. 84, 85, 86.

29. William Blake, "Milton," Book I, Plate 29, ll. 1–3, in *Writings*, p. 516.

30. *Collected Poems*, pp. 254–255.

31. *Plays*, p. 394.

32. *Ibid*.

33. *Vision*, B, p. 240.

34. *Plays*, p. 395.

35. *Ibid*., p. 208. Compare also the passage on terror in *Essays, 1931–36* quoted by Peter Ure on p. 118 of *Towards a Mythology* (London, 1946): "I think profound philosophy must come from terror. An abyss opens under our feet; inherited convictions, the presuppositions of our thoughts, those Fathers of the Church Lionel Johnson expounded, drop into the abyss. Whether we will or no we must ask the ancient questions: Is there reality anywhere? Is there a God? Is there a Soul?"

36. *Plays*, p. 395.

37. *Collected Poems*, p. 336. See also "Words," pp. 88–89.

38. Wilson, *Yeats and Tradition*, pp. 90, 92, 86, 87.

39. *Plays*, p. 396.

40. *Letters*, pp. 845, 904.

41. See, for example, "Poetry and Tradition," in W. B. Yeats, *The Cutting of an Agate*, p. 130.

42. *Ibid*., p. 70.

43. Wilson asserts (*Yeats and Tradition*, pp. 106, 115–117) with some justification, that the Great Herne consummates his union with Attracta "through the agency" of Congal and his men. Yeats nowhere suggests such a clear solution, however: it is possible that Attracta deludes herself.

44. *Ibid*., pp. 95–136.

45. W. B. Yeats, *Letters to Dorothy Wellesley*, p. 46.

46. See, for example, *Yeats and Tradition*, pp. 126, 128.

47. *Plays*, p. 419.

48. *Ibid*.

49. *Ibid*., p. 413.

50. Stevens, *Poems*, p. 87.

51. *Plays*, p. 419.
52. Wilson, *Yeats and Tradition*, pp. 125–126.
53. *Plays*, pp. 416–417.
54. *Ibid.*, p. 410.
55. *Ibid.*, p. 409.
56. "What will you do, God, when I die?" Rainer Maria Rilke, *Das Stundenbuch*.
57. *Plays*, p. 409.
58. *Vision*, B, p. 189.
59. *Plays*, p. 412.
60. *Ibid.*, p. 424.
61. In Corney's speech, *ibid.*, p. 421.
62. *Ibid.*, p. 426.
63. *Ibid.*, p. 427.

Chapter VIII. Plays of Death, Purgation, and Resurrection.

1. See "The Vision of Hanrahan the Red" in *The Secret Rose*, where in the tale of Dermond and Dervadilla we recognize the Diarmuid and Dervorgilla of the play.
2. W. B. Yeats, *Wheels and Butterflies*, p. 22; *Autobiographies*, p. 277.
3. Edwin John Ellis and William Butler Yeats, eds., *The Works of William Blake* (London, 1893), I, 142–143, 152. I have corrected Yeats's punctuation from the *Diary, Reminiscences, and Correspondence of Henry Crabb Robinson*, Boston, 1869, II, 25.
4. "William Blake and His Illustrations to *The Divine Comedy*," in *Ideas of Good and Evil*, p. 213; W. B. Yeats, ed., *The Poems of William Blake*, Modern Library Edition (New York, undated), p. xxvi.
5. *Collected Poems*, p. 206.
6. *Four Plays for Dancers*, pp. 135–137. I cannot understand, in the face of Yeats's explicit antithesis between Christ and the birds, why Peter Ure insists on their similarity ("Yeats's Christian Mystery Plays," *Review of English Studies*, New Series, 11:176 (May 1960). Like F. A. C. Wilson, Ure equates Yeats with the Greek in *Resurrection*, an unjustified identification. I agree, however, with Ure (p. 174) on the significance of Christ's "Dreaming Back" in *Calvary*: it serves as a distancing device, and the emphasis is certainly not on Christ's mental state.
7. John Rees Moore, "Evolution of Myth in the Plays of W. B. Yeats." Unpublished dissertation (Columbia University, 1957), p. 121.
8. *Autobiographies*, p. 171.
9. *Ibid.*, pp. 171–172.
10. The aesthetic interpretation is partially justified by Yeats's use

of the word "daemon" in the manuscript of the play, as reported by
Wilson (*Yeats's Iconography*, p. 200).

11. Wilson, I think, misreads the opening song (*Yeats's Iconography*, pp. 187–188), as well as other important parts of the play.
"The full," for instance, in the song represents the height of *Christ's*
power, now waning. An objective cycle has a Phase 15, and consequently a full moon, too.

12. *Plays*, pp. 288–289.

13. *Ibid.*, p. 289.

14. *Ibid.*, p. 290.

15. *Ibid.*, p. 291.

16. *Vision*, B, p. 178.

17. *Yeats's Iconography*, pp. 190–191.

18. *Four Plays for Dancers*, p. 138.

19. *Yeats's Iconography*, p. 203.

20. *Plays*, pp. 293–294.

21. See MS *On the Road to Calvary* in Houghton Library, Harvard University (Catalog No. MS Eng 338.8).

22. *Collected Poems*, pp. 129–130.

23. *Plays*, p. 371.

24. Ellmann, *The Identity of Yeats*, pp. 260–263.

25. *Plays*, p. 364.

26. Wilson seems to agree with this view in *Yeats's Iconography*,
pp. 167–168, but to disagree with it on pp. 185 and 191, where he
(mistakenly, I think) declares that Yeats saw Christ's rule "as something essentially sordid." That rule produced, after all, the mosaics
of Byzantium.

27. Jeffares, *W. B. Yeats*, p. 270.

28. *Plays*, pp. 364–365.

29. Percy Bysshe Shelley, *Hellas*, the final chorus.

30. E. M. W. Tillyard, *Poetry Direct and Oblique* (London, 1948),
p. 74, quoted in Jeffares, p. 335n.

31. Ellmann, *The Identity of Yeats*, p. 261.

32. *Plays*, p. 365.

33. *Wheels and Butterflies*, p. 98.

34. Ellmann, *The Identity of Yeats*, p. 260. Italics mine.

35. Wilson, *Yeats and Tradition*, p. 63.

36. *Plays*, p. 369.

37. Wilson, *Yeats and Tradition*, p. 64; see also *Yeats's Iconography*, p. 193.

38. *Plays*, pp. 372–373. It should be noticed that Christ's beating
heart has resemblances to the beating heart of another phantom —
Fand, in *The Only Jealousy of Emer*.

39. *Letters*, pp. 780, 715.

40. Blake, "The Four Zoas," ll. 20–21, in *Writings*, p. 264.

41. *Plays*, p. 373.

42. Ellmann, *The Identity of Yeats*, p. 262.

43. *Plays*, p. 373.

44. *Four Plays for Dancers*, pp. 129–130.

45. *Collected Poems*, p. 143.

46. *Four Plays for Dancers*, pp. 130, 131.

47. *Irish Fairy and Folk Tales*, p. 138.

48. *The Secret Rose*, p. 183.

49. *Ibid.*, p. 182.

50. Notes to *The Wind Among the Reeds* (London, 1899), quoted in *The Variorum Poems*, p. 803.

51. *The Secret Rose*, pp. 176, 177.

52. *Collected Poems*, p. 187.

53. *Plays*, p. 276.

54. *Ibid.*, pp. 278–279.

55. *Ibid.*, p. 284.

56. *Ibid.*, pp. 279–280.

57. *Ibid.*, p. 282.

58. Wilson, *Yeats's Iconography*, pp. 238–239.

59. *Plays*, p. 282.

60. *Ibid.*, p. 284.

61. *Collected Poems*, p. 338.

62. *Ibid.*, p. 232.

63. *Ibid.*, p. 107.

64. *Plays*, pp. 284–285.

65. *Letters*, p. 913.

66. Wilson, *Yeats and Tradition*, p. 137.

67. *Letters to Dorothy Wellesley*, p. 195.

68. T. S. Eliot, "The Poetry of W. B. Yeats," in *The Permanence of Yeats*, p. 338; Eliot, *After Strange Gods* (New York, 1934), p. 50.

69. John Heath-Stubbs, *The Darkling Plain* (London, 1950), p. 205, quoted in Wilson, *Yeats and Tradition*, p. 153. Donald R. Pearce agrees with the political interpretation of Mr. Heath-Stubbs (see his article "Yeats' Last Plays: an Interpretation," in *ELH* 18:67–76, March 1951). He adds nationalistic readings of *The Herne's Egg* and *The Death of Cuchulain*, in all cases painfully limiting the plays and ignoring their tone.

70. W. B. Yeats, "Swedenborg, Mediums, and the Desolate Places," in Lady Gregory, *Visions and Beliefs in the West of Ireland* (New York and London, 1920), II, 300–301.

71. *Per Amica*, pp. 74–75.

72. *Plays*, p. 431.

73. *Ibid.*, p. 432.

74. See, for example, Wilson, *Yeats and Tradition*, chapter 4.

75. *Plays*, p. 433.

76. *Ibid.*, p. 434.
77. *Collected Poems*, p. 309.
78. *Plays*, p. 435.
79. *Ibid.*, p. 436.
80. *Collected Poems*, pp. 337–338.

Chapter IX. The Saga of Cuchulain.

1. As *The Golden Helmet*, a prose version.
2. See Birgit Bjersby, *The Interpretation of the Cuchulain Legend in the Works of W. B. Yeats* (Upsala, 1950), p. 43.
3. *Letters*, p. 293n.
4. Standish O'Grady, *Selected Essays and Passages* (Dublin, undated), pp. 72, 339.
5. Bjersby, *The Cuchulain Legend*, p. 43.
6. *Plays*, p. 139.
7. Bjersby, *The Cuchulain Legend*, p. 44; the quotation from Yeats: *Ideas of Good and Evil*, pp. 72–73.
8. Bjersby, *The Cuchulain Legend*, p. 92; Richard Ellmann, *Yeats, the Man and the Masks* (London, 1949), pp. 218–219.
9. Wilson, *Yeats's Iconography*, p. 61 and note 80.
10. *Plays*, p. 137.
11. *Ibid.*
12. *Ibid.*, pp. 138–139.
13. *Ibid.*, p. 140.
14. *Ibid.*
15. *Ibid.*
16. *Ibid.*, p. 141.
17. Bjersby, *The Cuchulain Legend*, pp. 87–91.
18. *Plays*, p. 168.
19. Oliver St. John Gogarty, *It Isn't This Time of Year At All!* (New York, 1954), p. 245, quoted in George Brandon Saul, *Prolegomena to the Study of Yeats's Plays* (Philadelphia, 1958), p. 49.
20. Ellmann, *Yeats, the Man and the Masks*, p. 219.
21. *Plays*, p. 142.
22. *Ibid.*, p. 143.
23. *Ibid.*
24. *Ibid.*
25. Lady Gregory, *Cuchulain of Muirthemne* (London, 1902), pp. 11, 12.
26. *Plays*, p. 144.
27. Wilson, *Yeats's Iconography*, pp. 71–72.
28. *On Baile's Strand*, in *Plays*, p. 172.
29. *Plays*, p. 140.
30. *Plays*, pp. 144–145.
31. Bjersby, *The Cuchulain Legend*, p. 93.

32. *Yeats's Iconography*, pp. 63–67.

33. For the sources of *The Only Jealousy of Emer*, see the tale of that name in Lady Gregory's *Cuchulain of Muirthemne*, pp. 276–293, and, for a version closer to the original, see "The Sick-Bed of Cu Chulainn" in Tom Peete Cross and Clark Harris Slover, eds., *Ancient Irish Tales* (New York, 1936), pp. 176–198.

34. *Yeats's Iconography*, pp. 107–110.

35. This was first brought to my attention by Professor John V. Kelleher.

36. *Collected Poems*, pp. 177, 176.

37. *Plays*, pp. 184–185.

38. So given in its earliest printing and in the manuscript draft of the play in the Houghton Library at Harvard University (Catalog No. MS Eng 338.7).

39. *Plays*, p. 185.

40. *Four Plays for Dancers*, p. 46.

41. Wilson wrongly says (*Yeats's Iconography*, pp. 113–114) that in the final version Cuchulain turns from Fand of his own volition, for "Emer is no more than the voice of his own conscience." She is not: she is a separate dramatic character acting as an agent for Bricriu.

42. Bricriu has all the characteristics of the Fomoroh, misshapen sea gods of night and death and cold; see Yeats's notes on them in the *Variorum Poems*, p. 795. Many of the notes on bewitchment collected in the Variorum Poems (pp. 800–802) are interesting in regard to *Emer*.

43. Bricriu always presented difficulties. As early as 1916, when the conception of the play first took shape in Yeats's mind, he wrote to Lady Gregory: "I want to follow *The Hawk's Well* with a play on *The Only Jealousy of Emer* but I cannot think who should be the changeling put in Cuchulain's place when he is taken to the other world . . . Who should it be — Cuchulain's grandfather, or some god or devil or woman?" (*Letters*, p. 612).

44. *Plays*, p. 189.

45. Peter Ure, *Towards a Mythology*, p. 21.

46. *Plays*, p. 190.

47. *Ibid.*

48. *Ibid.*, pp. 191–192.

49. *Yeats's Iconography*, p. 111.

50. *Vision*, A, p. 241.

51. *Ibid.*, p. 242.

52. *Per Amica*, p. 84.

53. *Plays*, p. 190.

54. *Ibid.*

55. *Ibid.*, pp. 171–172.

56. *Ibid.*, p. 191.

57. *Wheels and Butterflies*, p. 61.

58. *Plays*, p. 191.

59. *Ibid.*, p. 192.

60. *Ibid.*

61. *Ibid.*, pp. 192–193.

62. *Ibid.*, p. 193.

63. *Four Plays for Dancers*, pp. 45–46.

64. *Plays*, pp. 193–194.

65. Harvard MS Eng 338.7. I am not entirely certain of my transcription of Yeats's difficult handwriting, but the substance is correct. The angle brackets enclose cancellations.

66. *Ibid.* These and later transcriptions are similar to the version of *Emer* printed in *Two Plays for Dancers* (Dundrum, Ireland, 1919).

67. *Ibid.*

68. *Plays*, p. 190.

69. It is clear that my view of this lyric differs from the interpretation offered by Wilson (*Yeats's Iconography*, pp. 123–126). His ingenuity is perhaps greater than mine, but the necessity for such contortions testifies to Yeats's poetic confusion. The difference turns partly on the symbolic meaning of "stars" in the third stanza, and although I have checked Yeats's other uses of the word in the forthcoming Cornell concordance to Yeats's poetry, I find no conclusive evidence either way. Wilson would have "stars" mean "intellectual love, the emanation from the superior spheres," but it seems to me that stars, most brilliant at the dark of the moon, are a symbol for the primary forces (in the case of *Emer*, the communal force of marriage). In "Byzantium" stars and moon are set against each other as alternatives; both perfect primary and perfect antithetical are "superhuman" and one excludes the other:

> A starlit or a moonlit dome disdains
> All that man is.

Wilson gives no reason for calling starlight intellectual love.

70. Cf. *Collected Poems*, p. 144, "The stars fade out where the moon comes."

71. Wilson (*Yeats's Iconography*, p. 111) quotes "The Phases of the Moon" to show that Emer is "deformed," being an "honest wife." This would lend probability to her strange alliance with Bricriu.

72. W. B. Yeats, "Preface" to Lady Gregory's *Cuchulain of Muirthemne*, pp. xii–xiv.

73. The poem was later retitled "Cuchulain's Fight with the Sea."

74. George Moore, *Hail and Farewell* (New York, 1914), III (*Vale*), 187.

75. See Wilson, *Yeats and Tradition*, pp. 166–171, for relevant legendary material.

76. See the early typescript version of the play in the MS collection of Harvard's Houghton Library (Catalog No. MS Eng 338.3).

77. *Plays*, p. 439.

78. T. R. Henn, *The Lonely Tower* (London, 1950), p. 258.

79. *Plays*, p. 438.

80. *Ibid.*, p. 439.

81. *Ibid.*, p. 438.

82. *Ibid.*

83. *Ibid.*, p. 440.

84. *Ibid.* Wilson (*Yeats and Tradition*, p. 168) believes that these lines refer to the Morrigu, but this is syntactically impossible (the antecedent of "her" is Maeve).

85. *Collected Poems*, p. 328.

86. *Ibid.*, p. 291.

87. *Plays*, p. 441.

88. *Ibid.*, p. 442.

89. *Ibid.*, p. 444.

90. Wilson, *Yeats and Tradition*, p. 185.

91. *Collected Poems*, pp. 296–297.

92. *Plays*, p. 445.

93. *Ibid.*, pp. 445, 446.

94. *Ibid.*, p. 446.

95. *Ibid.*

96. Wilson, *Yeats and Tradition*, pp. 176–180.

97. I am aware that in the sources, Maeve and the Morrigu never "belonged" to Cuchulain at all, and therefore can scarcely be said to desert him. Nevertheless, since the Morrigu is represented as the Goddess of War in the play, she may be said to have been the supernatural being favoring Cuchulain in previous battles, his Muse of battle, so to speak; and Yeats invented, for the purpose of the play, a previous affair between Maeve and Cuchulain in order to make her treachery more striking.

98. *Collected Poems*, p. 336.

99. *Ibid.*, p. 335.

100. *Yeats and Tradition*, p. 246.

101. *Ibid.*, p. 246, and *Yeats's Iconography*, p. 305.

102. *Letters to Dorothy Wellesley*, pp. 212–213. The passage from Dante which Yeats's lines resemble reads, in Longfellow's translation,

> Then he turned round, and seemed to be of those
> Who at Verona run for the Green Mantle
> Across the plain; and seemed to be among them
> The one who wins, and not the one who loses.

103. *Collected Poems*, p. 340.

104. *Ibid.*, p. 192.

105. *Vision*, A, pp. 229–231.

106. *Collected Poems*, pp. 339–340.
107. *Yeats and Tradition*, p. 248.
108. *Collected Poems*, p. 292.
109. *On the Boiler* (Dublin, 1939), p. 35.
110. Bjersby, *The Cuchulain Legend*, p. 105.
111. *Collected Poems*, p. 291.

Conclusion

1. I. P. Sturm, letter to Yeats, quoted in Hone, *W. B. Yeats*, p. 436.
2. George Russell (A.E.), "Heavenly Geometry," in *The Living Torch*, ed. Monk Gibbon (London, 1937), p. 261.
3. Quoted by Horace Reynolds, ed., in W. B. Yeats, *Letters to the New Island*, p. 50.
4. Donald Pearce, "Philosophy and Phantasy: Notes on the Growth of Yeats's 'System,'" *University of Kansas City Review*, 18:177 (Spring 1952).
5. Quoted by T. S. Eliot in *After Strange Gods*, pp. 49–50, from *Science and Poetry* (New York, 1926), pp. 86–87. This is an early comment, granted, but its conclusions are still widely shared.

Index

DATE DUE